Astounding Stories of Super-Science, May, 1930

by Various

ISBN: 9781318923069

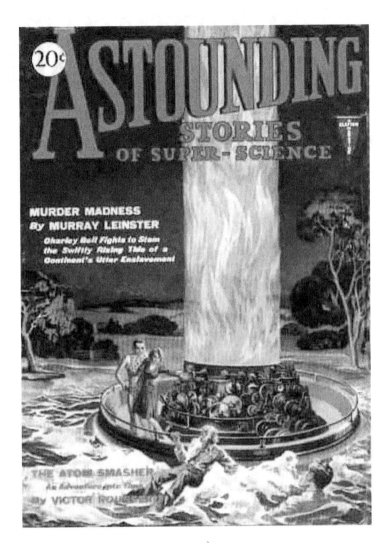

20¢

ASTOUNDING
STORIES
OF SUPER-SCIENCE

ELETION

MURDER MADNESS
By **MURRAY LEINSTER**

*Charley Bell Fights to Stem
the Swiftly Rising Tide of a
Continent's Utter Enslavement*

THE ATOM SMASHER
An Adventure into Time
By VICTOR ROUSSEAU

ASTOUNDING

STORIES
OF SUPER-SCIENCE

20¢

On Sale the First Thursday of Each Month

W. M. CLAYTON, Publisher   HARRY BATES, Editor   DR. DOUGLAS M. DOLD, Consulting Editor

---

The Clayton Standard on a Magazine Guarantees

That the stories therein are clean, interesting, vivid, by leading writers of the day and purchased under conditions approved by the Authors' League of America;

That such magazines are manufactured in Union shops by American workmen;

That each newsdealer and agent is insured a fair profit;

That an intelligent censorship guards their advertising pages.

The other Clayton magazines are:

ACE-HIGH MAGAZINE, RANCH ROMANCES, COWBOY STORIES, CLUES, FIVE-NOVELS MONTHLY, ALL STAR DETECTIVE STORIES, RANGELAND LOVE STORY MAGAZINE, and WESTERN ADVENTURES.

More than Two Million Copies Required to Supply the Monthly Demand for Clayton Magazines.

VOL. II, No. 2 CONTENTS MAY, 1930

O
C
E
A
N
'
S
D
E
P
T
H
S

E
A
S
L
E
E
W
R
I
G
H
T

To Save Imee's Race of Men-
Who-Returned-To-The-Sea,
Two Land-Men Answer the
Challenge of the Dreaded
Rorn, Corsairs of the Under-
Seas.

M
U
R
D
E
R
M
A
D

M
U
R
R
A
Y
L
E
I

N   N
E   S
S   T
S   E
                R

*Murder Madness! Seven
Secret Service Men Had
Completely Disappeared.
Another Had Been Found a
Screaming, Homicidal
Maniac, Whose Fingers
Writhed Like Snakes. So Bell,
of the Secret "Trade," Plunges
into South America After The
Master—the Mighty,
Unknown Octopus of Power
Whose Diabolical Poison
Threatens a Continent!
(Beginning a Four-part
Novel.)*

B   R
R   A
I   Y
G   C
A   U
N   M
D   M
S   I

1
9
5

O
F
T
H
E
M
O
O
N

N
G
S

*Gregg and Anita Risk Quick,
Sure Death in a Desperate
Bluff on the Ruthless Martian
Brigands. (Part Three of a
Four-part Novel.)*

T
H
E
J
O
V
I
A
N
J
E
S
T

L
I
L
I
T
H
L
O
R
R
A
I

N
E

There Came to Our Pigmy
Planet a Radiant Wanderer
with a Message—and a
Jest—from the Vasty
Universe.

THE ATOM-SMASHER

VICTOR ROUSSEAU

2
3
4

Four Destinies Rocket
Through the Strange Time-
Space of the Fourth
Dimension in Tode's

Marvelous Atom-Smasher. (A
Complete Novelette.)

THE READERS' CORNER

ALL OF US

277

A Meeting Place for Readers
of Astounding Stories.

Single Copies, 20 Cents (In Canada, 25 Cents) Yearly Subscription, $2.00

Issued monthly by Publishers' Fiscal Corporation, 80 Lafayette St., New York, N. Y. W. M. Clayton, President; Nathan Goldmann,

Secretary. Application for entry as second-class mail pending at the Post Office at New York, under Act of March 3, 1879. Title registered as a Trade Mark in the U. S. Patent Office. Member Newsstand Group—Men's List. For advertising rates address E. R. Crowe & Co., Inc., 25 Vanderbilt Ave., New York; or 225 North Michigan Ave., Chicago.

---

[151]

The two shark-faced creatures were dragging at my arms and legs.

Into the Ocean's Depths

A Sequel to "From the Ocean's Depths"

By Sewell Peaslee Wright

I

read the telegram for the second time. Then I folded it up, put it in my pocket, and pressed the little button on my desk. My mind was made up.

> To save Imee's race of Men-Who-Returned-To-The-Sea, two Land-Men answer the challenge of the dreaded Rorn, corsairs of the under-seas.

"Miss Fentress, I'm leaving this afternoon on an extended trip. The Florida address will reach me after Thursday. Tell Wade and Bennett to carry on. I think you have everything in hand? Is everything clear to you?"

"Yes, Mr. Taylor." Miss Fentress was not in the least surprised. She was used to my sudden trips. The outfit got along perfectly without me; sometimes I think my frequent absences are good for the business. The boys work like the devil to make a fine showing while I'm away. And Miss Fentress is a perfect gem of a secretary. I had nothing to worry about there.

"Fine! Will you get my diggings on the phone?" I hurriedly put my few papers in place, and signed a couple of letters. Then Josef was on the wire.

"Josef? Pack my bags right away, will you? For Florida. The usual things.... Yes, right away. I'll be leaving by noon.... Yes, driving through."[152]

―――――――――――――――――――――――――――――――

T

hat was that. There were a few more letters to sign, a few hasty instructions to be given regarding one or two matters that were hanging fire. Then, on my way to my bachelor apartments, I read the telegram through again:

THINK IT WORTH WHILE IF YOU FEEL ADVENTUROUS AND HAVE NOTHING PRESSING TO COME TO THE MONSTROSITY STOP MAKE YOUR WILL FIRST STOP SHALL LOOK FOR YOU ANY DAY AS I KNOW YOU ARE ALWAYS LOOKING FOR EXCITEMENT AND NEVER HAVE ANYTHING IMPORTANT TO DO SO DON'T BOTHER TO WIRE STOP PERHAPS WE SHALL SEE HER AGAIN

MERCER

I smiled at Mercer's frank opinion of my disposition and my importance to my business. But I frowned over the admonition to make my will, and the last telling statement in the wire: "Perhaps we shall see her again." I knew whom he meant by "her."

Josef had my bags waiting for me. A few hurried instructions, most of them shouted over my shoulder, and I was purring down the main drag, my duffel in the rumble, and the roadster headed due south.

"Perhaps we shall see her again." Those words from the telegram kept coming before my eyes. Mercer knew what he was about, if he wanted my company, when he put that line in his wire.

―――――――――――――――――――――――――――――――

I

have already told the story of our first meeting with the strange being from the ocean's depths that, wounded and senseless, had been flung up on the beach near Warren Mercer's Florida estate. In all the history of civilization, no stranger bit of flotsam had ever been cast up by a storm.

Neither of us would ever forget that slim white creature, swathed in her veil of long, light golden hair, as she crouched on the bottom of Mercer's swimming pool, and pictured for us, by means of Mercer's thought-telegraph (my own name for the device; he has a long and scientific title for it with as many joints as a centipede), the story of her people.

They had lived in a country of steaming mist, when the world was very young. They had been forced into the sea to obtain food, and after many generations they had gone back to the sea as man once emerged from it. They had grown webs on their hands and feet, and they breathed oxygen dissolved in water, as fishes do, instead of taking it from the atmosphere. And under the mighty Atlantic, somewhere, were their villages.

The girl had pictured all these things for us, and then—nearly a year ago, now—she had pleaded with us to let her return to her people. And so we had put her back into the sea, and she had bade us farewell. But just before she disappeared, she had done a strange thing.

S

he had pointed, under the water, out towards the depth, and then, with a broad, sweeping motion of her arm, she had indicated the shore, as though to promise, it seemed to me, that she intended to return.

And now, Mercer said, we might see her again! How? Mercer, conservative and scientific, was not the man to make rash promises. But how...?

The best way to solve the riddle was to reach Mercer, and I broke the speed laws of five states three days running.

I did not even stop at my own little shack. It was only four miles from there to the huge, rather neglected estate, built in boom times by some newly-rich promoter, and dubbed by Mercer "The Monstrosity."

Hardly bothering to slow down, I turned off the concrete onto the long, weed-grown gravel drive, and shot between the two massive, stuccoed pillars that guarded the drive. Their corroded bronze plates, bearing the original title of the estate, "The Billows," were a promise that my long, hard drive was nearly at an end.[153]

---

s soon as the huge, rambling structure was fairly in sight, I pressed the flat of my hand on the horn button. By the time I came to a locked-wheel halt, with the gravel rattling on my fenders, Mercer was there to greet me.

"It's ten o'clock," he grinned as he shook hands. "I'd set noon as the hour of your arrival. You certainly must have made time, Taylor!"

"I did!" I nodded rather grimly, recalling one or two narrow squeaks. "But who wouldn't, with a wire like this?" I produced the crumpled telegram rather dramatically. "You've got a lot to explain."

"I know it." Mercer was quite serious now. "Come on in and we'll mix highballs with the story."

Locked arm in arm, we entered the house together, and settled ourselves in the huge living room.

Mercer, I could see at a glance, was thinner and browner than when we had parted, but otherwise, he was the same lithe, soft-mannered little scientist I had known for years; dark-eyed, with an almost beautiful mouth, outlined by a slim, closely cropped and very black moustache.

"Well, here's to our lady from the sea," proposed Mercer, when Carson, his man, had brought the drinks and departed. I nodded, and we both sipped our highballs.

"Briefly," said my friend, "this is the story. You and I know that somewhere beneath the Atlantic there are a people who went back to whence they came. We have seen one of those people. I propose that, since they cannot come to us, we go to them. I have made preparations to go to them, and I wanted you to have the opportunity of going with me, if you wish."

"But how, Mercer? And what—"

H

e interrupted with a quick, nervous gesture.

"I'll show you, presently. I believe it can be done. It will be a dangerous adventure, though; I was not joking when I advised you to make your will. An uncertain venture, too. But, I believe, most wonderfully worth while." His eyes were shining now with all the enthusiasm of the scientist, the dreamer.

"It sounds mighty appealing," I said. "But how...."

"Finish your drink and I'll show you."

I downed what was left of my highball in two mighty gulps.

"Lead me to it, Mercer!"

He smiled his quiet smile and led the way to what had been the billiard room of "The Billows," but which was the laboratory of "The Monstrosity." The first thing my eyes fell upon were two gleaming metal objects suspended from chains let into the ceiling.

"Diving suits," explained Mercer. "Rather different from anything you've ever seen."

They were different. The body was a perfect globe, as was the head-piece. The legs were cylindrical, jointed at knee and thigh with huge discs. The feet were solid metal, curved rocker-like on the bottom, and at the ends of the arms were three hooked talons, the concave sides of two talons facing the concave side of the third. The arms were hinged at the elbow just as the legs were hinged, but there was a huge ball-and-socket joint at the shoulder.

"B

ut Mercer!" I protested. "No human being could even stand up with that weight of metal on and around him!"

"You're mistaken, Taylor," smiled Mercer. "That is not solid metal, you see. And it is an aluminum alloy that is not nearly as heavy as it looks. There are two walls, slightly over an inch apart, braced by innumerable trusses. The fabric is nearly as strong as that much solid metal, and infinitely lighter. They work all right, Taylor. I know, because I've tried them."

"And this hump on the back?" I asked, walking around the odd, dangling figures, hanging like bloated[154] metal skeletons from their chains. I had thought the bodies were perfect globes; I could see now that at the rear there was a humplike excrescence across the shoulders.

"Air," explained Mercer. "There are two other tanks inside the globular body. That shape was adopted, by the way, because a globe can withstand more pressure than any other shape. And we may have to go where pressures are high."

"And so," I said, "we don these things and stroll out into the Atlantic looking for the girl and her friends?"

"Hardly. They're not quite the apparel for so long a stroll. You haven't seen all the marvels yet. Come along!"

H

e led the way through the patio, beside the pool in which our strange visitor from the depths had lived during her brief stay with us, and out into the open again. As we neared the sea, I became aware, for the first time, of a faint, muffled hammering sound, and I glanced at Mercer inquiringly.

"Just a second," he smiled. "Then—there she is, Taylor!"

I stood still and stared. In a little cove, cradled in a cunning, spidery structure of wood, a submarine rested upon the ways.

"Good Lord!" I exclaimed. "You're going into this right, Mercer!"

"Yes. Because I think it's immensely worth while. But come along and let me show you the *Santa Maria*—named after the flagship of Columbus' little fleet. Come on!"

Two men with army automatics strapped significantly to their belts nodded courteously as we came up. They were the only men in sight, but from the hammering going on inside there must have been quite a sizeable crew busy in the interior. A couple of raw pine shacks, some little distance away, provided quarters for, I judged, twenty or thirty men.

"Had her shipped down in pieces," explained Mercer. "The boat that brought it lay to off shore and we lightered the parts ashore. A tremendous job. But she'll be ready for the water in a week; ten days at the latest."

"You're a wonder," I said, and I meant it.

---

ercer patted the red-leaded side of the submarine affectionately. "Later," he said, "I'll take you inside, but they're busy as the devil in there, and the sound of the hammers fairly makes your head ring. You'll see it all later, anyway—if you feel you'd like to share the adventure with me?"

"Listen," I grinned as we turned back towards the house, "it'll take more than those two lads with the pop-guns to keep me out of the *Santa Maria* when she sails—or dives, or whatever it is she's supposed to do!"

Mercer laughed softly, and we walked the rest of the way in silence. I imagine we were both pretty busy with our thoughts; I know that I was. And several times, as we walked along, I looked back over my shoulder towards the ungainly red monster straddling on her spindling wooden legs—and towards the smiling Atlantic, glistening serenely in the sun.

M

ercer was so busy with a thousand and one details that I found myself very much in the way if I followed him around, so I decided to loaf.

For weeks after we had put our strange girl visitor back into the sea from whence Mercer had taken her, I had watched from a comfortable seat well above the high-water mark that commanded that section of shore. For I had felt sure by that last strange gesture of hers that she meant to return.

I located my old seat, and I found that it had been used a great deal since I had left it. There were whole winnows of cigarette butts, some of them quite fresh, all around. Mercer, cold-blooded scientist as he was, had hoped[155] against hope that she would return too.

It was a very comfortable seat, in the shade of a little cluster of palms, and for the next several days I spent most of my time there, reading and smoking—and watching. No matter how interesting the book, I found myself, every few seconds, lifting my eyes to search the beach and the sea.

I am not sure, but I think it was the eighth day after my arrival that I looked up and saw, for the first time, something besides the smiling beach and the ceaseless procession of incoming rollers. For an instant I doubted what I saw; then, with a cry that stuck in my throat, I dropped my book unheeded to the sand and raced towards the shore.

S

he was there! White and slim, her pale gold hair clinging to her body and gleaming like polished metal in the sun, she stood for a moment, while the spray frothed at her thighs. Behind her, crouching below the surface, I could distinguish two other forms. She had returned, and not alone!

One long, slim arm shot out toward me, held level with the shoulder: the well-remembered gesture of greeting. Then she too crouched below the surface that she might breathe.

As I ran out onto the wet sand, the waves splashing around my ankles all unheeded, she rose again, and now I could see her lovely smile, and her dark, glowing eyes. I was babbling—I do not know what. Before I could reach her, she smiled and sank again below the surface.

I waded on out, laughing excitedly, and as I came close to her, she bobbed up again out of the spray, and we greeted each other in the manner of her people, hands outstretched, each gripping the shoulder of the other.

She made a quick motion then, with both hands, as though she placed a cap upon the shining glory of her head, and I understood in an instant what she wished: the antenna of Mercer's thought-telegraph, by the aid of which she had told us the story of herself and her people.

I

nodded and smiled, and pointed to the spot where she stood, trying to show her by my expression that I understood, and by my gesture, that she was to wait here for me. She smiled and nodded in return, and crouched again below the surface of the heaving sea.

As I turned toward the beach, I caught a momentary glimpse of the two who had come with her. They were a man and a woman, watching me with wide, half-curious, half-frightened eyes. I recognized them instantly from the picture she had impressed upon my mind nearly a year ago. She had brought with her on her journey her mother and her father.

Stumbling, my legs shaking with excitement, I ran through the water. With my wet trousers flapping against my ankles, I sprinted towards the house.

I found Mercer in the laboratory. He looked up as I came rushing in, wet from the shoulders down, and I saw his eyes grow suddenly wide.

I

opened my mouth to speak, but I was breathless. And Mercer took the words from my mouth before I could utter them.

"She's come back!" he cried. "She's come back! Taylor—she has?" He gripped me, his fingers like steel clamps, shaking me with his amazing strength.

"Yes." I found my breath and my voice at the same instant. "She's there, just where we put her into the sea, and there are two others with her—her mother and her father. Come on, Mercer, and bring your thought gadget!"

"I can't!" he groaned. "I've built an improvement on it into the diving armor, and a central instrument on the sub, but the old apparatus is strewn all over the table, here, just as it was[156] when we used it the other time. We'll have to bring her here."

"Get a basin, then!" I said. "We'll carry her back to the pool just as we took her from it. Hurry!"

And we did just that. Mercer snatched up a huge glass basin used in his chemistry experiments, and we raced down to the shore. As well as we could we explained our wishes, and she smiled her quick smile of understanding. Crouching beneath the water, she turned to her companions, and I could see her throat move as she spoke to them. They seemed to protest, dubious and frightened, but in the end she seemed to reassure them, and we picked her up, swathed in her hair as in a silken gown, and carried her, her head immersed in the basin of water, that she might breathe in comfort, to the pool.

It all took but a few minutes, but it seemed hours. Mercer's hands were shaking as he handed me the antenna for the girl and another for myself, and his teeth were chattering as he spoke.

"Hurry, Taylor!" he said. "I've set the switch so that she can do the sending, while we receive. Quickly, man!"

I

leaped into the pool and adjusted the antenna on her head, making sure that the four electrodes of the crossed curved members pressed against the front and back and both sides of her head. Then, hastily, I climbed out of the pool, seated myself on its edge, and put on my own antenna.

Perhaps I should say at this time that Mercer's device for conveying thought could do no more than convey what was in the mind of the person sending. Mercer and I could convey actual words and sentences, because we understood each other's language, and by thinking in words, we conveyed our thoughts in words. One received the impression, almost, of having heard actual speech.

We could not communicate with the girl in this fashion, however, for we did not understand her speech. She had to convey her thoughts to us by means of mental pictures which told her story. And this is the story of her pictures unfolded.

First, in sketchy, half-formed pictures, I saw her return to the village, of her people; her welcome there, with curious crowds around her, questioning her. Their incredulous expressions as she told them of her experience were ludicrous. Her meeting with her father and mother brought a little catch to my throat, and I looked across the pool at Mercer. I knew that he, too, was glad that we bad put her back into the sea when she wished to go.

T

hese pictures faded hastily, and for a moment there was only the circular swirling as of gray mist; that was the symbol she adopted to denote the passing of time. Then, slowly, the picture cleared.

It was the same village I had seen before, with its ragged, warped, narrow streets, and its row of dome-shaped houses, for all the world like Eskimo igloos, but made of coral and various forms of vegetation. At the outskirts of the village I could see the gently moving, shadowy forms of weird submarine growths, and the quick darting shapes of innumerable fishes.

Some few people were moving along the streets, walking with oddly springy steps. Others, a larger number, darted here and there above the roofs, some hovering in the water as gulls hover in the air, lazily, but the majority apparently on business or work to be executed with dispatch.

Suddenly, into the midst of this peaceful scene, three figures came darting. They were not like the people of the village, for they were smaller, and instead of being gracefully slim they were short and powerful in build. They were not white like the people of the girl's village, but swarthy, and they were dressed in a sort of tight-fitting shirt of gleaming leather—shark-skin, I learned later. They carried, tucked[157] through a sort of belt made of twisted vegetation, two long, slim knives of pointed stone or bone.

B

ut it was not until they seemed to come close to me that I saw the great point of difference. Their faces were scarcely human. The nose had become rudimentary, leaving a large, blank expanse in the middle of their faces that gave them a peculiarly hideous expression. Their eyes were almost perfectly round, and very fierce, and their mouths huge and fishlike. Beneath their sharp, jutting jaws, between the angle of the jaws and a spot beneath the ears, were huge, longitudinal slits, that intermittently showed blood-red, like fresh gashes cut in the sides of their throats. I could see even the hard, bony cover that protected these slits, and I realized that these were gills! Here were representatives of a people that had gone back to the sea ages before the people of the girl's village.

Their coming caused a sort of panic in the village, and the three noseless creatures strode down the principal street grinning hugely, glancing from right to left, and showing their sharp pointed teeth. They looked more like sharks than like human beings.

A committee of five gray old men met the visitors, and conducted them into one of the larger houses. Insolently, the leader of the three shark-faced creatures made demands, and the scene changed swiftly to make clear the nature of those demands.

T

he village was to give a number of its finest young men and women to the shark-faced people; about fifty of each sex, I gathered, to be servants, slaves, to the noseless ones.

The scene shifted quickly to the interior of the house. The old men were shaking their heads, protesting, explaining. There was fear on their faces, but there was determination, too.

One of the three envoys snarled and came closer to the five old men, lifting a knife threateningly. I thought for an instant that he was about to strike down one of the villagers; then the picture dissolved into another, and I saw that he was but threatening them with what he could cause to happen.

The fate of the village and the villagers, were the demands of the three refused, was a terrible one. Hordes of the noseless creatures came swarming. They tore the houses apart, and with their long, slim white weapons they killed the old men and women, and the children. The villagers fought desperately, but they were outnumbered. The shark-skin kirtles of the invaders turned their knives like armor, and the sea grew red with swirling blood that spread like scarlet smoke through the water. Then, this too faded, and I saw the old men cowering, pleading with the three terrible envoys.

The leader of the three shark-faced creatures spoke again. He would give them time—a short revolving swirl of gray that indicated only a brief time, apparently—and return for an answer. Grinning evilly, the three turned away, left the dome-shaped house, and darted away over the roofs of the village into the dim darkness of the distant waters.

I

saw the girl, then, talking to the elders. They smiled sadly, and shook their heads hopelessly. She argued with them earnestly, painting a picture for them: Mercer and myself, as she viewed us, tall and very strong and with great wisdom in our faces. We too walked along the streets of the village. The hordes of shark-faced ones came, like a swarm of monstrous sharks, and—the picture was very vague and nebulous, now—we put them to rout.

She wished us to help her, she had convinced the elders that we could. She, her mother and father, started out from the village. Three times they had fought with sharks, and each time they had killed them. They had found the shore, the very spot where we had put her back into the sea. Then there was[158] a momentary flash of the picture she had called up, of Mercer and I putting the shark-faced hordes to rout, and then, startlingly, I was conscious of that high, pleading sound—the sound that I had heard once before, when she had begged us to return her to her people.

The sound that I knew was her word for *"Please!"*

There was a little click. Mercer had turned the switch. He would transmit now; she and I would listen.

n the center of the village—how vaguely and clumsily he pictured it!—rested the *Santa Maria*. From a trap in the bottom two bulging, gleaming figures emerged. Rushing up, a glimpse through the face-plates revealed Mercer and myself. The shark-faced hordes descended, and Mercer waved something, something like a huge bottle, towards them. None of the villagers were in sight.

The noseless ones swooped down on us fearlessly, knives drawn, pointed teeth revealed in fiendish grins. But they did not reach us. By dozens, by scores, they went limp and floated slowly to the floor of the ocean. Their bodies covered the streets, they sprawled across the roofs of the houses. And in a few seconds there was not one alive of all the hundreds who had come!

I looked down at the girl. She was smiling up at me through the clear water, and once again I felt the strange, strong tug at my heart-strings. Her great dark eyes glowed with a perfect confidence, a supreme faith.

We had made her a promise.

I wondered if it would be possible to keep it.

I

n the day following, the *Santa Maria* was launched. Two days later, trial trips and final adjustments completed, we submerged for the great adventure.

It sounds very simple when recorded thus in a few brief lines. It was not, however, such a simple matter. Those three days were full of hectic activity. Mercer and I did not sleep more than four hours any of those three nights.

We were too busy to talk. Mercer worked frantically in his laboratory, slaving feverishly beside the big hood. I overlooked the tests of the submarine and the loading of the necessary supplies.

The girl we had taken back to her parents, giving her to understand that she was to wait. They went away, but every few hours returned, as though to urge us to greater haste. And at last we were ready, and the girl and her two companions seated themselves on the tiny deck of the *Santa Maria*, just forward of the conning tower, holding themselves in place by the chains. We had already instructed the girl in her duties: we would move slowly, and she should guide us, by pointing either to the right or the left.

I

will confess I gave a last long, lingering look at the shore before the hatch of the conning tower was clamped down. I was not exactly afraid, but I wondered if I would ever step foot on solid land again.

Standing in the conning tower beside Mercer, I watched the sea rise at an angle to meet us, and I dodged instinctively as the first green wave pelted against the thick porthole through which I was looking. An instant later the water closed over the top of the conning tower, and at a gentle angle we nosed towards the bottom of the sea.

An account of the trip itself, perhaps, does not belong in this record. It was not a pleasant adventure in itself, for the *Santa Maria*, like every undersea craft, I suppose, was close, smelly, and cramped. We proceeded very slowly, for only by so doing could our guide keep her bearings, and how she found the way was a mystery to all of us. We could see but very little, despite the clearness of the water.

It was by no means a sight-seeing[159] trip. For various reasons, Mercer had cut our crew to the minimum. We had two navigating officers, experienced submarine men both, and five sailors, also experienced in undersea work. With such a short crew, Mercer and I were both kept busy.

B

onnett, the captain, was a tall, dark chap, stooped from years in the low, cramped quarters of submarines. Duke, our second-officer, was a youngster hardly out of his 'teens, and as clever as they come. And although both of them, and the crew as well, must have been agog with questions, neither by word nor look did they express their feelings. Mercer had paid for obedience without curiosity, and he got it.

We spent the first night on the bottom, for the simple reason that had we come to the surface, we might have come down into territory unfamiliar to our guide. As soon as the first faint light began to filter down, however, we proceeded, and Mercer and I crowded together into the conning tower.

"We're close," said Mercer. "See how excited they are, all three of them."

The three strange creatures were holding onto the chains and staring over the bulging side of the ship. Every few seconds the girl turned and looked back at us, smiling, her eyes shining with excitement. Suddenly she pointed straight down, and held out her arm in unmistakable gesture. We were to stop.

M

ercer conveyed the order instantly to Bonnett at the controls, and all three of our guides dived gracefully off the ship and disappeared into the depths below.

"Let her settle to the bottom, Bonnett," ordered Mercer. "Slowly ... slowly...."

Bonnett handled the ship neatly, keeping her nicely trimmed. We came to rest on the bottom in four or five seconds, and as Mercer and I stared out eagerly through the round glass ports of the conning tower, we could see, very dimly, a cluster of dark, rounded projections cropping out from the bed of the ocean. We were only a few yards from the edge of the girl's village.

The scene was exactly as we had pictured it, save that it was not nearly as clear and well lighted. I realized that our eyes were not accustomed to the gloom, as were those of the girl and her people, but I could distinguish the vague outlines of the houses, and the slowly swaying shapes of monstrous growths.

"Well, Taylor," said Mercer, his voice shaking with excitement, "here we are! And here"—peering out through the glass-covered port again—"are her people!"

T

he whole village was swarming around us. White bodies hovered around us as moths around a light. Faces pressed against the ports and stared in at us with great, amazed eyes.

Then, suddenly the crowd of curious creatures parted, and the girl came darting up with the five ancients she had showed us before. They were evidently the council responsible for the government of the village, or something of the sort, for the other villagers bowed their heads respectfully as they passed.

The girl came close to the port through which I was looking, and gestured earnestly. Her face was tense and anxious, and from time to time she glanced over her shoulder, as though she feared the coming of an enemy.

"Our time's short, I take it, if we are to be of service," said Mercer. "Come on, Taylor; into the diving suits!"

I signaled the girl that we understood, and would hurry. Then I followed Mercer into our tiny stateroom.

"Remember what I've told you," he said, as we slipped into the heavy woolen undergarments we were to wear inside the suits. "You understand how[160] to handle your air, I believe, and you'll have no difficulty getting around in the suit if you'll just remember to go slowly. Your job is to get the whole village to get away when the enemy is sighted. Get them to come this way from the village, towards the ship, understand. The current comes from this direction; the way the vegetation bends shows that. And keep the girl's people away until I signal you to let them return. And remember to take your electric lantern. Don't burn it more than is necessary; the batteries are not large and the bulb draws a lot of current. Ready?"

I

was, but I was shaking a little as the men helped me into the mighty armor that was to keep the pressure of several atmospheres from crushing my body. The helmet was the last piece to be donned; when it was screwed in place I stood there like a mummy, almost completely rigid.

Quickly we were put into the air lock, together with a large iron box containing a number of things Mercer needed. Darkness and water rushed in on us. The water closed over my head. I became aware of the soft, continuous popping sounds of the air-bubbles escaping from the relief valve of the head-piece.

For a moment I was dizzy and more than a little nauseated. I could feel the cold sweat pricking my forehead. Then there was a sudden glow of light from before me, and I started walking towards it. I found I could walk now; not easily, but, after I caught the trick of it, without much difficulty. I could move my arms, too, and the interlocking hooks that served me for fingers. When my real fingers closed upon a little cross-bar at the end of the armored arms, and pulled the bars towards me, the steel claws outside came together, like a thumb and two fingers.

n a moment we stood upon the bottom of the ocean. I turned my head inside the helmet, and there, beside me, was the sleek, smooth side of the *Santa Maria*. On my other side was Mercer, a huge, dim figure in his diving armor. He made an awkward gesture towards his head, and I suddenly remembered something.

Before me, where I could operate it with a thrusting movement of my chin, was a toggle switch. I snapped it over, and heard Mercer's voice: "—n't forget everything I tell him."

"I know it," I said mentally to him. "I was rather rattled. O.K. now, however. Anything I can do?"

"Yes. Help me with this box, and then get the girl to put on the antenna you'll find there. Don't forget the knife and the light."

"Right!" I bent over the box with him, and we both came near falling. We opened the lid, however, and I hooked the knife and the light into their proper places outside my armor. Then, with the antenna for the girl, so that we could establish connections with her, and through her, with the villagers, I moved off.

This antenna was entirely different from the one used in previous experiments. The four cross-members that clasped the head were finer, and at their junction was a flat black circular box, from which rose a black rod some six inches in height, and topped by a black sphere half the size of my fist.

———

T

hese perfected thought-telegraphs (I shall continue to use my own designation for them, as clearer and more understandable than

Mercer's) did not need connecting wires; they conveyed their impulses by Hertzian waves to a master receiver on the *Santa Maria*, which amplified them and re-broadcast them so that each of us could both send and receive at any time.

As I turned, I found the girl beside me, waiting anxiously. Behind her were the five ancients. I slipped the antenna over her head, and instantly she began telling me that danger was imminent.[161]

To facilitate matters, I shall describe her messages as though she spoke; indeed, her pictures were as clear, almost, as speech in my native tongue. And at times she did use certain sound-words; it was in this way that I learned, by inference, that her name was *Imee*, that her people were called *Teemorn* (this may have been the name of the community, or perhaps it was interchangeable—I am not sure) and that the shark-faced people were the *Rorn*.

"The Rorn come!" she said quickly. "Two days past, the three came again, and our old men refused to give up the slaves. Today they will return, these Rorn, and my people, the Teemorn will all be made dead!"

T

hen I told her what Mercer had said: that she and every one of her people must flee swiftly and hide, beyond the boat, a distance beyond the village. Mercer and I would wait here, and when the Rorn came, it was they who would be made dead, as we had promised. Although how, I admitted to myself, being careful to hide the thought that she might not sense it, I didn't know. We had been too busy since the girl's arrival to go into details.

She turned and spoke quickly to the old men. They looked at me doubtfully, and she urged them vehemently. They turned back towards the village, and in a moment the Teemorn were stalking by obediently, losing their slim white forms in the gloom behind the dim bulk of the *Santa Maria*, resting so quietly on the sand.

They were hardly out of sight when suddenly Mercer spoke through the antenna fitted inside my helmet.

"They're coming!" he cried. "Look above and to your right! The Rorn, as Imee calls them, have arrived!"

I looked up and beheld a hundred—no, a thousand!—shadowy forms darting down on the village, upon us. They, too, were just as the girl had pictured them: short, swart beings with but the suggestion of a nose, and with pulsing gill-covers under the angles of their jaws. Each one gripped a long, slim white knife in either hand, and their tight-fitting shark-skin armor gleamed darkly as they swooped down upon us.

E

agerly I watched my friend. In the clasping talons of his left hand he held a long, slim flask that glinted even in that dim, confusing twilight. Two others, mates to the first, dangled at his waist. Lifting it high above his head, he swung his metal-clad right arm, and shattered the flask he held in his taloned left hand.

For an instant nothing happened, save that flittering bits of broken glass shimmered their way to the sand. Then the horde of noseless ones seemed to dissolve, as hundreds of limp and sprawling bodies sank to the sand. Perhaps a half of that great multitude seemed struck dead.

"Hydrocyanic acid, Taylor!" cried Mercer exultantly. "Even diluted by the sea water, it kills almost instantly. Go back and make sure that none of the girl's people come back before the current has washed this away, or they'll go in the same fashion. Warn her to keep them back!"

I

hurried toward the *Santa Maria*, thinking urgent warnings for Imee's benefit. "Stay back! Stay back, Imee! The Rorn are falling to the sand, we have made many of them dead, but the danger for you and your people is still here. Stay back!"

"Truly, do the Rorn become dead? I would like to see that with my own eyes. Be careful that they do not make you dead also, and your friend, for they have large brains, these Rorn."

"Do not come to see with your own eyes, or you will be as the Rorn!" I hurried around the submarine, to keep her back by force, if that were necessary. "You must—"

"Help, Taylor!" cut in a voice—Mercer's. "These devils have got me!"[162]

"Right with you!" I turned and hurried back as swiftly as I could, stumbling over the bodies of dead Rorn that had settled everywhere on the clean yellow sand.

I found Mercer in the grip of six of the shark-faced creatures. They were trying desperately to stab him, but their knives bent and broke against the metal of his armor. So busy were they with him that they did not notice me coming up, but finding their weapons useless, they suddenly snatched him up, one at either arm and either leg, and two grasping him by the head-piece, and darted away with him, carrying his bulging metal body between them like a battering ram, while he kicked and struggled impotently.

"They are taking him to the Place of Darkness!" cried Imee suddenly, having read my impressions of the scene. "Oh, go quickly, quickly, toward the direction of your best hand—to your right! I shall follow!"

"No! No! Stay back!" I warned her frantically. All but these six Rorn had fallen victims of Mercer's hellish poison, and while they seemed to be suffering no ill effects, I thought it more than likely that some sly current might bring the deadly poison to the girl, did she come this way, and kill her as surely as it had killed these hundreds of Rorn.

T

o the right, she had said. Towards the Place of Darkness. I hurried out of the village in the direction she indicated, towards the distant gleam of Mercer's armor, rapidly being lost in the gloom.

"I'm coming, Mercer!" I called to him. "Delay them as much as you can. You're going faster than I can."

"I can't help myself much," replied Mercer. "Doing what I can. Strong—they're devilish strong, Taylor. And, at close range, I can see you were right. They have true gill-covers; their noses are rudimentary and—"

"The devil take your scientific observations! Drag! Slow them down. I'm losing sight of you. For heaven's sake, drag!"

"I'm doing what I can. Damn you, if I could only get a hand free—" I realized that this last was directed at his captors, and plunged on.

H

uge, monstrous growths swirled around me like living things. My feet crunched on shelled things, and sank into soft and slimy creeping things on the bottom. I cursed the water that held me back so gently yet so firmly; I cursed the armor that made it so hard for me to move my legs. But I kept on, and at last I began to gain on them; I could see them quite distinctly, bending over Mercer, working on him....

"Do your best, Taylor," urged Mercer desperately. "We're on the edge of a sort of cliff; a fault in the structure of the ocean bed. They're tying me with strong cords of leather. Tying a huge stone to my body. I think they—" I had a momentary flash of the scene as Mercer saw it at that instant: the horrid noseless face close to his, the swart bodies moving with amazing agility. And at his very feet, a yawning precipice, holding nothing but darkness, leading down and down into nothingness.

"Run quickly!" It was Imee. She, too, had seen what I had seen. "That is the Place of Darkness, where we take those whom the Five deem worthy of the Last Punishment. They will tie the stone to him, and bear him out above the Blackness, and then they will let him go! Quickly! Quickly!"

I was almost upon them now, and one of the six turned and saw me. Three of them darted towards me, while the others held Mercer flat upon the edge of the precipice. If they had only realized that by rolling his armored body a foot or two, he would sink ... without the stone.... But they did not. Their brains had little reasoning power, apparently. The attaching of a stone was necessary, in their experience; it was necessary now.[163]

ith my left hand I unhooked my light; I already gripped my knife in my right hand. Swinging the light sharply against my leg, I struck the toggle-switch, and a beam of intense brilliancy shot through the gloom. It aided me, as I had thought it would; it blinded these large-eyed denizens of the deep.

Swiftly I struck out with the knife. It hacked harmlessly into the shark-skin garment of one of the men, and I stabbed out again. Two of the men leaped for my right arm, but the knife found, this time, the throat of the third. My beam of light showed palely red, for a moment, and the body of the Rorn toppled slowly to the bed of the ocean.

The two shark-faced creatures were hammering at me with their fists, dragging at my arms and legs, but I plunged on desperately towards Mercer. Myriads of fish, all shapes and colors and sizes, attracted by the light, swarmed around us.

"Good boy!" Mercer commended. "See if you can break this last flask of acid, here at my waist. See—"

---

ith a last desperate plunge, fairly dragging the two Rorn who tugged at me, I fell forward. With the clenched steel talons of my right hand, I struck at the silvery flask I could see dangling from Mercer's waist. I hit it, but only a glancing blow; the flask did not shatter.

"Again!" commanded Mercer. "It's heavy annealed glass— hydrocyanic acid—terrible stuff—even the fumes—"

I paid but slight heed. The two Rorn dragged me back, but I managed to crawl forward on my knees, and with all my strength, I struck at the flask again.

This time it shattered, and I lay where I fell, sobbing with weakness, looking out through the side window of my head-piece.

The five Rorn seemed to suddenly lose their strength. They struggled limply for a moment, and then floated down to the waiting sand beneath us.

"Finish," remarked Mercer coolly. "And just in time. Let's see if we can find our way back to the *Santa Maria*."

e were weary, and we plodded along slowly, twin trails of air-bubbles like plumes waving behind us, rushing upwards to the surface. I felt strangely alone at the moment, isolated, cut off from all mankind, on the bottom of the Atlantic.

"Coming to meet you, all of us," Imee signaled us. "Be careful where you step, so that you do not walk in a circle and find again the Place of Darkness. It is very large."

"Probably some uncharted deep," threw in Mercer. "Only the larger ones have been located."

For my part, I was too weary to think. I just staggered on.

A crowd of slim, darting white shapes surrounded us. They swam before us, showing the way. The five patriarchs walked majestically before us; and between us, smiling at us through the thick lenses of our headpieces, walked Imee. Oh, it was a triumphal procession, and had I been less weary, I presume I would have felt quite the hero.

I

mee pictured for us, as we went along, the happiness, the gratefulness of her people. Already, she informed us, great numbers of young men were clearing away the bodies of the dead Rorn. She was so happy she could hardly restrain herself.

A dim skeleton shape bulked up at my left. I turned to look at it, and Imee, watching me through the lights of my head-piece, nodded and smiled.

Yes, this was the very hulk by which she had been swimming when the shark had attacked her, the shark which had been the cause of the accident. She darted on to show me the very rib upon which her head had struck, stunning her so that she had drifted, unconscious and storm-tossed, to the shore of Mercer's estate.[164]

I studied the wreck. It was battered and tilted on its beam ends, but I could still make out the high poop that marked it as a very old ship.

"A Spanish galleon, Mercer," I conjectured.

"I believe so." And then, in pictured form, for Imee's benefit, "It has been here while much time passed?"

"Yes." Imee came darting back to us, smiling. "Since before the Teemorn, my people were here. A Rorn we made prisoner once told us his people discovered it first. They went into this strange skeleton, and inside were many blocks of very bright stone." She pictured quite clearly bars of dully-glinting bullion. Evidently the captive had told his story well.

hese stones, which were so bright, the Rorn took to their city, which is three swims distant." How far that might be, I could not even guess. A swim, it seemed, was the distance a Teemorn could travel before the need for rest became imperative. "There were many Rorn, and they each took one stone. And of them, they made a house for their leader." The leader, as she pictured him, being the most hideous travesty of a thing in semi-human form that the mind could imagine: incredibly old and wrinkled and ugly and gray, his noseless face seamed with cunning, his eyes red rimmed and terrible, his teeth gleaming, white and sharp, like fangs.

"A whole house, except the roof," she went on. "It is there now, and it is gazed at with much admiration by all the Rorn. All this our prisoner told us before we took him, with a rock made fast to him, out over the Place of Darkness. He, too, was very proud of their leader's house."

"Treasure!" I commented to Mercer. "If we could find the city of the Rorn, we might make the trip pay for itself!"

I could sense his wave of amusement.

"I think," he replied, "I'd rather stand it myself. These Rorn don't appeal to me."

It was over half an hour before we were at last free of our diving suits.

The first thing Captain Bonnett said:

"We've got to get to the surface, and that quickly. Our air supply is running damnably low. By the time we blow out the tanks we'll be just about out. And foul air will keep us here until we rot. I'm sorry, sir, but that's the way matters stand."

M

ercer, white-faced and ill, stared at him dazedly.

"Air?" he repeated groggily—I knew just how he felt—"We should have lots of air. The specifications—"

"But we're dealing with facts, not specifications, sir," said Captain Bonnett. "Another two hours here and we won't leave ever."

"Then it can't be helped, Captain," muttered Mercer. "We'll go up. And back. For more compressed air. We must remember to plot our course exactly. You kept the record on the way out as I instructed you?"

"Yes, sir," said Captain Bonnett.

"Just a minute, then," said Mercer.

Weakly he made his way forward to the little cubbyhole in which was housed the central station of his thought-telegraph. I didn't even inspect the gleaming maze of apparatus. I merely watched him dully as he plugged in an antenna similar to the one we had left with Imee, and adjusted the things on his head.

H

is eyes brightened instantly. "She's still wearing her antenna," he said swiftly over his shoulder. "I'll tell her that something's happened; we must leave, but that we will return."

He sat there, frowning intently for a moment, and then dragged the antenna wearily from his head. He touched a switch somewhere, and several softly glowing bulbs turned slowly red and then dark.

"You and I," he groaned, "had better go to bed. We overdid it. She understands, I think. Terribly sorry,[165] terribly disappointed. Some sort of celebration planned, I gather. Captain Bonnett!"

"Yes, sir?"

"You may proceed now as you think best," said Mercer. "We're retiring. Be sure and chart the course back, so we may locate this spot again."

"Yes, sir!" said Captain Bonnett.

hen I awoke we were at anchor, our deck barely awash, before the deserted beach of Mercer's estate. Still feeling none too well, Mercer and I made our way to the narrow deck.

Captain Bonnett was waiting for us, spruce in his blue uniform, his shoulders bowed as always.

"Good morning, gentlemen," he offered, smiling crisply. "The open air seems good, doesn't it?"

It did. There was a fresh breeze blowing in from the Atlantic, and I filled my lungs gratefully. I had not realized until that instant just how foul the air below had been.

"Very fine, Captain," said Mercer, nodding. "You have signaled the men on shore to send out a boat to take us off?"

"Yes, sir; I believe they're launching her now."

"And the chart of our course—did the return trip check with the other?"

"Perfectly, sir." Captain Bonnett reached in an inner pocket of his double-breasted coat, extracted two folded pages, and extended them, with a little bow, to Mercer.

Just as Mercer's eager fingers touched the precious papers, however, the wind whisked them from Bonnett's grasp and whirled them into the water.

Bonnett gasped and gazed after them for a split second; then, barely pausing to tear off his coat, he plunged over the side.

H

e tried desperately, but before he could reach either one of the tossing white specks, they were washed beneath the surface and disappeared. Ten minutes later, his uniform bedraggled and shapeless, he pulled himself on deck.

"I'm sorry, sir," he gasped, out of breath. "Sorrier than I can say. I tried—"

Mercer, white-faced and struggling with his emotions, looked down and turned away.

"You don't remember the bearings, I suppose?" he ventured tonelessly.

"I'm sorry—no."

"Thank you, Captain, for trying so hard to recover the papers," said Mercer. "You'd better change at once; the wind is sharp."

T

he captain bowed and disappeared down the conning tower. Then Mercer turned to me, and a smile struggled for life.

"Well, Taylor, we helped her out, anyway," he said slowly. "I'm sorry that—that Imee will misunderstand when we don't come back."

"But, Mercer," I said swiftly, "perhaps we'll be able to find our way back to her. You thought before, you know, that—"

"But I can see now what an utterly wild-goose chase it would have been." Mercer shook his head slowly. "No, old friend, it would be impossible. And—Imee will not come again to guide us; she will think we have deserted her. And"—he smiled slowly up into my eyes—"perhaps it is as well. After all, the photographs and the data I wanted would do the world no practical good. We did Imee and her people a good turn; let's content ourselves with that. I, for one, am satisfied."

"And I, old timer," I said, placing my hand affectionately upon his shoulder. "Here's the boat. Shall we go ashore?"

We did go ashore, silently. And as we got out of the boat, and set foot again upon the sand, we both turned and looked out across the smiling Atlantic, dancing brightly in the sun.

The mighty, mysterious Atlantic—home of Imee and her people!

[166]

The heads leveled the revolver in spite of him, while he flung his head from side to side in a frantic attempt to disturb their aim.

Murder Madness

BEGINNING A FOUR-PART NOVEL

By Murray Leinster

CHAPTER I

The engines of the *Almirante Gomez* were going dead slow. Away up beside her monster funnels her siren blew dismally, *Whoo-oo-oo-oo!* and was silent for the regulation period, and blew desolately again into the clinging gray mist that ringed her all about.

> Murder Madness! Seven Secret Service men had completely disappeared. Another had been found a screaming, homicidal maniac, whose fingers writhed like snakes. So Bell, of the secret "Trade," plunges into South America after The Master—the mighty, unknown octopus of power whose diabolical poison threatens a continent!

Her decks were wet and glistening. Droplets of water stood upon the deck-stanchions, and dripped from the outer edge of the roof above the promenade deck. A thin, swirling fog lay soggily upon the water and the big steamer went dead slow upon her course, sending dismal and depressing blasts from her horn from time to time. It was barely possible to see from one side of the ship to the other. It was surely impossible to see the bow from a point half astern.

Charley Bell[167] went forward along the promenade deck. He passed Senor Ortiz, ex-Minister of the Interior of the Argentine Republic. Ortiz bowed to him punctiliously, but Bell had a sudden impression that the Argentine's face was gray and ghastly. He checked himself and looked back. The little man was climbing the companion-ladder toward the wireless room.

B

ell slipped on toward the bow. He did not want to give an impression of furtiveness, but the *Almirante Gomez* was twelve days out of New York and Bell was still entirely ignorant of why he was on board. He had been called into the office of his chief in the State Department and told curtly that his request for leave of absence had been granted. And Bell had not asked for a leave of absence. But at just that moment he saw a rubber band on the desk of his immediate superior, a fairly thick rubber band which had been tied into a certain intricate knot. And Bell had kept quiet. He went to his apartment, found his bags packed and tickets to Rio via the *Almirante Gomez* in an envelope on his dressing-table, and went out and caught a train to the ship.

And that was all he knew. The siren up above blared dolefully into the fog. It was damp, and soggy, and depressing. The other passengers were under cover, and the decks seemed to be deserted. From the saloon came the sound of music. Bell pulled the collar of his light topcoat about his throat and strolled on toward the bow.

He faced a row of steamer chairs. There was a figure curled up in one of them. Paula Canalejas, muffled up against the dampness and staring somberly out into the mist. Bell had met her in Washington and liked her a great deal, but he swore softly at sight of her in his way.[168]

The afternoon before, he had seen a stoker on the *Almirante Gomez* pick up a bit of rope and absently tie knots in it while he exchanged Rabelasian humor with his fellows. He had not looked at Bell at all, but the knots he tied were the same that Bell had last seen tied in a rubber band on a desk in the State Department in Washington. And Bell knew a recognition signal when he saw one. The stoker would be off watch, just now, and by all the rules of reason he ought to be out there on the forecastle, waiting for Bell to turn up and receive instructions.

B

ut Bell paused, lit a cigarette carefully, and strolled forward.

"Mr. Bell."

He stopped and beamed fatuously at her. It would have been logical for him to fall in love with her, and it is always desirable to seem logical. He had striven painstakingly to give the impression that he had fallen in love with her—and then had striven even more painstakingly to keep from doing it.

"Hullo," he said in bland surprise. "What are you doing out on deck?"

Brown eyes regarded him speculatively.

"Thinking," she said succinctly. "About you, Mr. Bell."

Bell beamed.

"Thinking," he confided, "is usually a bad habit, especially in a girl. But if you must think, I approve of your choice of subjects. What were you thinking about me?"

The brown eyes regarded him still more speculatively.

"I was wondering—" said Paula, glancing to either side, "I was wondering if you happen to be—er—a member of the United States Secret Service."

Bell laughed with entire naturalness.

"Good Lord, no!" he said amusedly. "I have a desk in the State Department building, and I read consular reports all day long and write letters bedeviling the consuls for not including unavailable statistics in their communications. That's my work. I'm on leave now."

***

S

he looked skeptical and, it may be, disappointed.

"You look as if you didn't believe me," said Bell, smiling. "I give you my word of honor I'm not a member of the United States Secret Service. Will that do to relieve your suspicions?"

"I believe you," she said slowly, "but it does not relieve my mind. I shall think about other people. I have something important to tell a member of the United States Secret Service."

Bell shrugged.

"I'm sorry," he said amiably, "that I can't oblige you by tipping one of them off. That's what you wanted me to do, isn't it?"

She nodded, and the gesture was very much like a dismissal. Bell frowned, hesitated, and went on. He was anxious to meet the stoker, but this....

The siren droned dismally over his head. Fog lay deep about the ship. The washing of the waves and dripping of water on the decks was depressing. It seemed to be getting thicker. Four stanchions ahead, the mist was noticeable. He found that he could count five, six, seven.... The eighth was indefinite. But a bar materialized in the fog before him, and the grayness drew away before him and closed in behind. When he was at the forward end of the promenade, looking down upon the forecastle deck, he was isolated. He heard footsteps some distance overhead. The watch officer up on the bridge. Bell glanced up and saw him as an indistinct figure. He waited until the officer paced over to the opposite side of the bridge. The air throbbed and shook with the roaring of the siren.

Bell slipped over the edge of the rail and swung swiftly down the little ladder of iron bars set into the ship's structure. In seconds he had landed, and was down upon that terra incog[169]nita of all passengers, the deck reserved for the use of the crew.

A

mast loomed overhead, with its heavy, clumsy derrick-booms. A winch was by his side. Oddments of deck machinery, inexplicable to a landsman, formed themselves vaguely in the mist. The fog was thicker, naturally, since the deck was closer to the water's edge.

"Hey!" growled a voice close beside him. "Passengers ain't allowed down here."

An unshaven, soot-smeared figure loomed up. Bell could not see the man save as a blur in the mist, but he said cheerfully:

"I know it, but I wanted to look. Seafaring's a trade I'd like to know something about."

The figure grunted. Bell had just given his word of honor that he wasn't a member of the Secret Service. He wasn't. But he was in the Trade—which has no official existence anywhere. And the use of the word in his first remark was a recognition signal.

"What is your trade, anyways?" growled the figure skeptically.

"I sharpen serpents' teeth from time to time," offered Bell amiably. He recognized the man, suddenly. "Hullo, Jamison, you look like the devil."

J

amison drew nearer. He grunted softly.

"I know it. Listen closely, Bell. Your job is getting some information from Canalejas, Minister of War in Rio. He sent word up to Washington that he'd something important to say. It isn't treachery to Brazil, because he's a decent man. Seven Secret Service men have disappeared in South America within three months. They've found the eighth, and he's crazy. Something has driven him mad, and they say it's a devilish poison. He's a homicidal maniac, returning to the United States in a straight-jacket. Canalejas knows what's happened to the Service men. He said so, and he's going to tell us. His daughter brought the news to Washington, and then instead of going on to Europe as she was supposed to do, she started back to Rio. You're to get this formation and pass it on to me, then try to keep your skin whole and act innocent. You were picked out because, as a State Department man, hell could be raised if you vanished. Understand?"

Bell nodded.

"Something horrible is going on. Secret Service can't do anything. The man in Asunción isn't dead—he's been seen—but he's cut loose. And Service men don't often do that. He don't report. That means the Service code may have been turned over, and hell to pay generally. It's up to the Trade."

"I've got it," said Bell. "Here are two items for you. Miss Canalejas just said she suspected I was Secret Service. I convinced her I wasn't. She says she has important information for a Service man."

T

he brawny figure of the stoker growled.

"Damn women! She was told somebody'd be sent to see her father. She was shown a recognition-knot with the outsider's variation. Given one, for father. That'll identify you to him. But she shouldn't have talked. Now, be careful. As nearly as we know, that chap in the straight-jacket was given some poison that drove him insane. There are hellish drugs down there. Maybe the same thing happened to others. Look out for yourself, and give me the information Canalejas gives you as quickly as God will let you. If anything happens to you, we want the stuff to get back. Understand?"

"Of course," said Bell. He carefully did not shiver as he realized what Jamison meant by anything happening to him. "The other item is that Ortiz, ex-Minister of the Interior of the Argentine, is scared to death about something. Sending radios right and left."

"Umph," growled Jamison. "One of[170] our men vanished in Buenos Aires. Watch him. You're friendly?"

"Yes."

"Get friendlier. See what he's got. Now shoo."

Bell swung up the ladder again. Mist opened before him and closed again behind. He climbed over the rail to the promenade deck, and felt a little flare of irritation. There was a figure watching him.

He slipped to the deck and grinned sheepishly at Paula Canalejas. She stood with her hands in the pockets of her little sport coat, regarding him very gravely.

"I

suppose," said Charley Bell sheepishly, "that I look like a fool. But I've always wanted to climb up and down that ladder. I suppose it's a survival from the age of childhood. At the age of seven I longed to be a fireman."

"I wonder," said Paula quietly. "Mr. Bell"—she stepped close to him—"I am taking a desperate chance. For the sake of my father, I wish certain things known. I think that you are an honorable man, and I think that you lied to me just now. Go and see Senor Ortiz. Your government will want to know what happens to him. Go and see him quickly."

Bell felt the same flare of irritation as before. Women do not follow rules. They will not follow rules. They depend upon intuition, which is sometimes right, but sometimes leads to ungodly errors. Paula was right this time, but she could have been wholly and hopelessly wrong. If she had talked to anyone else....

"My child," said Bell paternally—he was at least two years older than Paula—"you should be careful. I did not lie to you just now. I am not Secret Service. But I happen to know that you have a tiny piece of string to give your father, and I beg of you not to show that to anyone else. And—well—you are probably watched. You must not talk seriously to me!"

He lifted his hat and started astern. He was more than merely irritated. He was almost frightened. Because the Trade, officially, does not exist at all, and everybody in the Trade is working entirely on his own; and because those people who suspect that there is a Trade and dislike it are not on their own, but have plenty of resources behind them. And yet it is requisite that the Trade shall succeed in its various missions. Always.

T

he Government of the United States, you understand, will admit that it has a Secret Service, which it strives to identify solely with the pursuit of counterfeiters, postal thieves, and violators of the prohibition laws. Strongly pressed, it will admit that some members of the Secret Service work abroad, the official explanation being that they work abroad to forestall smugglers. And at a pinch, and in confidence, it may concede the existence of diplomatic secret agents. But there is no such thing as the Trade. Not at all. The funds which members of the Trade expend are derived by very devious bookkeeping from the appropriations allotted to an otherwise honestly conducted Department of the United States Government.

Therefore the Trade does not really exist. You might say that there is a sort of conspiracy among certain people to do certain things. Some of them are government officials, major and minor. Some of them are private citizens, reputable and otherwise. One or two of them are in jail, both here and abroad. But as far as the Government of the United States is concerned, certain fortunate coincidences that happen now and then are purely coincidences. And the Trade, which arranges for them, does not exist. But it has a good many enemies.

T

he fog-horn howled dismally overhead. Mist swirled past the ship, and an oily swell surged vaguely overside and disappeared into a gray[171] oblivion half a ship's length away. Bell moved on toward the stern. It was his intention to go into the smoking-room and idle ostentatiously. Perhaps he would enter into another argument with that Brazilian air pilot who had so much confidence in Handley-Page wing-slots. Bell had, in Washington, a small private plane that, he explained, had been given him by a wealthy aunt, who hoped he would break his neck in it. He considered that wing-slots interfered with stunting.

He had picked out the door with his eye when he espied a small figure standing by the rail. It was Ortiz, the Argentine ex-Cabinet Minister, staring off into the grayness, and seeming to listen with all his ears.

Bell slowed up. The little stout man turned and nodded to him, and then put out his hand.

"Senor Bell," he said quietly, "tell me. Do you hear airplane motors?"

Bell listened. The drip-drip-drip of condensed mist. The shuddering of the ship with her motors going dead slow. The tinkling, muted notes of the piano inside the saloon. The washing and hissing of the waves overside. That was all.

"Why, no," said Bell. "I don't. Sound travels freakishly in fog, though. One might be quite close and we couldn't hear it. But we're a hundred and fifty miles off the Venezuelan coast, aren't we?"

O

rtiz turned and faced him. Bell was shocked at the expression on the small man's face. It was drained of all blood, and its look was ghastly. But the rather fine dark eyes were steady.

"We are," agreed Ortiz, very steadily indeed, "but I—I have received a radiogram that some airplane should fly near this ship, and it would amuse me to hear it."

Bell frowned at the fog.

"I've done a good bit of flying," he observed, "and if I were flying out at sea right now, I'd dodge this fog bank. It would be practically suicide to try to alight in a mist like this."

Ortiz regarded him carefully. It seemed to Bell that sweat was coming out upon the other man's forehead.

"You mean," he said quietly, "that an airplane could not land?"

"It might try," said Bell with a shrug. "But you couldn't judge your height above the water. You might crash right into it and dive under. Matter of fact, you probably would."

Ortiz's nostrils quivered a little.

"I told them," he said steadily, "I told them it was not wise to risk...."

---

e stopped. He looked suddenly at his hands, clenched upon the rail. A depth of pallor even greater than his previous terrible paleness seemed to leave even his lips without blood. He wavered on his feet, as if he were staggering.

"You're sick!" said Bell sharply. Instinctively he moved forward.

The fine dark eyes regarded him oddly. And Ortiz suddenly took his hands from the railing of the promenade deck. He looked at his fingers detachedly. And Bell could see them writhing, opening and closing in a horribly sensate fashion, as if they were possessed of devils and altogether beyond the control of their owner. And he suddenly realized that the steady, grim regard with which Ortiz looked at his hands was exactly like the look he had seen upon a man's face once, when that man saw a venomous snake crawling toward him and had absolutely no weapon.

Ortiz was looking at his fingers as a man might look at cobras at the ends of his wrists. Very calmly, but with a still, stunned horror.

e lifted his eyes to Bell.

"I have no control over them," he said quietly. "My hands are useless to me, Senor Bell. I wonder if you will be good enough to assist me to my cabin."[172]

Again that deadly pallor flashed across his face. Bell caught at his arm.

"What is the matter?" he demanded anxiously. "Of course I'll help you."

Ortiz smiled very faintly.

"If any airplane arrives in time," he said steadily, "something may be done. But you have rid me of even that hope. I have been poisoned, Senor Bell."

"But the ship's doctor...."

Ortiz, walking rather stiffly beside Bell, shrugged.

"He can do nothing. Will you be good enough to open this door for me? And"—his voice was hoarse for an instant—"assist me to put my hands in my pockets. I cannot. But I would not like them to be seen."

Bill took hold of the writhing fingers. He saw sweat standing out upon Ortiz's forehead. And the fingers closed savagely upon Bell's hands, tearing at them. Ortiz looked at him with a ghastly supplication.

"Now," he said with difficulty, "if you will open the door, Senor Bell...."

Bell slid the door aside. They went in together. People were making the best of boresome weather within, frankly yawning, most of them. But the card-room would be full, and the smoking-room steward would be busy.

"My cabin is upon the next deck below," said Ortiz through stiff lips. "We—we will descend the stairs."

B

ell went with him, his face expressionless.

"My cabin should be unlocked," said Ortiz.

It was. Ortiz entered, and, with his hands still in his pockets, indicated a steamer-trunk.

"Please open that." He licked his lips. "I—I had thought I would have warning enough. It has not been so severe before. Right at the top...."

Bell flung the top back. A pair of bright and shiny handcuffs lay on top of a dress shirt.

"Yes," said Ortiz steadily. "Put them upon my wrists, please. The poison that has been given to me is—peculiar. I believe that one of your compatriots has experienced its effects."

Bell started slightly. Ortiz eyed him steadily.

"Precisely." Ortiz, with his face a gray mask of horror, spoke with a steadiness Bell could never have accomplished. "A poison, Senor Bell, which has made a member of the Secret Service of the United States a homicidal maniac. It has been given to me. I have been hoping for its antidote, but—Quick! Senor Bell! Quick! The handcuffs!"

CHAPTER II

The throbbing of the engines went on at an unvarying tempo. There was the slight, almost infinitesimal tremor of their vibration. The electric light in the cabin wavered rhythmically with its dynamo. From the open porthole came the sound of washing water. Now and then a disconnected sound of laughter or of speech came down from the main saloon.

Ortiz lay upon the bed, exhausted.

"It is perhaps humorous, Senor Bell," he said presently, in the same steady voice he had used upon the deck. "It is undoubtedly humorous that I should call upon you. I believe that you are allied with the Secret Service of your government."

Bell started to shake his head, but was still. He said nothing.

"I am poisoned," said Ortiz. He tried to smile, but it was ghastly. "It is a poison which makes a man mad in a very horrible fashion. If I could use my hands—and could trust them—I would undoubtedly shoot myself. It would be entirely preferable. Instead, I hope—"

He broke off short and listened intently. His forehead beaded.

"Is that an airplane motor?"

Bell went to the port and listened. The washing of waves. The throbbing of the ship's engines. The dismal,[173] long-drawn-out moaning of the fog-horn. Nothing else.... Yes! A dim and distant muttering. It drew nearer and died away again.

"That is a plane," said Bell. "Yes, It's out of hearing now."

Ortiz clamped his jaws together.

"I was about to speak," he said steadily, "to tell you—many things. Which your government should know. Instead, I ask you to go to the wireless room and have the wireless operator try to get in touch with that plane. It is a two-motored seaplane and it has a wireless outfit. It will answer the call M.S.T.R. Ask him to use his directional wireless and try to guide it to the ship. It brings the antidote to the poison which affects me."

Bell made for the door. Ortiz raised his head with a ghastly smile.

"Close the door tightly," he said quietly. "I—I feel as if I shall be unpleasant."

C

losing the door behind him, Bell felt rather like a man in a nightmare. He made for the stairway, bolted for the deck, and fairly darted up the ladder to the wireless room.

"Ortiz sent me," he said to the operator. "You heard that plane just now. See if you can get it."

The operator looked up at him beneath a green eyeshade and grinned crookedly.

"Talking to 'em now," he said.

The key flicked up and down, and a tiny dancing spark leaped into being and vanished beneath its contact-point. The wireless room was dark save for the bright, shaded light above the sending table. A file of sent messages by an elbow. A pad for messages received was by a hand. Stray wreaths of tobacco smoke floated about the room, leaping into view as they drifted beneath the lamp.

"Is he bad?" asked the operator fascinatedly, his eyes fixed on his key.

Bell felt his eyelids flicker.

"Very bad," he said shortly.

"They tell me," said the operator and shuddered, "your hands get working and you can't stop 'em.... I'm playing, I am! I'm playing The Master's game!"

T

he key stopped. He listened.

"They're going to try to swoop over the ship and drop it," he said a moment later. "I don't think they can. But tell Ortiz they're going to try."

Bell's eyes were narrow. It is not customary for a radio operator on a passenger ship to speak of an ex-Cabinet Minister of the Argentine Republic by his surname only. It bespeaks either impertinence or a certain very peculiar association. Bell frowned imperceptibly for an instant, thinking.

"You've—had it?" he asked sharply.

"God, no! I never took the chance! I saw the red spots once, and I went to Rib—Say! You got a password?"

He was staring up at Bell. Bell shrugged.

"I'm trying to help Senor Ortiz now."

The operator continued to stare, his eyes full of suspicion. Then he grimaced.

"All right. Go tell him they're going to drop it."

B

ell went out. Gray fog, and washing seas, and the big ship ploughing steadily on toward the south.... The horn blared, startlingly loud and unspeakably doleful. Bell listened for other sounds. There were none.

Down the steep ladder to the promenade deck. Paula Canalejas nodded to him.

"I saw you speak to Senor Ortiz," she said quietly. "You see?"

Bell was beginning to have a peculiar, horrible suspicion. It was incredible, but it was inevitable.

"I think I see," he said harshly. "But I don't dare believe it. Keep quiet and don't speak to me unless I give you some sign it's safe! It's—hellish!"

He went inside and swiftly down[174] the stairs. He found a steward hesitating outside the door of Ortiz's cabin. He touched Bell's arm anxiously as he was about to go in.

"Beg pardon, sir," he said, and stammered. "I—I heard Mr. Ortiz making some—very strange noises, sir. I—I thought he was sick...."

"He is," said Bell grimly. "He told me he does not want a doctor, though. I'm looking after him."

He closed the door behind him, and Ortiz grinned at him. It was a horrible, a terrible grin, and Ortiz fought it from his face with a terrific effort of will. There was foam about his lips.

"D

ios! It was—it was devilish!" he gasped. "Senor Bell, *amigo mio*, for the love of the good God get my revolver from my trunk. Give it to me...."

Bell said shortly: "The airplane just radioed that it's going to try to swoop overhead and drop a package on board the steamer. It doesn't dare alight in this fog."

"I think," gasped Ortiz, "I think it would be well to tie my feet. Tie them fast! If—if the package comes, if I—if I am unpleasant, knock me unconscious and pour it into my mouth. I fear it is too late now. But try it...."

Through the port came the muttering of a seaplane's engines. The noise died away. Almost instantly the siren boomed hoarsely.

"Ah, *Dios!*" said Ortiz unsteadily. "There it is! Senor Bell, I think it is too late. Would you—would you assist me to go out on deck, where I might fling myself overboard? I—think I can control my legs so long."

"Steady!" said Bell, wrenched by the sight of the man before him fighting against unnameable horror. "Tell me—"

"It is poison," said Ortiz, his features fixed in a terrible effort of will. "A ghastly, a horrible poison of the *Indios* of Matto Grosso, in Brazil. It drives a man mad, murder mad. It is as if he were possessed by a devil. His hands first refuse to obey him. His feet next. And then his body. It is as if a devil had seized hold of his body and carried it about doing murder with it. A part of the brain is driven insane, and a man goes about shrieking with the horror of what crimes his body commits until the poison reaches that portion of his brain as well. Then he is mad forever. That is what I face, *amigo mio*. That is why I beg you, I implore you, to kill me or assist me to the side of the ship so that I may fling myself overboard! The Master had it administered to me secretly, and demanded treason as the price of the antidote. He deman—"

S

teady and strong, rising from a muttering to a steady roar, the sound of airplane motors came through the port. Bell started up.

"Hold fast," he snapped savagely. "I'll go get that package when it lands. Hold fast, I tell you! Fight it!"

He flung out of the cabin and raced up the stairs. The door to the deck was open. He crowded through a group of passengers who had discounted the dampness for the sake of a novelty—an airplane far out at sea—and raced up to the upper deck. The roaring noise was receding. The siren roared hoarsely. Then the noise came back.

For minutes, then, the ship seemed to play hide-and-seek with the invisible fliers. The roaring noise overhead circled about, now near, now seeming very far away. And the siren sent its dismal blasts out into the grayness all about. Then, for an instant, a swiftly scudding shadow was visible overhead. It banked steeply and vanished, and seemed to have turned and come lower when it reappeared a moment later. It was not distinct, at first. It was merely a silhouette of darker gray against the all-enveloping mist. But its edges sharpened and became clear. One could make out struts, an aileron's trailing edge.[175]

"Got nerve, anyhow," said Bell grimly.

It swept across the ship and disappeared, but the noise of its engines did not dwindle more than a little. The blast of the siren seemed to summon it back again. Once more it came in sight, and this time it dived steeply, flashed across the forecastle deck amid a hideous uproar, desperately, horribly close to the dangling derrick-cables, and was gone.

B

ell had seen it more clearly than anyone else on the ship, perhaps. He saw a man in the pilot's cockpit between wings and tail reach high and fling something downward, something with a long streamer attached to it. Bell had an instant's glimpse of the goggled face. Then he was darting forward, watching the thing that fell.

It took only a second. Two at most. But the thing seemed to fall with infinite deliberation, the streamer shivering out behind it. It fell at a steep slant, the forward momentum of the plane's speed added to its own drop. It swooped down, slanting toward the rail....

Bell groaned. It struck the rail itself, and bounced. A sailor flung himself toward it. The streamer slipped from his fingers and slithered over the side.

Bell was at the railing just in time to see it drop into the water. He opened his mouth to shout, and saw it sink. The last of the streamer followed the dropped object down into the green water when it was directly below him.

His hands clenched. Bell stared sickly at the spot where it had vanished. An instant later he had whirled and was thrusting wide the wireless room door. The operator was returning to his key, grinning crookedly. He looked up sidewise.

"Tell them it went overside," snapped Bell. "Tell them to try it again. Ortiz is in hell! To try again! He's dying!"

T

he operator looked up fascinatedly, his fingers working his key.

"Is he—bad?" he asked with a shuddering interest.

"He's dying!" snarled Bell, in a rage because of his helplessness. He had forgotten everything but the fact that a man below decks was facing the most horrible fate that can overtake a man, and facing it with a steadfast gameness that made Bell's heart go out to him.

"They don't die," said the operator. He shuddered. "They don't die of it."

His key stopped. He listened. His key clicked again.

"They only had two packages," he said a moment later. "They don't dare risk the other one. They say the fog ends twenty miles farther on. They're going to land up there and taxi back on the surface of the water. It shouldn't be more than half an hour."

He pushed himself back from the table with an air of finality.

"That's all. They've signed off."

Bell felt rage sweeping over him. The operator grinned crookedly.

"Better go down and tie him up," he said, and licked his lips with the fascinated air of one thinking of a known and terrifying thing. "Better tie him up tight. It'll be half an hour more."

B

ell went down the companion-ladder. The promenade was crowded with passengers now, asking questions of each other. Some, frowning portentously, thought the plane an unscheduled ocean flier who had lost his way in the fog.

Paula Canalejas was close to Bell as he shouldered his way through the crowd.

"That was for him?" she asked, without moving her lips.

Bell nodded.

"Tell him," she said quietly, "I—pray for him."

Bell nodded abruptly and went into the saloon. It was nearly empty. He wiped the sweat off his face. It was horrible to have to go down to Ortiz[176] and tell him that at best it would be half an hour more....

Then there was a sudden scream below him, and then a shot. Bell jumped for the stairs, his heart in his throat, and saw Ortiz coming out of his stateroom door. His eyes were wide and agonized. His body....

Even in the incredibly short time before he reached the bottom of the steps, Bell had time to receive the ghastly impression that Ortiz was sane, but that his body had gone mad. Ortiz's face was white and horrified. His hands and arms were writhing savagely, working at the handcuffs on his wrists. His legs were carrying him at a curious, padding trot down the hallway. One of the hands held a glittering revolver. A steward was crouched behind a couch, his face white and filled with stark terror. And Ortiz held his head back, as if struggling to hold back and control his body, which was under the control of a malignant demon.

"Out of the way!" cried Ortiz in a voice of terrible despair. "Get someone to shoot me! Kill me! I cannot—ah, *Dios!*"

T

he hands leveled the revolver in spite of him, while he flung his head from side to side in a frantic attempt to disturb their aim.

"Close your eyes!" panted Bell, and hurled himself upon—whom? It was not Ortiz. It was Ortiz's body, gone mad and raging. The manacled arms flailed about frenziedly. The gun went off. Again. Again....

Bell struck. He knocked the Thing that possessed Ortiz's body off its feet. The hands groped for him. They clubbed at him with the revolver. The feet kicked....

"Keep your eyes closed," gasped Bell, struggling to get the gun away from those horrible hands. "It—it can't see when you keep your eyes closed!"

Fighting insanely as the Thing was fighting, he could not identify it with Ortiz himself. One of the hands unclosed from about the revolver and clawed at his throat. It seemed to abandon that effort and attacked Ortiz's face in a frenzy of rage, struggling to claw his eyes open. The other held the weapon fast with maniacal strength.

At the horror of feeling one of his own manacled hands attacking his face savagely as if it were itself a sensate thing, Ortiz opened his eyes. They were wide with despair.

The hand with the revolver made a sudden movement, and Bell flung his weight upon it as the clutching hand pulled the trigger. There was a deafening report....

T

he body seemed to weaken suddenly in Bell's grip. It fought less and less terribly, though with no lessening of its savagery. He managed to get the revolver away from the hands that shook with unspeakable rage. He flung it away and stood panting.

There was a crowd of people suddenly all about the place. Staring, stunned, incredulous people who regarded Bell with a dawning, damning suspicion.

Ortiz spoke suddenly. His voice was weak, but it was steady, and it was full of a desperate relief.

"I wish to make a statement," he said sharply. "I—I wished to commit suicide for personal reasons. Senor Bell tried to dissuade me. The handcuffs upon my wrists were placed there with my consent. Senor Bell is my friend and has done me no wrong. I shot myself, with intention."

Bell beckoned to the ship's doctor.

"Get him bandaged up," he ordered harshly. "There's no need for him to die."

The body was writhing only feebly, now. Ortiz looked up at him, and managed a smile. Again there was that incredible impression of the body not belonging to Ortiz, or Ortiz as a sane and whole and honorable, ad[177]mirable man, and the feebly writhing body with its clutching hands as some evil thing that had properly been defeated and killed.

T

he doctor bent down. It was useless, of course. He made futile movements.

"I wish to speak to my friend, Senor Bell," said Ortiz weakly. "I—I have not long."

Bell knelt beside him.

"The Master's—deputy in Rio," panted Ortiz weakly, almost in a whisper, "is—is Ribiera. In Buenos Aires I—I do not know. There was a man—the one who poisoned me—but I killed him. Secretly. I do not think—the Master knows. I pray that—"

He stopped. He could not speak again. But he smiled, and a few seconds later Bell clenched his hands. Ortiz was gone.

Someone touched his arm. Paula Canalejas. He stared down at her and managed to smile. It was not a very successful smile. He drew a deep breath.

"I would like," said Bell wryly, "to think that, when I die, I will die as well as this man did. But I'm afraid I shan't."

But Paula said:

"The airplane can be heard outside. It seems to be moving on the surface."

nd ten minutes later the plane loomed up out of the mist, queerly ungainly on the surface of the water. Its motors roared impatiently as if held in leash. It swung clumsily about, heading off out of sight in the fog to turn. It came back, sliding along the top of the water with its wing-tip floats leaving alternate streaks of white foam behind them. A man stood up in its after cockpit.

Bell crowded to the rail. The man—goggled and masked—held up a package as if to fling it on board. Bell watched grimly. But he saw that the pilot checked himself and looked up at the upper deck. Bell craned his neck. The wireless operator was waving wildly to the seaplane. He writhed his hands, and held his hand to his head is if blowing out his brains, and waved the plane away, frantically.

The pilot of the plane sat down. A moment later its motors roared more thunderously. It is not safe to alight on either land or water when fog hangs low, but there is little danger in taking off.

The seaplane shot away into the mist, its motors bellowing. The sound of its going changed subtly. It seemed to rise, and grow more distant.... It died away.

Bell halted at the top of the companion-ladder and saw the wireless operator, with a crooked, nervous grin upon his face.

CHAPTER III

Bell saw what he was looking for, out in the throng of traffic that filled the Avenida do Acre, in Rio. He'd seen it over the heads of the crowd, which was undersized, as most Brazilian crowds are, and he managed to get through the perpetual jam on the mosaic sidewalk and reach the curb.

He stood there and regarded the vehicles filling the broad avenue, wearing exactly the indifferent, half-amused air of a tourist with no place in particular to go and a great deal of time in which to go there. Taxis chuffed past, disputing right of way with private cars which were engaged in more disputes with other cars, all in the rather extraordinary bad temper and contentiousness which comes to the Latin-American when he takes the wheel of an automobile.

As if coming to an unimportant decision, Bell raised his hand to an approaching cab. It had two men on the chauffeur's seat. Of course. All taxis in Rio carry two men in front. One drives, and the other lights his cigarettes, makes witty comments upon passing ladies, and helps in collecting[178] the fares from recalcitrant passengers. The extra man is called the "secretary," and he assists materially in giving an impression of haughty pride.

The taxi ground to the curb. The secretary reached behind him indifferently and opened the door. Bell did not glance at him. He stepped inside and settled down languidly.

"The Beira Mar," he said listlessly.

The taxi started off with a jolt. It is the invariable custom in Rio de Janeiro. And besides, it reminds the passenger that he is merely a customer, admitted to the cab on suffrance, and that he must be suitably meek to those who will presently blandly ignore the amount registered by the meter and demand a fare of from eight to twenty-seven times the indicated amount.

T

he cab went shooting down the Avenida do Acre toward the harbor. The Avenida do Acre is officially the Avenida Rio Blanco, and it should be called by that name, only people forget. The Beira Mar, however, is named with entire propriety. It is actually the edge of the sea, and it is probably one of the two or three most beautiful driveways in the world.

The cab whirled past the crowded sidewalks. Incredible numbers of people, with an incredible variation in the shades of their complexions, moved to and from with the peculiar aimlessness of a Brazilian crowd. A stout and pompous negro politician from Bahia, wearing an orchid in his button-hole, rubbed elbows with a striking blonde lady of the sidewalks on his left, and forced a wizened little silk-hatted *parda*—approximately an octoroon—to dodge about him in order to progress. A young and languid person, his clothes the very last expiring gasp of fashion, fingered his stick patiently. He wore the painstakingly cultivated expression of bored disillusionment your young Brazilian dandy considers aristocratic. It was very probable that he shared a particularly undesirable bedroom with four or five other young men in order to purchase such clothing, but then, *farenda fita*—making a picture—is the national Brazilian sport.

Bell lighted a cigarette. It was not wise to regard the secretary of this particular taxi too closely, but if his face had been thickly smeared with coal dust, and if he had had a two weeks' beard, and if he had been seen on the forecastle of the *Almirante Gomez*, one would have deduced him to be a stoker who had not used the name of Jamison.

T

he cab reached the Beira Mar, and turned to take the long route about the bay. It is one of the most beautiful views to be found anywhere, and tall apartment houses have been built along its whole length to capitalize the scenery. True, the more brightly-colored ladies of the capital have established themselves in vast numbers among these apartment houses, but in their languid promenades they add—let us say—the beauties of art to those of nature.

A voice spoke from the chauffeur's seat.

"Bell."

"Right," said Bell without moving. His eyes flickered, however, and he found the device Jamison had inserted. A speaking-tube of sorts. Not especially efficient, but inconspicuous enough. He stirred listlessly and got his lips near it.

"All right to talk?" he asked briefly.

"Shoot," said Jamison from the secretary's seat beside the chauffeur. "This man doesn't understand English, and he thinks I'm in a smuggling gang. He expects to make some money out of me eventually."

Bell spoke curtly, while the taxi rolled past the Morro da Gloria with its quaint old church and went along the winding, really marvelous driveway past many beaches, with the incredibly blue water beyond.

"Canalejas is out of town," he said. "It isn't known when he'll be back. I[179] met his daughter at a dance at our Embassy here, and she told me. We didn't dare to talk much, but she's frightened. Especially after what happened to Ortiz. And I've met Ribiera, whom Ortiz named."

"I've been looking him up," growled Jamison through the speaking-tube.

B

ell flicked the ash from his cigarette out the door, and went on quietly.

"He's trying to get friendly with me. I've promised to call at his house and have him take me out to the flying field. He has two planes, he tells me, a big amphibian and a two-seater. Uses them for commuting between Rio and his place back inland. He went out of his way to cultivate me. I think he suspects I'm trying to find out something."

"Which you are," said Jamison dryly. "You've found out that Ortiz was right at least about—"

Bell nodded, and frowned at himself for having nodded. He spoke into the mouthpiece by his head with an expressionless face.

"He's practically fawned upon by a bunch of important officials and several high ranking army officers. Suspecting what I do, I think he's got hold of a devil of a lot of power."

Jamison scowled in a lordly fashion upon a mere pedestrian who threatened to impede the movement of the taxicab by making it run over him.

"Ortiz," said Bell quietly, "told me he'd been poisoned, and treason asked as the price of the antidote. I've heard that the Brazilian Minister for Foreign Affairs went insane six months ago. I heard, also, that it was homicidal mania—murder madness. And I'm wondering if these people who fawn upon Ribiera aren't paying a price for—well—antidotes, or their equivalent. The Minister for Foreign Affairs may have refused."

"You're improving," said Jamison dryly. The taxi rounded a curve and a vista of sea and sand and royal palms spread out before it. "Yes, you're improving. But Ortiz spoke of Ribiera only as a deputy of The Master. Who is The Master?"

"God knows," said Bell. He stared languidly out of the window, for all the world to see. A tourist, regarding the boasted beauties of the Biera Mar.

"A deputy," said Jamison without emotion, "of some unknown person called The Master poisoned Ortiz in Buenos Aires. And Ortiz was an important man in the Argentine. Ribiera is merely the deputy of that same unknown Master in Rio, and he has generals and state presidents and the big politicians paying court to him. If deputies in two countries that we know of have so much power, how much power has The Master?"

S

ilence. The taxi chugged steadily past unnoticed beauties and colorings. Rio is really one of the most beautiful cities in the world.

"It's like this," said Jamison jerkily. "Seven Service men vanish and one goes mad. You get two tips that the fate of Ortiz is the fate of the seven men—eight, in fact. We find that two men dispense a certain ghastly poison in two certain cities, at the orders of a man they call The Master. We find that those two men wield an astounding lot of power, and we know they're only deputies, only subordinates of the Master. We know, also, that the Service men vanished all over the whole continent, not in just those two cities. How many deputies has The Master? What's it all about? He wanted treason of Ortiz, we know. What does he want of the other men his deputies have enslaved? Why did he poison the Service men? And why—especially why—do two honorable men, officials of two important nations, want to tip off the United States Government about the ghastly business? What's it got to do with our nation?"

Bell flung away his cigarette.

"That last question has occurred to[180] me too," he observed, and carefully repressed a slight shiver. "I have made a guess, which is probably insane. I'm going to see Ribiera this afternoon."

"He already suspects you know too much," said Jamison without expression.

"I am"—Bell managed the ghost of a mirthless smile—"I am uncomfortably aware of it. And I may need an antidote as badly as Ortiz. If I do, and can't help myself, I'll depend on you."

J

amison growled.

"I simply mean," said Bell very quietly, "that I'd really rather not be—er—left alive if I'm mad. That's all. But Ortiz knew what was the matter with him before he got bad off. I know it's a risk. I'm goose-flesh all over. But somebody's got to take the risk. The guess I've made may be insane, but if it's right one or two lives will be cheap enough as a price for the information. Suppose you chaps turn around and take me to Ribiera's house?"

There was a long pause. Then Jamison spoke in Portuguese to his companion. The taxi checked, swerved, and began to retrace its route.

"You're a junior in the Trade," said Jamison painstakingly. "I can't order you to do it."

Bell fumbled with his cigarette case.

"The Trade doesn't exist, Jamison," he said dryly. "And besides, nobody gives orders in The Trade. There are only suggestions. Now shut up a while. I want to try to remember some consular reports I read once, from the consul at Puerto Pachecho."

"What?"

"The consul there," said Bell, smiling faintly, "was an amateur botanist. He filled up his consular reports with accounts of native Indian medicinal plants and drugs, with copious notes and clinical observations. I had to reprove him severely for taking up space with such matters and not going fully into the exact number of hides, wet and dry, that passed through the markets in his district. His information will be entirely useless in this present emergency, but I'm going to try to remember as much of it as I can. Now shut up."

hen the taxi swung off the Biera Mar to thread its way through many tree-lined streets—it is a misdemeanor, punishable by fine, to cut down a tree in Rio de Janeiro—it carried a young American with the air of an accomplished idler, who has been mildly bored by the incomparable view from the waterside boulevard. When it stopped at the foot of one of the slum covered *morros* that dot all Rio, and a liveried doorman came out of a splendid residence to ask the visitor his name, the taxi discharged a young American who seemed to feel the heat, in spite of the swift motion of the cab. He wiped off his forehead with his handkerchief as he was assured that the Senhor Ribiera had given orders he was to be admitted, night or day. When the taxi drove off, it carried two men on the chauffeur's seat, of whom one had lost, temporarily, the manner of haughty insolence which is normally inseparable from the secretary of a taxicab chauffeur.

But though he wiped his forehead with his handkerchief, Bell actually felt rather cold when he followed his guide through ornately furnished rooms, which seemed innumerable, and was at last left to wait in an especially luxurious salon.

There was a pause. A rather long wait. A distinctly long wait. Bell lighted a cigarette and seemed to become mildly bored. He regarded a voluptuous small statuette with every appearance of pleased interest. A subtly decadent painting seemed to amuse him considerably. He did not seem to notice that no windows at all were visible, and that shaded lamps lit this room, even in broad daylight.

T

wo servants came in, a footman in livery and the major-domo. Your average *Carioca* servant is either[181] fawning or covertly insolent. These two were obsequious. The footman carried a tray with a bottle, glass, ice, and siphon.

"The Senhor Ribiera," announced the major-domo obsequiously, "begs that the Senhor Bell will oblige him by waiting for the shortest of moments until the Senhor Ribiera can relieve himself of a business matter. It will be but the shortest of moments."

Bell felt a little instinctive chill at sight of the bottle and glasses.

"Oh, very well," he said idly. "You may put the tray there."

The footman lifted the siphon expectantly. Bell regarded it indifferently. The wait before the arrival of this drink had been longer than would be required merely for the announcing of a caller and the tending of a tray, especially if such a tray were a custom of the place. And the sending of a single bottle only, without inquiry into his preferences....

"No soda," said Bell. He poured out a drink into the tinier glass. He lifted it toward his lips, hesitated vaguely, and drew out his handkerchief again.

He sneezed explosively, and the drink spilled. He swore irritably, put down the glass, and plied his handkerchief vigorously. A moment later he was standing up and pouring the drink out afresh, from the bottle in one hand to the glass in the other. He up-tilted the glass.

"Get rid of this for me," he said annoyedly of the handkerchief.

H

e saw a nearly imperceptible glance pass between the footman and the major-domo. They retired, and Bell moved about the room exactly like a young man who has been discomfited by the necessity of sneezing before servants. Anywhere else in the world, of course, such a pose would not have been convincing. But your Brazilian not only adopts *fazenda fita* as his own avocation, but also suspects it to be everybody else's too. And a young Brazilian of the leisure class would be horribly annoyed at being forced to so plebeian an exhibition in public.

He moved restlessly about the room, staring at the picture. Presently he blinked uncertainly and gazed about less definitely. He went rather uncertainly to the chair he had first occupied and sat down. He poured—or seemed to pour—another drink. Again he sneered, and looked mortified. He put down the glass with an air of finality. But he looked puzzledly about him. Then he sank back in his chair and gradually seemed to sink into a sort of apathetic indifference.

H

e looked, then, like a very bored young man on the verge of dozing off. But actually he was very much alert indeed. He had the feeling of eyes upon him for a while. Then that sensation ceased and he settled himself to wait. And meantime he felt a particular, peculiar gratitude to the late American consul at Puerto Pachecho for his interest in medicinal plants.

That gentleman had gone into the subject with the passionate enthusiasm of the amateur. He had described *icus*, *uirari* and *timbo*. He had particularized upon *makaka-nimbi* and *hervamoura*. And he had gone into a wealth of detail concerning *yagué*, on account of its probable value if used in criminology. As consul at Puerto Pachecho he was not altogether a success in some ways, but he had invented an entirely original method of experimentation upon those drugs and poisons which did not require to be introduced into the blood-stream. His method was simplicity itself. An alcoholic solution "carried" a minute quantity of the drug in its vapor, just as an alcoholic solution carries a minute quantity of perfuming essential oil. He inhaled the odor of the alcoholic solution. The effect was immediately, strictly temporary, and not dangerous. He was enabled to describe the odors, in some cases the tastes, and in a few instances the effects of the substances he listed, from personal experience.[182]

A

nd Bell had used his method as an unpromising but possible test for a drug in the drink that had been brought him. He inhaled the strangling odor of the spilled liquor on his handkerchief. And there was a drug involved. For an instant he was dizzy, and for an instant he saw the room through a vivid blue haze. And something clicked in his brain and said "It's *yagué*." And the relief of dealing with something which he knew—if only at second-hand—was so enormous that he felt almost weak.

Yagué, you see, is an extract from the leaves of a plant which is not yet included in materia medica. It has nearly the effect of scopolamine—once famous in connection with twilight sleep—and produces a daze of blue light, an intolerable sleepiness, and practically all the effects of hypnotism. A person under *yagué*, as under scopolamine or hypnosis, will seem to slumber and yet will obey any order, by whomever given. He will answer any question without reserve or any concealment. And on awakening he will remember nothing done under the influence of the potion. The effects are not particularly harmful.

Bell then, sat in an apparent half-daze, half-slumber, in the salon in which he waited for Ribiera to appear. He knew exactly what he was expected to do. Ribiera wanted to find out what he knew or suspected about Ortiz's death. Ribiera wanted to know many things, and he would believe what Bell told him because he thought Bell had taken enough *yagué* to be practically an hypnotic subject. Let Ribiera believe what he was told!

When he came into the room, bland and smiling, Bell did not stir. He was literally crawling, inside, with an unspeakable repulsion to the man and the things for which he stood. But he seemed dazed and dull, and when Ribiera began to ask questions he babbled his answers in a toneless, flat voice. He babbled very satisfactorily, in Ribiera's view.

hen Ribiera shook him roughly by the shoulder he started, and let his eyes clear. Ribiera was laughing heartily.

"Senhor! Senhor!" said Ribiera jovially. "My hospitality is at fault! You come to be my guest and I allow you to be so bored that you drop off to sleep! I was detained for five minutes and came in to find you slumbering!"

Bell stared ruefully about him and rubbed his eyes.

"I did, for a fact," he admitted apologetically. "I'm sorry. Up late last night, and I was tired. I dropped in to see those planes you suggested I'd be interested in. But I daresay it's late, now."

Ribiera chuckled again. He was in his late and corpulent forties and was something of a dandy. If one were captious, one might object to the thickness of his lips. They suggested sensuality. And there was a shade—a bare shade—more of pigment in his skin than the American passes altogether unquestioned. And his hair was wavy.... But he could be a charming host.

"We'll have a drink," he said bluntly, "while the car's coming around to the door, and then go out to the flying field."

"No drink," said Bell, lifting his hand. "I feel squeamish now. I say! Haven't you changed the lamps, or something? Everything looks blue...."

That was a lie. Things looked entirely normal to Bell. But he looked about him as if vaguely puzzled. If he had drunk the liquor Ribiera had sent him, things would have had a bluish tinge for some time after. But as it was....

Ribiera chaffed him jovially on the way to the flying field. And introducing him to fliers and officials of the field, he told with gusto of Bell's falling asleep while waiting for him. A very jolly companion, Ribiera.

But Bell saw two or three men looking at him very queerly. Almost sympathetically. And he noticed, a lit[183]tle later, that a surprising number of fliers and officials of the airport seemed to be concealing an abject terror of Ribiera. One or two of them seemed to hate him as well.

CHAPTER IV

B

ell stepped out of a tall French window to a terrace, and from the terrace to the ground. There was a dull muttering in the sky to the east, and a speck appeared, drew nearer swiftly, grew larger, and became a small army biplane. It descended steeply to earth behind a tall planting of trees. Bell lighted a cigarette and moved purposelessly down an elaborately formalized garden.

"More victims," he observed grimly to himself, of the plane.

Ribiera lifted a pigmented hand to wave languidly from a shaded chair. There were women about him, three of them, and it sickened Bell to see the frightened assiduity with which they flattered him. Bell had met them, of course. Madame the wife of the State President of Bahia—in the United States of Brazil the states have presidents instead of governors—preferred the title of "Madame" because it was more foreign and consequently more aristocratic than Senhora. And Madame the wife of the General—

"Senhor," called Ribiera blandly, "I have news for you."

Bell turned and went toward him with an air of pleased expectancy. He noticed for the first time the third of the women. Young, in the first flush of youthful maturity, but with an expression of stark terror lingering behind a palpably assumed animation.

"An acquaintance of yours, Senhor," said Ribiera, "is to be my guests."

Bell steeled himself.

"The Senhor Canalejas," said Ribiera, beaming, "and his daughter."

B

ell seemed to frown, and then seemed to remember.

"Oh, yes," he said carelessly, "I met her in Washington. She was on the *Almirante Gomez*, coming down."

The next instant he saw Ribiera's expression, and cursed himself for a fool. Ribiera's eyes had narrowed sharply. Then they half-closed, and he smiled.

"She is charming," said Ribiera in drowsy contentment, "and I had thought you would be glad to improve her acquaintance. Especially since, as my friend, you may congratulate me. A contract of marriage is under discussion."

Bell felt every muscle grow taut. The fat, pigmented man before him....

"Indeed," said Bell politely, "I do congratulate you."

Ribiera looked at him with an expression in which a sardonic admiration mingled with something else less pleasant.

"You are clever, Senhor Bell," he said heavily, seeming to sink more deeply into his chair. "Very clever." He shifted his eyes to the women who stood about him. "You may go," he said indifferently. His tone was exactly that of a despot dismissing his slaves. Two of them colored with instinctive resentment. His eyes lingered an instant on the third. Her face had showed only a passionate relief. "You, Senhora," he said heavily, "may wait nearby."

The terror returned to her features, but she moved submissively to a spot a little out of earshot. Bell found his jaws clenched. There is a certain racial taint widespread in Brazil which leads to an intolerable arrogance when there is the slightest opportunity for its exercise. Ribiera had the taint, and Bell felt a sickening wrath at the terrified submission of the women.

"*Si,*" said Ribiera, suddenly adverting to insolence. "You are clever, Senhor Bell. Where did you learn of *yagué?*"

B

ell inhaled leisurely. His muscles were tense, but he gave no outward sign. Instead, he sat down comfortably upon the arm of a chair[184] facing Ribiera's. The only way to meet insolence is with equal insolence and a greater calm.

"Ah!" said Bell pleasantly. "So you found out it didn't work, after all!"

Ribiera's eyes contracted. He became suddenly enraged.

"You are trifling with me," he said furiously. "Do you know the penalty for that?"

"Why, yes," said Bell, and smiled amiably. "A dose of—er—poison of The Master's private brand."

It was a guess, but based on a good deal of evidence. Ribiera turned crimson, then pale.

"What do you know?" he demanded in a deadly quietness. "You cannot leave this place. You are aware of that. The people here—guests and servants—are my slaves, the slaves of The Master. You cannot leave this place except also as my slave. I will have you bound and given *yagué* so that you cannot fail to tell me anything that I wish to know. I will have you tortured so that you will gladly say anything that I wish, in return for death. I will—"

"You will," said Bell dryly, "drop dead with seven bullets in your body if you give a signal for anyone to attack me."

R

ibiera stared at him as his hand rested negligently in his coat pocket. And then, quite suddenly Ribiera began to chuckle. His rage vanished. He laughed, a monstrous, gross, cackling laughter.

"You have been my guest for two days," he gasped, slapping his fat knees, "and you have not noticed that your pistol his been tampered with! Senhor Bell! Senhor Bell! My uncle will be disappointed in you!"

It seemed to impress him as a victory that Bell had been depending upon an utterly futile threat for safety. It restored his good humor marvelously.

"It does not matter," he said jovially. "Presently you will tell me all that I wish to know. More, perhaps. My uncle is pleased with you. You recall your little talk with the wireless operator on the *Almirante Gomez*? You tried to learn things from him, Senhor. He reported it. Of course. All our slaves report. He sent his report to my uncle, The

Master, and I did not have it until to-day. I will admit that you deceived me. I knew you had talked with Ortiz, who was a fool. I thought that in his despair he might have spoken. I gave you *yagué*, as I thought, and informed my uncle that you knew nothing. And he is very much pleased with you. It was clever to deceive me about the *yagué*. My uncle has high praise for you. He has told me that he desires your services."

Bell inhaled again. There was no question but that Ribiera was totally unafraid of the threat he had made. His gun must have been tampered with, the firing-pin filed off perhaps. So Bell said placidly:

"Well? He desires my services?"

R

ibiera chuckled, in his gross and horrible good humor.

"He will have them. Senhor. He will have them. When you observe your hands writhing at the ends of your wrists, you will enter his service, through me. Of course. And he will reward you richly. Money, much money, such as I have. And slaves—such as I have. The Senhora...."

Ribiera looked at the terrified girl standing thirty or forty feet away. He chuckled again.

"My uncle desires that you should be induced to enter his service of your own will. So, Senhor, you shall see first what my uncle's service offers. And later, when you know what pleasures you may some day possess as my uncle's deputy in your own nation, why, then the fact that your hands are writhing at the ends of your wrists will be merely an added inducement to come to me. And I bear you no ill will for deceiving me. You may go."

Bell rose.[185]

"And still," he said dryly, "I suspect that you are deceived. But now you deceive yourself."

He heard Ribiera chuckling as he walked away. He heard him call, amusedly, "Senhora." He heard the little gasp of terror with which the girl obeyed. He passed her, stumbling toward the gross fat man with the light brown skin and curly hair. Her eyes were literally pools of anguish.

B

ell threw away his cigarette and began to fumble for another. He was beginning to feel the first twinges of panic, and fought them down. Ribiera had not lied. Bell had been at this *fazenda* of his—which was almost a miniature Versailles three hundred miles from Rio— for two days. In all that time he had not seen one person besides himself who did not display the most abject terror of Ribiera. Ribiera had made no idle boast when he said that everyone about, guests and servants, were slaves. They were. Slaves of a terror vastly greater than mere fear of death. It—

"Senhor!... *Oh, Dios!*" It was the girl's voice, in despair.

Ribiera laughed. Bell felt a red mist come before his eyes.

He deliberately steadied his hands and lighted his cigarette. He heard stumbling footsteps coming behind him. A hand touched his arm. He turned to see the girl Ribiera had pointed out, her cheeks utterly, chalky white, trying desperately to smile.

"Senhor!" she gasped. "Smile at me! For the love of God, smile at me!"

In the fraction of a second, Bell was mad with rage. He understood, and he hated Ribiera with a corrosive hatred past conception. And then he was deathly calm, and wholly detached, and he smiled widely, and turned and looked at Ribiera, and Ribiera's whole gross bulk quivered as he chuckled. Bell took the girl's arm with an excessive politeness and managed—he never afterward understood how he managed it—to grin at Ribiera.

"Senhora," he said in a low tone, "I think I understand. Stop being afraid. We can fool him. Come and walk with me and talk. The idea is that he must think you are trying to fascinate me, is it not?"

She spoke through stiffened lips.

"Ah, that I could die!"

Bell had a horrible part to play while he walked the length of the formal garden with her, and found a pathway leading out of it, and led her out of sight. He stopped.

"Now," he said sharply, "tell me. I am not yet his slave. He has ordered you...."

She was staring before her with wide eyes that saw only despair.

"I—I am to persuade you to be my lover," she said dully, "or I shall know the full wrath of The Master...."

B

ell asked questions, crisply, but as gently as he could.

"We are his slaves," she told him apathetically. "I and *mi Arturo*—my husband. Both of us...." She roused herself little under Bell's insistent questioning. "We were guests at his house at dinner. Our friends, people high in society and in the Republic, were all about us. We suspected nothing. We had heard nothing. But two weeks later Arturo became irritable. He said that he saw red spots before his eyes. I also. Then Arturo's hands writhed at the ends of his wrists. He could not control them. His nerves were horrible. And mine. And we—we have a tiny baby.... And Senhor Ribiera called upon my husband. He was charming. He observed my husband's hands. He had a remedy, he said. He gave it to my husband. He became normal again. And then—my hands writhed. Senhor Ribiera told my husband that if he would bring me to him.... And I was relieved. We were grateful. We accepted the invitation of the Senhor Ribiera to this place. And he showed us a man, in chains. He—he went mad before our eyes. He was a member of the United[186] States Secret Service.... And then the Senhor Ribiera told us that we faced the same fate if we did not serve him...."

B

ell had thrust aside rage as useless, now. He was deliberately cold.

"And so?"

"It is a poison," she said unsteadily. "A deadly, a horrible poison which drives men murder mad in two weeks from the time of its administration. The Senhor Ribiera has an antidote for it. But mixed with the antidote, which acts at once, is more of the horrible poison, which will act in two weeks more. So that we are entrapped. If we disobey him...."

Bell began to smile slowly, and not at all mirthfully.

"I think," he said softly, "that I shall gain a great deal of pleasure from killing the Senhor Ribiera."

"*Dios*—" She strangled upon the word. "Do you not see, Senhor, that if he dies we—we—" She stopped and choked. "We—have a tiny baby, Senhor. We—we would...."

Again sick rage surged up in Bell. To kill Ribiera meant to drive his slaves mad, and mad in the most horrible fashion that can be imagined. To kill Ribiera meant to have these people duplicate the death of Ortiz, as their greatest hope, or to fill madhouses with snarling animals lusting to kill....

"It is—it is not only I, Senhor," said the girl before him. She was utterly listless, and in the agony of despair. "It is Arturo, also. The Senhor Ribiera has said that if I do not persuade you, that both Arturo and I.... And our little baby, Senhor!... Our families also will be entrapped some day. He has said so.... He will give that poison to our baby.... And it will grow up either his slave, or—"

Her eyes were pools of panic.

"Oh, God!" said Bell very quietly. "And he's offering me this power! He's trying to persuade me to become like him. He's offering me pleasures!"

H

e laughed unpleasantly. And then he went sick with helplessness. He could kill Ribiera, perhaps, and let only God know how many people go mad. Perhaps. Or perhaps Ribiera would merely be supplanted by another man. Ortiz had said that he killed The Master's deputy in Buenos Aires, but that another man had taken his place. And the thing went on. And The Master desired a deputy in the United States....

"Somehow," said Bell very softly, "this has got to be stopped. Somehow. Right away. That devilish stuff! Can you get hold of a bit of the antidote?" he asked abruptly. "The merest drop of it?"

She shook her head.

"No, Senhor. It is given in food, in wine. One never knows that one has had it. It is tasteless, and we have only Senhor Ribiera's word that it has been given."

Bell's hands clenched.

"So devilish clever.... What are we going to do?"

The girl stuffed the corner of her handkerchief into her mouth.

"I am thinking of my little baby," she said, choking. "I must persuade you, Senhor. I—I have been tearful. I—I am not attractive. I will try. If I am not attractive to you...."

B

ell cursed, deeply and savagely. It seemed to be the only possible thing to do. And then he spoke coldly.

"Listen to me, Senhora. Ribiera talked frankly to me just now. He knows that so far I am not subdued. If I escape he cannot blame you. He cannot! And I am going to attempt it. If you will follow me...."

"There is no escape for me," she said dully, "and if he thinks that I knew of your escape and did not tell him...."

"Follow me," said Bell, smiling queerly. "I shall take care that he does not suspect it."

He gazed about for an instant, orienting himself. The plane that had just landed—the last of a dozen or[187] more that had arrived in the past two days—had dipped down on the private landing field to the north.

There was a beautifully kept way running from the landing field to the house, and he went on through the thick shrubbery amid a labyrinth of paths, choosing the turnings most likely to lead him to it.

H

e came out upon it suddenly, and faced toward the field. There were two men coming toward the house, on foot. One was a flying pilot, still in his flying clothes. The other was a tall man, for a Brazilian, with the lucent clarity of complexion that bespeaks uncontaminated white descent. He was white-haired, and his face was queerly tired, as if he were exhausted.

Bell looked sharply. He seemed to see a resemblance to someone he knew in the tall man. He spoke quickly to the girl beside him.

"Who is the man to the left?"

"Senhor Canalejas," said the girl drearily. "He is the Minister of War. I suppose he, too...."

Bell drew a deep breath. He walked on, confidently. As the two others drew near he said apologetically:

"Senhores."

They halted with the instinctive, at least surface, courtesy of the Brazilian. And Bell was fumbling with his handkerchief, rather nervously tying a knot in it. He held it out to Canalejas.

"Observe."

It was, of course, a recognition-knot such as may be given to an outsider by one in the Trade. The tall man's face changed. And Bell swung swiftly and suddenly and very accurately to the point of the other man's jaw.

He collapsed.

---

enhor Canalejas," said Bell politely, "I am about to go and steal an airplane to take what I have learned to my companion for transmission. If you wish to go with me...."

Canalejas stared for the fraction of a second. Then he said quietly:

"But of course."

He turned to retrace his steps. Bell turned to the girl.

"If you are wise," he said gently, "you will go and give the alarm. If you are kind, you will delay it as much as you dare."

She regarded him in agonized doubt for a moment, and nodded. She fled.

"Now," said Bell casually, "I think we had better hasten. And I hope, Senhor Canalejas, that you have a revolver. We will need one. Mine has been ruined."

Without a word, the white-haired man drew out a weapon and offered it to him.

"I had intended," he said very calmly, "to kill the Senhor Ribiera. His last demand is for my daughter."

They went swiftly. The plane Bell had seen alight some fifteen or twenty minutes before was just being approached by languid mechanics. It was, of course, still warm. Canalejas shouted and waved his arm imperiously. It is probable that he gave the impression of a man returning for some forgotten thing, left in the cockpit of the plane.

hat happened then, happened quickly. A few crisp words in a low tone. A minor hubbub began suddenly back at the house. Canalejas climbed into the passenger's seat as if looking for something. And

Bell presented his now useless automatic pleasantly at the head of the nearest staring mechanic, and while he froze in horror, scrambled up into the pilot's cockpit.

"Contact!" he snapped, and turned on the switch. The mechanic remained frozen with fear. "Damnation!" said Bell savagely. "I don't know the Portuguese for 'Turn her over'!"

He fumbled desperately about in the cockpit. Something whirred. The propeller went over.... Canalejas shot with painstaking accuracy, twice. The[188] motor caught with a spluttering roar.

As a horde of running figures, servants and guests, running with the same desperation, came plunging out on the flying field from the shrubbery. Bell gave the motor the gun. The fast little plane's tail came up off the ground as she darted forward. Faster and faster, with many bumpings. The bumpings ceased. She was clear.

And Bell zoomed suddenly to lift her over the racing, fear-ridden creatures who clutched desperately at the wheels, and then the little ship shot ahead, barely cleared the trees to the east of the field, and began to roar at her topmost speed toward Rio.

CHAPTER V

The Trade—which does not exist—has its obligations and its code, but also it has its redeeming features. When a man has finished his job, he has finished it. And as far as the Trade was concerned, Bell had but little more to do. But after that—and his eyes burned smokily in their depths—there was much that he intended to do. He sat in one of the *bondes* of the Botanical Garden half of the street railway system of Rio, and absent mindedly regarded the scenery. This particular *bonde* was headed out toward the Lagoa Rodrigo de Freitas, by which salty mass of water Bell would meet Paula Canalejas. He would receive a package from her, which he would deliver to Jamison. And then he would be free, and it was his private intention to engage in an enterprise which was very probably a form of suicide. But there are some things one cannot dismiss with a sage reflection that they are not one's business. This matter of Ribiera was definitely one of them.

———

The escape from Ribiera's *fazenda* had been relatively easy, because so thoroughly unexpected. The little plane had climbed to five thousand feet and found a stratum of cloud that stretched for very many miles. Bell had emerged from it only twice in the first hour of flight, and the second time the sky was clear all about him. That he was pursued, he had no doubt. That Ribiera had wireless communications with Rio, he knew. And he knew that instant, and imperative orders would have gone out for his capture.

Rio would not be a healthy place for him. If Ribiera had power over high government officials, he had surely indirect power over the police, and a search for Bell would be in order at once. Yet Canalejas assuredly expected to return to Rio.

A shouted question with the motor cut out, and a nodded answer. Bell headed for Petropolis, which is Rio's only real summer resort and is high in the hills and only an hour and a half from it by train. It was surprisingly satisfactory to be handling a swift plane again, and Bell allowed himself what he knew was about the only pleasure he was likely to have for some time to come.

Something of his hatred of Ribiera, however, came back as he prepared to land. He managed to crack the plane up very neatly, so that it would be of no use to Ribiera any more. And at the same time, of course, the cracking-up provided an excellent excuse for Canalejas to continue on by train.

T

hey talked very briefly by the puffing engine.

"It is best," said Canalejas, "for you, Senhor, to remain here overnight. I believe Senhor Ribiera has given orders for us both to be looked for, yet as a Cabinet Minister I am still immune from arrest by the ordinary police. If I reach my home I shall be able to do all that is necessary."

"And you will prepare a message for me to carry," said Bell.

"It is ready," said Canalejas. He smiled faintly. "No, Senhor. I have instructions to give my daughter. She will deliver the information to you to-morrow. Let me see. At the edge[189] of the Lagao Rodrigo de Feitas, at nine o'clock. She is the only messenger I can trust. I think that is all."

Bell hesitated uncomfortably.

"But you, sir," he said awkwardly. "You have been poisoned, as Senor Ortiz was."

"But certainly," said Canalejas. His smile was ironic as before. "But, unlike Senor Ortiz, I have no hope. I have arranged for my daughter to conceal herself and escape from Brazil. I have prepared for everything, Senhor. As you know, I had intended to kill Senhor Ribiera. In returning with you I have merely delayed my own death by a few hours."

Still smiling, and with the air of one entering a train for the most casual of journeys, Canalejas entered the coach.

---

nd Bell, sitting in the *bonde* next morning, saw with an uncanny clarity the one weak point in Ribiera's hold upon his subjects. When they had courage to fear nothing more than death, they could defy him. And not many could attain to that courage. But a few....

"I'll have some help, anyway," muttered Bell savagely to himself.

It is a long ride to the Botanical Gardens, from which one half the surface lines of Rio take their name. On the way out to the Lagao

Rodrigo de Feitas, which, is close by the Garden itself, Bell had time to work over for the thousandth time the information he possessed, and realize its uselessness. Two things, only, might be of service. One was that Ribiera was the nephew of the person referred to as The Master, and yet was evidently as much subjected to him as his own victims to himself. The other was that the ultimate end of all the ghastly scheme was in some fashion political. If wealth alone had been Ribiera's aim, the gathering of his slaves would have had a different aspect. The majority of them would have been rich men, men of business, men who could pay out hundreds of thousands a month in the desperate hope of being permitted to remain sane. There would not have been politicians and officials and officers of the army.

"The key men of the country," growled Bell inaudibly, "enslaved to Ribiera. They give him the power he's after more than cash. And it's those key men who have more to lose than money. There's such a thing as honor...."

Three times the conductor stopped beside him and suggestively rattled the coins in his box. Three times Bell absent mindedly paid the fare for the zone. But the ride is a long one, and he had had time to realize the hopelessness of any single-handed attack upon the thing he faced long before the end.

Then he absently moved through the amazing collection of tropic and near tropic growths that is the Botanical Garden until he came at once to Paula and the Lagoa Rodrico de Freitas.

I

t was alive with birds, and they hopped and pecked and squabbled without acrimony within feet of her seated figure. Bell knew that she had been waiting for a long time. He looked quickly at her face. It was quite pale, but entirely tearless.

"Here is the message, Senhor Bell," she said quietly, "but I think I have been followed."

Bell growled in his throat.

"I did not discover it until I reached this spot," she said evenly. "And I did not know what to do. If I left, I would be seized and the message taken—and I think that someone would have waited here for you. So, in part to gain time, and in part because I hoped you might have some resource, I remained."

"How many of them?" asked Bell shortly.

"Two," she said quietly. She looked at him, her large eyes entirely calm and grave.

"Give me the package," said Bell briefly. "They'll be more anxious to[190] get it back than to bother you. And I'll either knock them cold or hold them in a scrap until you get away."

She reached in her pocket and handed him a small thick envelope. He stuffed it in the side pocket of his coat.

"I will walk away," he observed, "and they'll follow me. Can you arrange to give me some sign that you're safe?"

"By the gateway," she told him. "My handkerchief. I shall start as soon as you have vanished. If I am followed, I will drop this handkerchief, as it is. If I am not followed, I will tie a knot. But what can you do?"

"I'll do something," said Bell coldly. "Something!"

S

he smiled, with the same odd bitterness her father had shown.

"My father—shot himself," she said briefly. "I have no particular hope of doing better. But I shall not be Ribiera's slave."

She remained quite still. Bell moved away. He hurried. There was thick jungle ahead, a section of the Gardens that is painstakingly preserved untouched and undisturbed, that visitors to the capital of Brazil may observe a typical sample of the virgin interior. He dived into that jungle as if in flight.

And very shortly after, two men dived in after him. They hesitated, these men, because your policeman of Rio does not like to injure his uniform, and there are many thorns in jungle growths. But they entered it, having first drawn small glittering weapons. And then from the jungle came silence.

I

t seemed to be silence. But there may have been some small unusual noises. It would not be easy to tell if they were unusual or not, because there are peculiar flashes of charm in certain Brazilian institutions. The preservation of the spot of jungle itself is one. Another is the fact that in the Gardens all manner of wild things live at large and provide unexpected and delightful surprises to the usually foreign visitors.

So there were noises, after a bit. Such noises as some grunting wild thing might have made, perhaps. But they might also have been the gasping of a man as breath was choked out of him.... And there was a cracking sound a little later, which might—of course—have been any one of any number of accidental and perfectly natural causes. And it might have been a man upon whom another man had hurled himself, when the second man landed on his jaw. And thrashing noises a little later might have been anything.

But after what seemed a long time, Bell emerged. Alone. He was breathing quickly, and there were scratches on his face and hands which—well, which might have been made by thorns. He went swiftly back toward the spot where Paula had waited. He looked cautiously. She was gone.

And then Bell went leisurely, in the studious fashion of a person going through the Botanical Gardens because it was the thing to do, toward the gateway and the surface cars. As he neared the gate his eyes roved with apparent casualness all about. He saw a tiny speck of white on the edge of the roadway. It looked as if it had been flung from a car. Bell picked it up. It was Paula's handkerchief, and there was no knot whatever in it. In fact, its lacy edge was torn.

"They've got her," said Bell, apparently unmoved.

H

e waited for a car. A bulky figure wearing thick spectacles came placidly from the Gardens. It waited, also, for the car. The car arrived, in its two sections of first and second class; the first reserved for *cavalhieros*, which is to say persons wearing coat, shirt, collar, necktie, hat, shoes and socks, and carrying no parcel larger than a brief case. Lesser folk who[191] lacked any of the sartorial requirements for admission to the first class section, or wore *tomancos* instead of shoes, heaped themselves into the second section and paid one-third of the fare in the first.

Bell took his seat in the first section. It was comfortably filled. The bulky person with the thick spectacles wedged himself carefully into the space beside Bell. He unfolded a copy of the *Jornal do Commercio* and began to regard the advertisements. Presently he found what he was looking for. "*O Bicho,*" said medium-sized type. Beside it was a picture of a kangaroo. The gentleman with the thick spectacles resignedly fished into his pockets and found a lottery ticket. He tore it into scraps and threw them away. Then he began to gaze disinterestedly at the scenery and the other passengers in the car.

B

ell drummed on his knee. With one's forefinger representing a dot, and one's second finger serving as a dash, it is surprising how naturally and absentmindedly one may convey a perfectly intelligible message to a man sitting within a reasonable distance. When the man is alongside, the matter is absurdly simple.

Presently the man with the thick lenses got out his paper again, as if bored by vistas such as no other city in the world can offer. His paper was in the pocket which pressed against Bell. If in getting out his newspaper he also abstracted a thick fat envelope from Bell's pocket and placed it in his own, and if all this took place under a sign— even in the section reserved for *cavalhieros* of approved raiment—

solemnly warning passengers against "*batadores de carteiras,*" or pickpockets—well, it was an ironical coincidence whose humor Bell did not see.

He was busily tapping out on his knee the briefest possible account of what he had learned at Ribiera's *fazenda* up country.

"*One chance for me,*" he tapped off at the end. "*If I can kidnap Ribiera I can make him talk. Somehow. He has big amphibian plane kept fueled and ready for long trip. I think he is back in Rio to direct hunt for me. Paula kidnapped. My job finished. On my own now.*"

The man with thick spectacles did not nod. He seemed to be looking idly at his paper, but it was folded at an article very discreetly phrased, beneath a photograph of Senhor Teixeira Canalejas, Minister of War, who had very unfortunately been found dead that morning. He had been depressed, of late, but there were certain circumstances which made it as yet impossible to determine whether he had killed himself or was the victim of an assassin.

"*Getting set for me,*" tapped Bell grimly on his knee. "*Ribiera told me too much.*"

T he man with thick spectacles yawned and turned the paper over. Under a smaller headline—which would only find a place on a Brazilian sheet—"A Regrettable Incident"—an item of more direct importance was printed. It told of an unnamed Senhor from the United States of the North America, who as the guest of a widely known Brazilian gentleman had behaved most boorishly, had stolen an airplane from his host and broken it to bits on landing unskilfully, and had vanished with priceless heirlooms belonging to his host. It read, virtuously:

No names are mentioned because the American Senhor has been widely introduced in Rio society as a person with an official status in Washington. It is understood that an inquiry is to be made of the Ambassador as to the status of the young man, before any action is taken by the police. It is to be expected, however, that he will at least be requested to leave the country.

[192]

Bell managed the barest flicker of a smile. Arrest, of course. Detention, most courteously arranged, while the Ambassador was communicated with. And Ribiera.

"*Give me dismiss,*" he tapped on his knee.

The gentleman in the thick spectacles ran his finger thoughtfully about the edge of his collar. In the Trade that is a signal of many varied meanings. A hand across the throat in any fashion means, "Clear out, your job is finished," "Save your skin as best you can," and "Get away without trying to help me," according to circumstances. In this case it relieved Bell of all future responsibility.

He yawned, tapping his lips with the back of his hand, signaled for a stop of the car, and got out. Five minutes later he had signaled a taxicab and given Ribiera's address. In six minutes he was being whirled toward the one house in all Rio de Janeiro from which his chance of a safe departure was slightest. In little more than half an hour he had dismissed the cab and was gazing placidly into the startled eyes of the doorman. The doorman, like all of Rio where Ribiera was known and feared, knew that Bell was being hunted.

Bell handed over his card with an inscrutable air.

"The Senhor Ribiera," he said drily, "returned to the city last night. Present my card and say that I would like to speak to him."

T

he doorman ushered him inside and summoned the major-domo, still blinking his amazement. And the major-domo blinked again. But Bell followed with the air of an habitué, as he was again ushered into the luxurious salon in which he had once been offered a drugged drink.

Again he sank down in a softly padded chair and surveyed the pictures and the minor objects of decadent art about him. Again he lighted a cigarette with every appearance of ease, and again had the impression of eyes upon him. The major-domo appeared, somewhat agitated.

"The Senhor Ribiera," he said harshly, "will see you only if you are not armed. He requires your word of honor."

Bell smiled lazily.

"I'll do better than that," he said languidly. "I haven't had time to buy a revolver. But the automatic he had put out of commission is in my pocket. Present it to him with my compliments."

He handed over the weapon, butt first. The major-domo blinked, and took it. Bell sat down and smiled widely. He had been expected to be uproarious, to attempt to force the major-domo to lead him to Ribiera. And, of course, he would have been led past a perfectly planned ambush for his capture—but he might have killed the major-domo. Which would not disturb Ribiera, but had disturbed the servant.

B

ell smoked comfortably. And suddenly hangings parted, and Ribiera came into the room. He smiled nervously, and then, as Bell blew a puff of smoke at him and nodded casually, he scowled.

"I came," said Bell deliberately, "to make a bargain. Frankly, I do not like to break my word. I was under obligations to deliver a package from Senhor Canalejas to a certain messenger who will take it to my government. I have done it. But I am not, Senhor Ribiera, a member of the Secret Service. I am entirely a free agent now, and I am prepared to consider your proposals, which I could not in honor do before."

He smiled pleasantly. Effrontery, properly managed, is one of the most valuable of all qualities. Especially in dealing with people who themselves are arrogant when they dare.

R

ibiera purpled with rage, and then controlled it.

"Ah!" he rumbled. "You are prepared to consider my proposals. There[193] are no proposals. The Master may be amused at your cleverness in escaping. I do not know. I do know that I am ordered to make you my slave and send you to The Master. That, I shall do."

"Perhaps," said Bell blandly: "but I can go without food and drink for several days, which will delay the process. And while I cannot honorably tell you how to stop the man bearing Senhor Canalejas' package to my government, still ... If I willingly accepted a dose of *yagué* in token of my loyalty to The Master...."

Ribiera's good humor returned. He chuckled.

"You actually mean," he said jovially, "that you think you were given some of The Master's little compound, and that you wish to make terms before your hands begin to writhe at the ends of your wrists. Is not that your reason?"

Bell's eyes flickered. He had been horribly afraid of just that. But Ribiera's amusement was reassuring.

"Perhaps," said Bell. "Perhaps I am."

R

ibiera sat down and stretched his fat legs in front of him. He surveyed Bell with an obscene, horrible amusement.

"Ah, Senhor," he chuckled, "some day we will laugh together over this! You yet hope, and do not yet know how much better it will be for you if you cease to hope, and cultivate desires! The Master is pleased with you. You have just those qualities he knows are necessary in dealing with your nation. He is not angry with you. It is his intention to use you to extend his—ah—influence among the officials of your nation. You know, of course, that in but a little more time I will hold all Brazil—as I now hold this city—in the hollow of my hand. Four of the republics of this continent are already completely under the control of The Master's deputies, and of the rest, Brazil is not the most nearly subdued. A year or two, and The Master will become Emperor, and his deputies viceroys. And it is his whim to give you the opportunity of becoming the first deputy and the first viceroy of North America. And you come to me and offer—you, Senhor!—to make terms! I believe even The Master will laugh when he hears of it."

"But," said Bell practically, "do you accept my terms?"

Ribiera chuckled again.

"What are they, Senhor?"

"That you release the daughter of the Senhor Canalejas and pledge your word of honor that she will not be enslaved."

R

ibiera's word of honor, of course, would be worth rather less than the breath that was used to give it. But his reception of the proposal would be informative.

He chuckled again.

"No, Senhor. I do not accept. But I will promise you as a favor, because my uncle The Master admires you, that within a few weeks you shall enjoy her charms. I do not," he added with amused candor, "find that any one woman diverts me for a very long time."

"Oh," said Bell, very quietly.

He sat still for an instant, and then shrugged, and looked about as if for an ash tray in which to knock the ashes from his cigarette. He stood up, carrying the tube of tobacco gingerly, and moved toward one by Ribiera's elbow. He knocked off the ash, and crushed out the tiny coal. He fumbled in his pockets.

The next instant Ribiera choked with terror.

"Let me explain," said Bell softly. "I did not give your major-domo my word that I was unarmed. I merely gave him a weapon. I got these from two policemen who tried to arrest me an hour or so ago. And I also remind you, Senhor, that if the armed men you have posted to prevent my escape try to shoot me, that the inevitable contraction of my muscles will send[194] two bullets into your heart—even if I am dead. I am a dead man, Senhor, if you give the word, but so are you if you give it."

Ribiera gasped. His eyes rolled in his head.

"Send for her," said Bell very gently. "Send for her, Senhor. I estimate that she has been in this house for less than half an hour. Have her brought here at once, and if she has been harmed the three of us will perish very promptly, and half of Rio will go mad after our death."

And the muzzles of two revolvers bored into the fat flesh of Ribiera's body, and a gasp that was almost a wail of terror came from the watchers—armed watchers—who dared not kill the man they had been posted to guard Ribiera against.

Ribiera lifted his hand and croaked an order.

(To be continued.)

In The Next Issue

THE MOON MASTER
A Thrilling Novelet of Adventure on the Moon
By Charles W. Diffin

MURDER MADNESS
*The Second Instalment of the Gripping Story
of the Diabolical Genius Who Is Enslaving
All South America*
By Murray Leinster

THE CAVERN WORLD
An Amazing Sub-Earth Story
By James P. Olsen

BRIGANDS OF THE MOON
*The Exciting Conclusion of Our Splendid
Continued Story*
By Ray Cummings

—And Others!

Light-rays and silent flashes seemed to envelop us.

Brigands of the Moon

(The Book of Gregg Haljan)

PART THREE OF A FOUR-PART NOVEL

By Ray Cummings

WHAT HAS GONE BEFORE

O

ne day in 2075 the Interplanetary Space-Ship *Planetara* left the Earth for Mars. I, Gregg Haljan, was third officer.

> Gregg and Anita risk quick, sure death in a desperate bluff on the ruthless Martian brigands.

It was destined to be a tragic voyage. For in our midst were unscrupulous brigands, masquerading as harmless passengers, intent on seizing the secret treasure of radium ore Johnny Grantline of the Grantline Expedition had dug from the Moon. The *Planetara* was to stop on the Moon and pick the treasure up on her return trip from Mars.

Miko, a giant Martian, and his sister, Moa, were the ringleaders. With them were, as passengers, Sir Arthur Coniston and Ob Hahn, a Venus mystic. The whole crew was in their pay.

Miko struck. The captain was killed, as were the officers. Only Snap Dean, the radio-helio operator, Venza, a girl of Venus, and I were left. And, of course, Anita Prince, who had captivated my heart upon my first glimpse of her.

The brigands abandoned the other passengers on a small asteroid, and Miko signaled his space-ship far off on Mars to meet him on the Moon. I was forced to guide the *Planetara* to the Moon. We sighted the huts of the[196] Grantline Expedition, and suddenly, just as we started to descend, the controls, snapped, and the *Planetara* tumbled like a spent rocket! Desperately I tried to check her, but only partially succeeded. We crashed horribly against the barren gray rock of the Moon. Anita, Venza, Snap and I lived through it, but we could not find the bodies of Miko and Moa in the wreckage. Evidently they were still alive, somewhere.

We reached Johnny Grantline. The *Planetara* was a complete wreck. And, speeding to us from Mars, was Miko's brigand ship.

We were powerless—without means of leaving the Moon—and completely at the mercy of Miko's fast approaching brigands!

CHAPTER XXIII

The Prowling Watchman

"Try it again," Snap urged. "Good God, Johnny, we've got to raise some Earth station! Chance it! Use your power—run it up to the full. Chance it!"

We were gathered in Grantline's instrument room. The duty-man, with blanched grim face, sat at his senders. The Grantline crew shoved close around us, tense and silent.

Above everything we must make some Earth station aware of our plight. Conditions were against us. There were very few observers, in the high-powered Earth stations who knew that an exploring party was on the Moon. Perhaps none of them. The Government officials who had sanctioned the expedition—and Halsey and his confrères in the Detective Bureau—were not anticipating trouble now. The *Planetara* was supposed to be well on her course to Ferrok-Shahn. It was when she was due to return that Halsey would be alert.

And it seemed, too, that nature was against us. The bulging half-Earth[1] hung poised near the zenith over our little crater. Its rotation through the hours was clearly visible. We timed our signals when the western hemisphere was facing us. But nature was against us. No clouds, no faintest hint of mist could fog the airless Lunar surface. But there were continuous clouds over the Americas.

[1] Between the half and the full illumined disc, the complete Earth now was some ten days old.

"Try it again," Snap urged.

T

hese bulging walls! Grantline used his power far beyond the limits of safety. He cut down his lights; the telescope intensifiers were permanently disconnected; the ventilators were momentarily stilled, so that the air here in the little room crowded with men rapidly grew fetid. All to save power pressure, that the vital Erentz system might survive.

Even so it was strained to the danger point. The walls seemed to bulge outward with the pressure of the room, the aluminite braces straining and creaking. And our heat was radiating away; the deadly chill of space crept in.

"Again!" ordered Grantline.

The duty-man flung on the power in rhythmic pulses. In the silence the tubes hissed. The light sprang through the banks of rotating prisms, intensified up the scale until, with a vague, almost invisible beam, it left the last swaying mirror and leaped through our overhead dome into space.

"Commander!" The duty-man's voice carried an appeal. These bulging walls! If they cracked, or even sprung a serious leak, the camp would be uninhabitable....

"Enough," said Grantline. "Switch it off. We'll let it go at that for now."

It seemed that every man in the room had been holding his breath in the darkness. The lights came on again: the Erentz motors accelerated to normal. The strain on the walls eased up, and the room began warming.

Had the Earth caught our signal? We did not want to waste the power to find out. Our receivers were dis[197]connected. If an answering signal came, we could not know it. One of the men said:

"Let's assume they saw us." He laughed, but it was a high-pitched, tense laugh. "We don't dare even use the telescope. Our rescue ship will be right overhead, visible to the naked eye before we see it. Three days more—that's what I'll give it."

B

ut the three days passed, and no rescue ship came. The Earth was almost at the full. We tried signaling again. Perhaps it got through— we did not know. But our power was weaker now. The wall of one of the rooms sprang a leak, and the men were hours repairing it. I did not say so, but never once did I feel that our signals were seen on Earth. Those cursed clouds! The Earth almost everywhere seemed to have poor visibility.

Four of our eight days of grace were all too soon passed. The brigand ship must be half-way here by now.

They were busy days for us. If we could have captured Miko and his band, our danger would have been less imminent. With the treasure insulated so that its Gamma rays could not betray us, and our camp in darkness, the arriving brigand ship might never find us. But Miko knew our location: he would signal his oncoming ship when it was close and lead it to us.

Three times during those days—and the days which followed them—Grantline sent out searching parties. But it was unavailing.

Miko, Moa and Coniston, with their five underlings, could not be found. We searched all the territory from the camp to the *Planetara*, and off to the foot-crags of Archimedes, and a score of miles into the flatness of the Mare Imbrium. There was no sign of the brigands. Yet we knew they could be near here—it was so easy to hide amid the tumbled crags, the ravines, the gullies, the numberless craters and pit-holes: or underground in the vast honeycombed subterranean recesses.

e had at first hoped that the brigands might have perished. But that was soon dispelled! I went—about the third day—with the party that was sent to the *Planetara*. We wanted to salvage such of its equipment, its unbroken power units, as might be available. And Snap and I had worked out an idea which we thought might be of service. We needed some of the *Planetara's* smaller gravity-plate sections. Those in Grantline's wrecked little *Comet* had stood so long that their radiations had gone dead. But the *Planetara's* were still efficacious.

We secured the fragments of Newtonia.[2] But our hope that Miko might have perished was dashed. He too had returned to the *Planetara*! The evidence was clear before us. The vessel was stripped of all its power units save those which were dead and useless. The last of the food and water stores was taken. The weapons in the chart-room—the Benson curve-lights, bullet projectors, and heat-rays—had vanished.

[2] An allusion to the element Newtonia, named in memory of the great founder of celestial mechanics, Sir Isaac Newton. Artificially electronized,

this metal element may be charged either positively or negatively, thus to attract or repel other masses of matter. The gravity plates of all space-ships were built of it.

Other days passed. The Earth reached the full, and began waning. The twenty-eight day Lunar night was in its last half. No rescue ship came from Earth. We had ceased our efforts to signal, for we needed all our power to maintain ourselves. The camp would be in a state of siege. That was the best we could hope for. We had a few short-range weapons, such as Bensons, heat-rays and rifles. A few hundred feet of effective range was the most any of them could obtain. The heat-rays—in giant form one of the most deadly weapons on Earth—were only slowly efficacious on the airless Moon. Striking an intensely cold surface, their warming radiations, without [198]atmosphere to aid them, were slow to act. Even in a blasting heat-beam a man in his Erentz helmet-suit could withstand the ray for several minutes.

---

e were, however, well equipped with explosives. Grantline had brought a large supply for his mining operations, and much of it was still unused. We had, also, an ample stock of oxygen fuses, and a variety of oxygen light flares in small fragile glass-globes.

It was to use these explosives against the brigands that Snap and I were working out our scheme with the gravity-plates. The brigand ship would come with giant projectors and with some thirty men. If we could hold out against them for a time, the fact that the *Planetara* was missing would bring us help from Earth.

"A month," said Grantline. "A month at the most. If we can hold them off that long—even in a week or two help may come."

Another day. A tenseness fell on us all, despite the absorption of our feverish activities. To conserve the power, the camp was almost dark, we lived in dim, chill rooms, with just a few weak spots of light outside to mark the watchmen on their rounds. We did not use the telescope,[3] but there was scarcely an hour when one or the other of the men was not sitting on a cross-piece up in the dome of the little instrument room, casting tense searching gaze into the black, starry firmament. A ship might appear at any time now—a rescue ship from Earth, or the brigands from Mars.

A

nita and Venza during these days could aid us very little save by their cheering words. They moved about the rooms, trying to inspire us; so that all the men, when they might have been humanly sullen and cursing their fate, were turned to grim activity, or grim laughter, making a joke of this coming siege. The morale of the camp now was perfect. An improvement indeed over the inactivity of the former peaceful weeks!

[3] An old-fashioned telescope, of limited field and needing no electronic power, would have been immensely serviceable to Grantline, but his was of the more modern type.

Grantline mentioned it to me. "We'll put up a good fight, Haljan. These fellows from Mars will know they've had a task before they ever sail off with this treasure."

I had many moments alone with Anita. I need not mention them. It seemed that our love was crossed by the stars, with an adverse fate dooming it. And Snap and Venza must have felt the same. Among the men we were always quietly, grimly active. But alone.... I came upon Snap once with his arms around the little Venus girl. I heard him say:

"Accursed luck! That you and I should find each other too late, Venza. We could have a mighty lot of fun in Great-New York together."

"Snap, we will!"

As I turned away, I murmured: "And, pray God, so will Anita and I."

The girls slept together in a small room of the main building. Often during the time of sleep, when the camp was stilled except for the night watch, Snap and I would sit in the corridor near the girls' door-grid, talking of that time when we would all be back on our blessed Earth.

ur eight days of grace were passed. The brigand ship was due—now, to-morrow, or the next day.

I recall, that night, my sleep was fitfully uneasy. Snap and I had a cubby together. We talked, and made futile plans. I went to sleep, but awakened after a few hours. Impending disaster lay heavily on me. But there was nothing abnormal nor unusual in that!

Snap was asleep. I was restless, but I did not have the heart to awaken him. He needed what little repose he could get. I dressed, left our cubby and wandered out into the corridor of the main building.[199]

It was cold in the corridor, and gloomy with the weak blue light. An interior watchman passed me.

"All as usual, Haljan."

"Nothing in sight?"

"No. They're looking."

I went through the connecting corridor to the adjacent building. In the instrument-room several of the men were gathered, scanning the vault overhead.

"Nothing, Haljan."

I stayed with them awhile, then wandered away. The outside man met me near the admission lock-chambers of the main building. The duty-man here sat at his controls, raising the air-pressure in the locks through which the outside watchman was coming. The relief sat here in his bloated suit, with his helmet on his knees. It was Wilks.

"Nothing yet, Haljan. I'm going up to the peak of the crater to see if anything is in sight. I wish that damnable brigand ship would come and get it over with."

Instinctively we all spoke in half whispers, the tenseness bearing in on us.

The outside man came out of his helmet. He was white and grim, but he grinned at Wilks.

"All is usual." He tried the familiar jest at Wilks, but his voice was flat: "Don't let the Earthlight get you!"

Wilks went out through the portes—a process of no more than a minute. I wandered away again through the corridors.

I

suppose it was half an hour later that I chanced to be gazing through a corridor window. The lights along the rocky cliff-edge were tiny blue spots. The head of the stairway leading down to the abyss of the crater floor was visible. The bloated figure of Wilks was just coming up. I watched him for a moment making his rounds. He did not stop to inspect the lights. That was routine; I thought it queer that he passed them.

Another minute passed. The figure of Wilks went with slow bounds over toward the back of the ledge where the glassite shelter housed the treasure. It was all dark off there. Wilks went into the gloom, but before I lost sight of him he came back. As though he had changed his mind he headed for the foot of the staircase which led up the cliff-face to where, at the peak of the little crater, five hundred feet above us, the narrow observatory platform was perched. He climbed with easy bounds, the light on his helmet bobbing in the gloom.

I stood watching. I could not tell why there seemed to be something queer about Wilks' actions. But I was struck with it, nevertheless. I watched him disappear over the peak of the summit.

Another minute went by. Wilks did not reappear. I thought I could make out his light on the platform up there. Then abruptly a tiny white beam was waving from the observatory platform! It flashed once or twice, then was extinguished. And now I saw Wilks plainly, standing in the Earthlight, gazing down.

Queer actions! Had the Earthlight touched him? Or was that a local signal-call which he had sent out? Why should Wilks be signalling? What was he doing with a hand-helio? Our watchmen, I knew, had no reason to carry one.

And to whom could Wilks be signalling across this Lunar desolation? The answer stabbed at me: to Miko's band!

I waited another moment. No further light. Wilks was still up there!

I

went back to the lock entrance. Spare suits and helmets were here beside the keeper. He gazed at me inquiringly.

"I'm going out, Franck, just for a minute." It struck me that perhaps I was a meddlesome fool. Wilks, of all Grantline's men, was, I knew, most in his commander's trust. The signal could have been some part of this[200] night's ordinary routine, for all I knew.

I was hastily donning an Erentz suit. I added, "Let me out. I just got the idea Wilks is acting queerly." I laughed. "Maybe the Earthlight has touched him."

With my helmet on I went through the locks. Once outside, with the outer panel closed behind me, I dropped the weights from my belt and shoes and extinguished my helmet-light.

Wilks was still up there. Apparently he had not moved. I bounded off across the ledge to the foot of the ascending stairs. Did Wilks see me coming? I could not tell. As I approached the stairs the platform was cut off from my line of vision.

I mounted with bounding leaps. In my flexible gloved hand I carried my only weapon, a small bullet projector with oxygen firing caps for use in this outside near-vacuum. The leaden bullet with its slight mass would nevertheless pierce a man at the distance of twenty feet.

I held the weapon behind me. I would talk to Wilks first.

I went slowly up the last hundred feet. Was Wilks still up there? The summit was bathed in Earthlight. The little metal observatory platform came into view above my head.

Wilks was not there. Then I saw him standing on the rocks nearby, motionless. But in a moment he saw me coming.

I waved my left arm with a gesture of greeting. It seemed to me that he started, made as though to leap away, then changed his mind and waited for me.

I sailed from the head of the staircase with a twenty-foot leap and landed lightly beside him. I gripped his arm for audiphone contact.

"Wilks!"

Through the visors his face was visible. I saw him, and he saw me. And I heard his voice.

"You, Haljan! How nice!"

It was not Wilks, but the brigand Coniston!

CHAPTER XXIV

Imprisoned!

T he duty-man at the exit locks of the main building stood at his window and watched me curiously. He saw me go up the spider-stairs. He could see the figure he thought was Wilks, standing at the top. He saw me join Wilks, saw us locked together in combat.

For an instant the duty-man stood amazed. There were two fantastic, misshapen figures swaying in the Earthlight five hundred feet above the camp, fighting desperately at the very brink. They were small, dwarfed by distance, alternately dim and bright as they swayed in and out of the shadows. Soon the duty-man could not tell one from the other. Haljan and Wilks—fighting to the death!

The duty-man recovered himself and sprang into action. An interior siren-call was on the instrument panel near him. He rang it, alarming the camp.

The men came rushing to him, Grantline among them.

"What's this? Good God, Franck!"

They saw the silent, deadly combat up there on the cliff. The two figures had fallen together from the observatory platform, dropped twenty feet to a lower landing on the stairs. They lay as though stunned for a moment, then fought on.

Grantline stood stricken with amazement. "That's Wilks!"

"And Haljan," the duty-man gasped. "Went out—something wrong with Wilks—acting strangely—"

The interior of the camp was in a turmoil. The men awakened from sleep, ran out into the corridors, shouted questions.

"An attack?"

"Is it an attack?"

"The brigands?"

B

ut it was Wilks and Haljan in a fight out there on the cliff. The men crowded at the bulls'-eye windows.

And over all the confusion the alarm[201] siren, with no one thinking to shut it off, was screaming with its electrical voice.

Grantline, stricken for that moment of inactivity, stood gazing. One of the figures broke away from the other, bounded up to the summit from the stair-platform to which they had fallen. The other followed. They locked together, swaying at the brink. For an instant it seemed to Grantline that they would go over; then they surged back, momentarily out of sight.

Grantline found his wits. "Stop them! I'll go out to stop them! What fools!"

He was hastily donning one of the Erentz suits which stood at the lock entrance. "Shut off that siren, Franck!"

Within a minute Grantline was ready. The duty-man called from the window:

"Still at it! By the infernal, such fools! They'll kill themselves!"

The figures had swayed back into view, then out of sight again.

"Franck, let me out."

Grantline was ready. He stood, helmet in hand.

"I'll go with you, Commander."

But the volunteer was not equipped. Grantline would not wait.

"I'm going at once. Hurry, Franck."

The duty-man turned to his panel. The volunteer shoved a weapon at Grantline. "Here, take this."

Grantline jammed on his helmet.

e moved the few steps into the small air-chamber which was the first of the three pressure locks. Its interior door-panel swung open for him. But the door did not close after him!

Cursing the duty-man's slowness, he waited a few seconds. Then he turned to the corridor. The duty-man came running.

Grantline took off his helmet. "What in hell—"

"Broken! Dead!"

"What!"

"Smashed from outside," gasped the duty-man. "Look there—my tubes—"

The control-tubes of the portes had flashed into a close-circuit and burned out. The admission portes would not open!

"And the pressure controls smashed! Broken from outside—!"

There was no way now of getting out through these pressure-locks. The doors, the entire pressure-lock system, was dead. Had it been tampered with from outside?

As though to answer Grantline's amazed question there came a chorus of shouts from the men at the corridor windows.

"Commander! By God—look!"

A figure was outside, close to the building! Clothed in suit and helmet, it stood, bloated and gigantic. It had evidently been lurking at the porte-entrance, had ripped out the wires there.

It moved past the windows, saw the staring faces of the men, and made off with giant bounds. Grantline reached the window in time to see it vanish around the building corner.

It was a giant figure, larger than a normal Earthman. A Martian?

---

p on the summit of the crater the two small figures were still fighting. All this turmoil had taken no more than a minute or two.

A lurking Martian outside? The brigand, Miko? More than ever, Grantline was determined to get out. He shouted to his men to don some of the other suits, and called for some of the hand bullet projectors.

But he could not get out through these main admission portes. He could have forced the panels open perhaps; but with the pressure-changing mechanisms broken, it would merely let the air out of the corridor. A rush of air, probably uncontrollable. How serious the damage was no one could tell as yet. It would perhaps take hours to repair it.

Grantline was shouting. "Get those weapons! That's a Martian outside![202] The brigand leader, probably! Get into your suits, anyone who wants to go with me! We'll go by the manual emergency exit!"

But the prowling Martian had found it! Within a minute Grantline was there. It was a smaller, two-lock gateway of manual control, so that the person going out could operate it himself. It was in a corridor at the other end of the main building. But Grantline was too late! The lever would not open the panels!

Had someone gone out this way and broken the mechanisms after him? A traitor in the camp? Or had someone come in from outside? Or had the skulking Martian outside broken this lock as he had broken the other?

The questions surged on Grantline. His men crowded around him. The news spread. The camp was a prison. No one could get out.

And outside, the skulking Martian had disappeared. But Wilks and Haljan were still fighting. Grantline could see the two figures up on the observatory platform. They bounded apart, then together again. Crazily swaying—bouncing—striking the rail.

T

hey went together in a great leap off the platform onto the rocks, and rolled in a bright patch of Earthlight. First one on top, then the other, they rolled, unheeding, to the brink. Here, beyond the midway ledge which held the camp, it was a sheer drop of a thousand feet, on down to the crater-floor.

The figures were rolling: then one shook himself loose, rose up, seized the other and, with a desperate lunge, shoved him—

The victorious figure drew back to safety. The other fell, hurtling down into the shadows past the camp-level—down out of sight in the darkness of the crater-floor.

Snap, who was in the group near Grantline at the windows, gasped.

"God! Was that Gregg Haljan who fell?"

No one could say. No one answered. Outside, on the camp-ledge, another helmeted figure now became visible. It was not far from the main building when Grantline first noticed it. It was running fast, bounding toward the spider-staircase. It began mounting.

And now still another figure became visible—the giant Martian again. He appeared from around the corner of the main Grantline building. He evidently saw the winner of the combat on the cliff, who now was standing in the Earthlight, gazing down. And he saw, too, no doubt, the second figure mounting the stairs. He stood quite near the window through which Grantline and his men were gazing, with his back to the building, looking up to the summit. Then he ran with tremendous leaps toward the ascending staircase.

Was it Haljan standing up there on the summit? Who was it climbing the staircase? And was the third figure Miko?

Grantline's mind framed the questions. But his attention was torn from them, and torn even from the swift silent drama outside. The corridor was ringing with shouts.

"We're imprisoned! Can't get out! Was Haljan killed? The brigands are outside!"

And then an interior audiphone blared a call for Grantline. Someone in the instrument room of the adjoining building was talking:

"Commander, I tried the telescope to see who got killed—"

But he did not say who got killed, for he had greater news.

"Commander! The brigand ship!"

Miko's reinforcements from Mars had come.

CHAPTER XXV

The Combat on the Crater-top

N

ot Wilks, but Coniston! His drawling, British voice:

"You, Gregg Haljan! How nice!"

His voice broke off as he jerked his arm from me. My hand with the bullet-[203]protector came up, but with a sweeping blow he struck my wrist. The weapon dropped to the rocks.

I fought instinctively, those first moments; my mind was whirling with the shock of surprise. This was not Wilks, but the brigand Coniston.

His blow wrenched him around. Awkward, fighting in the air-puffed suits, with only a body-weight of some thirty pounds! Coniston stumbled over the rocks. I had still scarce recovered my wits, but I avoided his outflung arms, and, stooping, tried to recover my revolver. It lay nearby. But Coniston followed my scrambling steps and fell upon me. My foot struck the weapon; it slid away and fell down a crag into a six-foot pit.

We locked together, and when I rose erect he had me around the middle. His voice jangled with broken syllables in my receiver.

"Do for you now, Haljan—"

It was an eery combat. We swayed, shoving, kicking, wrestling. His hold around my middle shut off the Erentz circulation; the warning buzz rang in my ears to mingle with the rasp of his curses. I flung him off, and my tiny Erentz motors recovered. He staggered away, but in a great leap came at me again.

I was taller, heavier and far stronger than Coniston. But I found him crafty, and where I was awkward in handling my lightness, he seemed more skilfully agile.

I became aware that we were on the twenty-foot square grid of the observatory platform. It had a low metal railing. We surged against it. I caught a dizzying glimpse of the abyss. Then it receded as we bounced the other way. And then we fell to the grid. His helmet bashed against mine, striking as though butting with the side of his head to puncture my visor-panel. His gloved fingers were trying to rip at the fabric around my throat.

As we regained our feet, I flung him off, and bounded, like a diver, head-first into him. He went backward, but skilfully kept his feet, gripped me again and shoved me.

I was tottering at the head of the staircase—falling. But I clutched at him.

We fell some twenty or thirty feet to the next lower spider landing. The impact must have dazed us both. I recall my vague idea that we had fallen down the cliff—my Erentz motors smashed—my air shut off. Then the air came again. The roaring in my ears was stilled; my head cleared, and I found that we were on the landing—fighting.

He presently broke away from me, bounded to the summit, with me after him. In the close confines of the suit I was bathed in sweat, and gasping. I had had no thought to increase the oxygen content of my air. But I sorely needed more oxygen for my laboring, pounding heart and my panting breath. I fumbled for the oxygen control-lever. I could not find it; or it would not operate.

I realized I was fighting sluggishly, almost aimlessly. But so was Coniston!

I

t seemed dreamlike. A phantasmagoria of blows and staggering steps. A nightmare with only the horrible vision of this goggled helmet always before my eyes.

It seemed that we were rolling on the ground, back on the summit. The unshadowed Earthlight was clear and bright. The abyss was beside me. Coniston, rolling, was now on top, now under me, trying to shove me over the brink. It was all like a dream—as though I were asleep, dreaming that I did not have enough air.

I strove to keep my senses. He was struggling to roll me over the brink. Ah, that would not do! But I was so tired. One cannot fight without oxygen!

I suddenly knew that I had shaken him off and gained my feet. He rose up, swaying. He was as tired, confused, half-asphyxiated as I.[204]

The brink of the abyss was behind us. I lunged, desperately shoving, avoiding his clutch.

He went over, and fell soundlessly, his body whirling end over end down into the shadows, far down.

I drew back. My senses faded as I sank panting to the rocks. But with inactivity, my thumping heart quieted. My respirations slowed. The Erentz circulation gained on my poisoned air. It purified.

That blessed oxygen! My head cleared again. Strength came to me. I felt better.

Coniston had fallen to his death. I was victor. I went to the brink, cautiously, for I was still dizzy. I could see, far down there on the crater-floor, a little patch of Earthlight in which a mashed human figure was lying.

I

staggered back again. A moment or two must have passed while I stood there on the summit, with my senses clearing and my strength renewed as the blood-stream cleared in my veins.

I was victor. Coniston was dead. I saw now, down on the lower staircase below the camp-ledge, another goggled figure lying huddled. That was Wilks, no doubt. Coniston had doubtless caught him there, surprised him, killed him.

My attention, as I stood gazing, went down to the camp-buildings. Another figure was outside! It bounded along the ledge, reached the foot of the ascending staircase at the top of which I was standing. With agile leaps, it came mounting at me!

Another brigand! Miko? No, it was not large enough to be Miko, not nearly large enough. I was still confused. I thought of Hahn. But that was absurd. Hahn was in the wreck of the *Planetara*. One of the stewards then....

The figure came up the staircase recklessly, to assail me. I took a step backward, bracing myself to receive this new antagonist.

And then I saw Miko! Unquestionably he: for there was no mistaking his giant figure. He was down on the camp-ledge, running toward the foot of the staircase, coming up to help this other man in advance of him.

I thought of my revolver. I turned to try and find it. I was aware that the first of my assailants was at the stairhead. I could not locate at once where the revolver had fallen. I would be caught, leaped upon from behind. Should I run?

I swung back to see what the oncoming brigand was doing. He had reached the summit. His arms went up, legs bent under him. With a sailing leap he launched for me. I could have bounded way, but with a last look to locate the revolver, I braced myself for the shock.

The figure hit me. It was small and light in my clutching arms. I recall I saw that Miko was half-way up the staircase. I gripped my assailant. The audiphone contact brought a voice.

"Gregg! Is it you?"

It was Anita clutching at me!

CHAPTER XXVI

At Bay

"Gregg, you're safe!"

She had heard the camp corridors resounding with the shouts that Wilks and Haljan were fighting. She had come upon a suit and helmet by the manual emergency lock, had run out through the lock, confused, with her only idea to stop Wilks and me from fighting. Then she had seen one of us killed. Impulsive, barely knowing what she was doing, she mounted the stairs, frantic to find if I were alive.

"Anita!"

Miko was coming! She had not seen him: for she had no thought of brigands—only the belief that either Wilks or I had been killed.

But now, as for an instant we stood together on the rocks near the observation platform, I could see the towering figure of Miko nearing the top of the stairs.[205]

"Anita, that's Miko! We must run."

Then I saw my bullet projector. It lay in a bowl-like depression quite near us. I jumped for it. And as I tore loose from Anita, she leaped down after me. It was a broken bowl in the rocks, some six feet deep. It was open on the side facing the staircase—a narrow, ravinelike gully, full of gray, broken, tumbled rock-masses. The little gully was littered with crags and boulders. But I could see out through it.

Miko had come to the head of the staircase. He stopped there, his great figure etched sharply by the Earthlight. I think he must have known that Coniston was the one who had fallen over the cliff, as my helmet and Coniston's were different enough for him to recognize which was which. He did not know who I was, but he did know me for an enemy.

H

e stood now at the summit, peering to see where we had gone. He was no more than fifty feet from us.

"Anita, lie down."

I pulled her down on the rocks. I took aim with the bullet projector. But I had forgotten our helmet-lights. Miko must have seen them just as I pulled the trigger. The flying bullet missed him as he jumped sidewise. He dropped, but I could see him moving in the shadows to where a jutting rock gave him shelter. I fired again.

"Gregg."

I had stood up to take aim. I saw the bullet chip a bit of rock. Anita pulled me sharply down beside her.

"Gregg, he's armed!"

It was his turn to fire. It came—the familiar vague flash of the paralyzing ray. It spat its tint of color on the rocks near us, but could not reach us.

Miko rose a moment later and bounded to another rock. I scrambled up, and shot at him, but missed. Then he crouched and returned my fire from his new angle; but Anita and I had shifted.

Time passed—only a few moments. I could not see Miko momentarily. Perhaps he was crouching; perhaps he had moved away again. He was, or had been, on slightly higher ground than the bottom of our bowl. It was dim down here where we were lying, but I feared that every moment Miko might appear and strike at us. His ray at any short range would penetrate our visor-panes, even though our suits might temporarily resist it.

"Anita—it's too dangerous here."

Had I been alone, I might perhaps have leaped up to lure Miko. But with Anita I did not dare chance it.

"We've got to get back to the camp," I told her. The audiphone brought her comment:

"Perhaps he has gone."

B

ut he had not. We saw him again, out in a distant patch of Earthlight. He was further from us than before, but on still higher ground. We had extinguished our small helmet-lights. But he knew we were here, and possibly he could see us. His projector flashed again. But we had again shifted, and were untouched. He was a hundred feet or more away now. His weapon was of longer range than mine. I did not answer his fire, for I could not hope to hit him at such a distance, and the flash of my weapon would help him with his aim.

I murmured to Anita, "We must get out of here."

Yet how did I dare take Anita from these concealing shadows? Miko could reach us so easily as we bounded away, in plain view in the

Earthlight of the open summit! We were caught, at bay in this little bowl.

The camp from here was not visible. But out through the broken gully, beyond the staircase top, a white beam of light suddenly came up from below.

"Haljan."

It spelled the signal.

"Haljan."

It was coming from the Grantline instrument room, I knew.

I could answer it with my helmet-[206]light, but I did not dare. I hesitated.

"Try it," urged Anita.

---

e crouched where we thought we might be safe from Miko's fire. My little light-beam shot up from the bowl. It was undoubtedly visible to the camp.

"Yes? I am Haljan."

And I added:

"Help! Send us help."

I did not mention Anita. Miko could doubtless read these signals. And in the camp they must have missed Anita by now. They answered:

"*Cannot—*"

I lost the rest of it. There came a flash from Miko's weapon. But it gave us confidence. He could not reach us at the moment.

The Grantline beam repeated:

"*Cannot come out. Portes broken. You cannot get in. Stay where you are—an hour or two. We may be able to repair portes.*"

The portes were broken! Stay here an hour or two! But I could not hold this position against Miko that long! Sooner or later he would find a place from where he could sweep this bowl beyond possibility of our hiding. I saw him running now, well beyond my range, to ferret out another point of vantage.

I extinguished my light. What use was it to tell Grantline anything further? Besides, my light was dangerous.

But the Grantline beam spelled another message:

"*The brigand ship is coming! It will be here before we can get out to you! No lights! We will try and hide our location.*"

And the signal-beam brought a last appeal to me:

"*Miko and his men will divulge where we are. Unless you can stop them—*"

The beam vanished. The lights of the Grantline camp made a faint glow that showed above the crater-edge. The glow died, as the camp now was plunged into darkness.

CHAPTER XXVII

Anita's Plan

e crouched in the shadows, the Earthlight filtering down to us. The skulking figure of Miko had vanished; but he was out there somewhere on the crags I was sure, lurking, maneuvering to where he could strike us with his ray. Anita's metal-gloved hand was on my arm; in my ear diaphragm her voice sounded eager and unmistakable:

"What was the signal, Gregg?"

She could not read the semaphore lights. I told her.

"Oh Gregg, the Martian ship coming!"

Her mind clung to that as the most important thing. But not so myself. To me there was only the realization that Anita was caught out here, almost at the mercy of Miko's ray. Grantline's men could not get out to help us, nor could I get Anita into the camp.

She added, "Where do you suppose the ship is? In telescopic view?"

"Yes—twenty or thirty thousand miles up, probably."

The stars and the Earth were visible over us. Somewhere up there disclosed by Grantline's instrument but not yet discernible to the naked eye, Miko's reinforcements were hovering.

I stood up cautiously to try and locate Miko. Immediately I saw him. He jumped as though fearing my coming bullet, and I dropped back, barely avoiding his flash, which swept across the top of our bowl.

"Gregg—Gregg, don't take such a chance!"

We lay for a moment in silence. It was horribly nerve-straining. Miko could be creeping up on us. Would he dare chance my sudden fire? Creeping—or would he make a swift, unexpected rush?

The feeling that he was upon us abruptly swept me. I jumped to my feet, against Anita's effort to hold me. But again Miko had vanished. Where was he now?[207]

I

sank back. "That ship will be here in a few hours."

I told her what Grantline's signal had suggested: the ship was hovering overhead. It must be fairly close; for Grantline's telescope had revealed its identity as a bandit flyer, unmarked by any of the standard code-identification lights. It was doubtless too far away as yet to have located the whereabouts of Grantline's camp. The Martian brigands knew that we were in the vicinity of Archimedes, but no more than that. Searching this glowing Moon surface, our little lights, the tiny local semaphore beams we had momentarily been using, could easily pass unnoticed.

But as the brigand ship approached now—dropping close to Archimedes as it probably would—our danger was that Miko and his men would then signal it, join it, and reveal the camp's location, and the brigand attack would be upon us.

I told this now to Anita. "The signal said, '*Unless you can stop them.*'"

It was an appeal to me. But how could I respond to it? What could I do, alone out here with Anita, to cope with this enemy?

Anita made no comment.

I added, "That ship will land near Archimedes I imagine, within an hour or two! If Grantline can repair his portes, and I can get you inside—"

Again she made no comment. Then suddenly she gripped me. "Gregg, look there!"

Out through the gully break in our bowl the figure of Miko showed! He was running. But not at us. Circling the summit, leaping to keep himself behind the upstanding crags. He passed the head of the staircase; he did not descend it, but headed off along the summit of the curving crater-rim.

I

stood up to watch him. He was making off. Abandoning us!

"He's going!"

I let her stand up beside me; cautiously, at first, for it occurred to me that this might be a ruse to cover some other of Miko's men who might be lurking up here.

But the summit seemed clear. The figure of Miko was a thousand feet away now. We could see the tiny blob of it bobbing over the rocks. Then it plunged down—not into the crater-valley, but out toward the open Moon surface.

Miko had abandoned his attack on us. The reason seemed plain. He had come here from his encampment with Coniston, had sent

Coniston ahead to lure and kill Wilks. When this was done, Coniston had flashed his brief signal to Miko, who was hiding nearby.

It was not like the brigand leader to remain in the background. Miko was no coward. But Coniston could impersonate Wilks, whereas Miko's giant stature at once would reveal his identity. Miko had been engaged in smashing the portes. He had looked up and seen me kill Coniston. He had come up to assail me. And then he had read Grantline's signal to me. It was his first knowledge that his ship was at hand. With the camp exits inoperative, Grantline and his men were imprisoned. Miko made an effort to kill me. He did not know my companion was Anita. The effort was taking too long: with the Grantline camp imprisoned and his ship at hand, it was Miko's best move to return to his own camp, rejoin his men, and await their opportunity to signal the ship.

At least, so I reasoned it. Anita and I stood alone. What could we do?

e went to the brink of the cliff. The unlighted Grantline buildings showed vaguely in the Earthlight.

I said, "We'll go down, I'll leave you there. You can wait at the porte. They'll repair it soon, perhaps, and let you in."

"And what will you do?" she demanded.

I was hurrying her down the stairs. But suddenly she stopped. "What are you going to do, Gregg?"[208]

I had not intended to tell her. "Hurry, Anita!"

"Why?" She stood stock still. Through the visors I could see her white face gazing at me rebelliously.

"Why should I hurry, Gregg?"

"Because I want to leave you at the porte. I'm going after Miko—try and locate where he and his men are camping."

I had indeed no specific plan as yet. But it seemed useless for me to sit at the porte waiting to be let in.

"But he's gone, Gregg."

She was right on that. Miko was already a mile or more away, down on the outer surface, making off. He would soon be out of sight. It would be impossible to follow him.

"Gregg, let me go with you."

She jerked away from me and bounded back up the staircase. I caught her on the summit.

"Anita!"

"I'm going with you."

"You're going to stay here."

"I'm not!"

This exasperating controversy! And time was so precious!

"Anita, please."

"I'll be safer with you than waiting here, Gregg."

I

t almost decided me. Perhaps she would. It was only my intention to follow Miko at a distance. And with much more of this delay here, he would be lost to me.

And she added, "Besides, I won't stay, and you can't make me."

We ran along the crater-top. At its distant edge the lower plain spread before us. Far down, and far away on the distant broken surface, the leaping figure of Miko showed.

We plunged down the broken outer slope, reached the level. Soon, as we ran, the little Grantline crater faded behind us.

Anita ran more skillfully than I. Ten minutes or so passed. We had seen Miko, and the direction he was taking, but down here on the plain we could no longer see him. It struck me that this was purposeless—and dangerous. Suppose Miko were to see us following? Suppose he stopped and lay in ambush to fire at us as we came leaping heedlessly by?

"Anita, wait," I said, checking her.

I drew her down amid a group of tumbled boulders. And then abruptly she clung to me.

"Gregg, I know what we can do! Gregg, don't tell me you won't let me try it!"

I

listened to her plan. Incredible! Incredibly dangerous! Yet, as I pondered it, the very daring of the thing seemed the measure of its possible success. The brigands would never imagine we could be so rash!

"But Anita—"

"Gregg, you're stupid!" It was her turn to be exasperated. In truth, I was indeed in no mood for daring, for my mind was obsessed with Anita's safety. I had been planning that we might see the glow of Miko's encampment, and then return to Grantline and hope that he would have the portes repaired.

"But Gregg—the safety of the treasure—of all the Grantline men...."

"To the infernal with that! It's you—your safety."

"My safety, then! If you put me in the camp and the brigands attack it and I am killed—what then? But this plan of mine, if we can do it, Gregg ... safety, in the end, for all of us."

And it seemed possible. We crouched, discussing it. So daring a thing!

The brigand ship would come down near Archimedes. That was fifty miles from Grantline. The brigands from Mars would not have seen the dark Grantline buildings hidden in the little crater-pit. They would wait for Miko and his men to make their whereabouts known.

M

iko's encampment was ahead of us now, undoubtedly. We had been following him toward the Mare Imbrium; we were at its borders now.[209] Archimedes from here was also about fifty miles.

And Anita proposed that we go to Archimedes, climb in slope and await the coming of the brigand ship. Miko would be off in the Mare Imbrium. Or at least, we hoped so. He would signal his ship. But Anita and I, closer to it, would also signal it—and, posing as brigands, could join it!

"Remember, Gregg, I am Anita Prince, George's sister." Her voice trembled as, she mentioned her dead brother. "They know that George was in Miko's pay, and I am his sister.... It will help convince them."

This daring scheme! If we could join the ship, we might be able to persuade its leader that Miko's distant signals were merely a ruse of Grantline to lure the brigands in that direction. A long-range projector from the ship would kill Miko and his men as they came forward to join it! And then we could falsely direct the brigands, lead them away from Grantline and the treasure.

"Gregg, we must try it."

Heaven help me, I yielded to her persuasion!

We turned at right angles and ran toward where the distant frowning walls of Archimedes loomed against the starlit sky.

CHAPTER XXVIII

The Ascent of Archimedes

T he broken shaggy ramparts of the giant crater rose above us. We toiled upward, out of the foothills, clinging now to the crags and pitted terraces of the main ascent. An hour had passed since we turned from the borders of the Mare Imbrium. Or was it two hours? I could not tell. I only know that we ran with desperate frantic haste.

Anita would not admit that she was tired. She was more skilful than I in this leaping over the broken rock masses. Yet I felt that her slight strength must give out. It seemed miles up the undulating slopes of the foothills with the black and white ramparts of the massive crater close before us.

And then the main ascent. There were places where, like smooth black frozen ice, the walls rose sheer. We avoided them, toiling aside, plunging into gullies, crossing pits where sometimes we perforce went downwards, and then up again; or sometimes we stood, hot and breathless, upon ledges, recovering our strength, selecting the best route upward.

This tumbled mass of rock! Honeycombed everywhere with caves and passages leading into darkness impenetrable. There were pits into which we might so easily have fallen; ravines to span, sometimes with a leap, sometimes by a long and arduous detour.

Endless climb! We came to a ledge, with the plains of the Mare Imbrium stretching out beneath us. We might have been upon this main ascent for an hour; the plains were far down, the broken surface down there smoothed now by the perspective of our height. And yet still above us the brooding circular wall went up into the sky. Ten thousand feet still above us—I think it was at least that, or more.

"You're tired, Anita. We'd better stay here."

"No! If we could only get to the top—the ship may land on the other side—they would see us if we were at the top."

T

here was as yet no sign of the brigand ship. With every stop for rest we searched the starry vault. The Earth hung over us, flattened beyond the full. The stars blazed to mingle with the Earthlight and illumine these massive crags of the Archimedes walls. But no speck appeared to tell us that the ship was up there.

We were on the curving side of the Archimedes wall which fronted the Mare Imbrium to the North. The plains lay like a great frozen sea, congealed ripples shining in the light of the[210] Earth, with dark patches to mark the hollows. Somewhere down there—six or eight thousand feet below us now, or even more than that, for all I could tell—Miko's encampment lay concealed. We searched for lights of it, but could see none.

Or had Miko rejoined his party, left his camp and come here like ourselves to climb Archimedes? Or was our assumption wholly wrong—perhaps the brigand ship would not land near here at all?

Sweeping around from the Mare Imbrium, the plains were less smooth—the shattered, crag-littered, crater-scarred region beyond which the distant Apennines raised their terraced walls. The little crater which concealed the Grantline camp was off that way. There was nothing to mark it from here.

"Gregg, do you see anything up there? There seems to be a blur."

H

er sight, sharper than mine, had picked it out. The descending brigand ship! A faintest tiny blur against the stars, a few of them occulted as though strangely an invisible shadow were upon them. A growing shadow, materializing into a blur—a blob, a shape faintly defined. Then sharper until we were sure of what we saw. It was the brigand ship. It came dropping slowly, silently down.

We crouched on the little ledge. A cave-mouth was behind us. A gully was beside us, a break in the ledge; and at our feet the wall dropped sheer.

We had extinguished our little lights. We crouched, silently gazing up into the stars.

The ship, when first we distinguished it was central over Archimedes. We thought for a while that it might descend into the crater. But it did not; it came sailing forward.

I whispered into the audiphone—whispering by instinct, as though out here in all this airless desolation someone might overhear us!

"It's coming over the crater."

Her hand pressed my arm in answer.

I recalled that when, from the *Planetara*, Miko had forced Snap to signal this brigand band on Mars, Miko's only information as to the whereabouts of the Grantline camp was that it lay between Archimedes and the Apennines. That was Grantline's first message to us, and Miko had relayed it to his men. The brigands from Mars now were following that information.

A tense interval passed. We could see the ship plainly above us now, a gray-black shape among the stars up beyond the shaggy, towering crater-rim. The vessel came upon a level keel, hull-down, slowly circling, looking for Miko's signal, no doubt, or for possible lights of Grantline. They were also picking a landing place.

---

e saw it soon as a cylindrical, cigarlike shape, rather smaller than the *Planetara*, but similar of design. It bore lights now. The ports of its hull were tiny rows of illumination, and the glow of light under its rounding upper dome was faintly visible.

A bandit ship, no doubt of that. Its identification keel-plate was empty of official pass-code lights. These brigands had not attempted to secure official sailing lights when leaving Ferrok-Shahn. It was an outlawed ship, unmistakably. And here upon the deserted Moon there was no need for secrecy. Its lights were openly displayed, that Miko might see it and join it.

It went slowly past us, only a few thousand feet higher than our level. We could see the whole outline of its pointed cylinder-hull, with the rounded dome on top. And under the dome was its open deck-space, with a little cabin superstructure in the center.

I thought for a moment that by some fortunate chance it might land quite near us. There was a wide ledge a quarter of a mile away.

"Anita, look."

But it went past. And then I saw[211] that it was heading for a level, plateau-like surface a few miles further on. It dropped, cautiously floating down.

There was still no sign of Miko. But I realized that haste was necessary. We must be the first to join the brigand ship.

I lifted Anita to her feet. "I don't think we should signal from here."

"No. Miko might see it."

We could not tell where he was. Down on the plains, perhaps? Or up here, somewhere in these miles of towering rocks?

"Are you ready, Anita?"

"Yes, Gregg."

I

stared through the visors at her white, solemn face.

"Yes, I'm ready," she repeated.

Her hand-pressure seemed to me suddenly like a farewell. Were we plunging rashly into what was destined to mean our death? Was this a farewell?

An instinct swept me not to do this thing. Why, in an hour or two I could have Anita back to the comparative safety of the Grantline buildings. The exit portes would doubtless be repaired by now. I could get her inside.

She had bounded away from me, leaped down some thirty feet into the broken gully, to cross it and then up on the other side. I stood for an instant watching her fantastic shape, with the great rounded, goggled, trunked helmet and the lump on her shoulders which held the little Erentz motors. Then I made after her.

It did not take us long—two or three miles of circling along the giant wall. The ship lay only a few hundred feet above our level.

We stood at last on a buttelike pinnacle. The hull-porte lights of the ship were close over us. And there were moving lights up there, tiny moving spots on the adjacent rocks. The brigands had come out, prowling around to investigate their location.

No signal yet from Miko. But it might come at any moment.

"I'll flash now," I whispered.

"Yes."

The brigands had probably not yet seen us. I took the lamp from my helmet. My hand was trembling. Suppose my signal were answered by a shot? A flash from some giant projector mounted on the ship?

Anita crouched behind a rock, as she had promised. I stood with my torch, and flung its switch.

My puny light-beam shot up. I waved it, touched the ship with its faint glowing circle of illumination.

They saw me. There was a sudden movement among the lights up there.

I

semaphored:

"*I am from Miko. Do not fire.*"

I used the open Universal Code. In Martian first, and then in English.

There was no answer, but no attack. I tried again.

"*This is Haljan, once of the* Planetara. *George Prince's sister is with me. There has been disaster to Miko.*"

A small light-beam came down from the brink of the overhead cliff beside the ship.

"*We read you.*"

I went steadily on: "*Disaster—the* Planetara *is wrecked. All killed but me and George Prince's sister. We want to join you.*"

I flashed off my light. The answer came: "*Where is the Grantline camp?*"

"*Near here. The Mare Imbrium.*"

As though to answer my lie, from down on the Earthlit plains, ten miles or so from the crater-base, a tiny signal-light shot up. Anita saw it and gripped me.

"There is Miko's light!"

It spelled in Martian, "*Come down. Land Mare Imbrium.*"

Miko had seen the signalling up here and was joining it! He repeated, "*Land Mare Imbrium.*"

I

flashed a protest up to the ship: "*Beware! That is Grantline! Trickery!*"

From the ship the summons came: "*Come up.*"[212]

We had won this first encounter! Miko must have realized his disadvantage. His distant light went out.

"Come, Anita."

There was no retreat now. But again I seemed to feel in the pressure of her hand that vague farewell.

Her voice whispered, "We must do our best, act our best to be convincing."

In the white glow of a search-beam we climbed the crags, reached the broad upper ledge. Helmeted figures rushed at us, searched us for weapons, seized our helmet lights. The evil face of a giant Martian peered at me through the visors. Two other monstrous, towering figures seized Anita.

We were shoved toward the port-locks at the base of the ship's hull. Above the hull bulge I could see the grids of projectors mounted in the dome-side, and the figures of men standing on the deck, peering down at us.

We went through the admission locks into a hull corridor, up an incline passage, and reached the lighted deck. Our helmets were taken off. The Martian brigands crowded around us.

CHAPTER XXIX

On the Brigand Ship

nita's words echoed in my memory: "We must act our best to be convincing." It was not her ability that I doubted as much as my own. She had played the part of George Prince cleverly, unmasked only by an evil chance.

I steeled myself to face the searching glances of the brigands as they shoved around us. This was a desperate game into which we had plunged! For all our acting, how easy it would be for some small chance thing abruptly to undo us! I realized it, and now, as I gazed into the peering faces of these men from Mars, I cursed my witless rashness which had brought Anita into this!

The brigands—some ten or fifteen of them here on the deck—stood in a ring around us. They were all big men, nearly of a seven-foot average, dressed in leather jerkins and short leather breeches, with bare knees and flaring leatherboots. Piratical swaggering fellows, knife-blades mingled with small hand-projectors fastened to their belts. Gray, heavy faces, some with scraggling, unshaved beard. They plucked at us, jabbering in Martian.

One of them seemed the leader. I said sharply, "Are you the commander here? I speak not Ilton[4] well. You speak the Earth English?"

[4] Ilton, the ruling race and official language of the Martian Union.

"Yes," he said readily, "I am Commander here." He spoke English with the same freedom and accent of Miko. "Is this George Prince's sister?"

"Yes. Her name is Anita Prince. Tell your men to take their hands off her."

He waved his men away. They all seemed more interested in Anita than in me. He added:

"I am Set Potan." He addressed Anita. "George Prince's sister? You are called Anita? I have heard of you. I knew your brother—indeed, you look very much like him."

He swept his plumed hat to the grid with a swaggering gesture of homage. A courtierlike fellow this, debonair as a Venus cavalier!

He accepted us. I realized that Anita's presence was immensely valuable in making us convincing. Yet there was about this Potan— as with Miko—a disturbing suggestion of irony. I could not make him out. I decided that we had fooled him. Then I remarked the steely glitter of his eyes as he turned to me.

"You were an officer of the *Planetara*?"

T

he insignia of my rank was visible on my white jacket-collar which showed beneath the Erentz suit, now that my helmet was off.

"Yes, I was supposed to be. But a [213]year ago I embarked upon this adventure with Miko."

He was leading us to his cabin. "The *Planetara* wrecked? Miko dead?"

"And Hahn and Coniston. George Prince, too—we are the only survivors."

While we divested ourselves of our Erentz suits at his command, I told him briefly of the *Planetara's* fall. All had been killed on board save Anita and me. We had escaped, awaited his coming. The treasure was here; we had located the Grantline camp, and were ready to lead him to it.

Did he believe me? He listened quietly. He seemed not shocked at the death of his comrades. Nor yet pleased: merely imperturbable.

I added with a sly, sidelong glance, "There were too many of us on the *Planetara*. The purser had joined us, and many of the crew. And there was Miko's sister, the Setta Moa—too many. The treasure divides better among less."

An amused smile played on his thin gray lips. But he nodded. The fear which had leaped in me was allayed by his next words.

"True enough, Haljan. He was a domineering fellow, Miko. A third of it all was for him alone. But now...."

The third would go to this sub-leader, Potan! The implication was obvious.

I said, "Before we go any further—I can trust you for my share?"

"Of course."

I

figured that my very boldness in bargaining so prematurely would convince him. I insisted, "And Miss Prince? She will have her brother's share?"

Clever Anita! She put in swiftly, "I give no information until you promise! We know the location of the Grantline camp, its weapons, its defense, the amount and location of the ore. I warn you, if you do not play us fair...."

He laughed heartily. He seemed to like us. He spread his huge legs as he lounged in his settle, and drank of the bowl which one of his men set before him.

"Little tigress! Fear me not—I play fair!" He pushed two of the bowls across the table. "Drink, Haljan. All is well with us, and I am glad to hear it. Miss Prince, drink my health as your leader."

I waved it away from Anita. "We need all our wits; your strong Martian drinks are dangerous. Look here, I'll tell you just how the situation stands—"

I plunged into a glib account of our supposed wanderings to find the Grantline camp; its location off in the Mare Imbrium—hidden in a cavern there. Potan, with the drink, and under the gaze of Anita's eyes, was in a high good humor. He laughed when I told him that we had dared to invade the Grantline camp, had smashed its exit portes, had even gotten up to have a look at where the ore was piled.

"Well done, Haljan! You're a fellow to my liking!" But his gaze was on Anita. "You dress like a man, or a charming boy."

She still wore the dark clothes of her brother. She said, "I am used to action—man's garb pleases me. You shall treat me like a man, give me my share of the gold-leaf."

H

e had already demanded of us the meaning of that signal from the Mare Imbrium. Miko's signal! It had not come again, though any moment I feared it. I told him that Grantline had doubtless repaired his damaged portes and sallied out to assail me in reprisal. And seeing the brigand ship landing on Archimedes, had tried to lure it.

I wondered if my explanation were very convincing. It did not sound so. But he was flushed now with the drink. And Anita added:

"Grantline knows the territory near his camp very well. He is equipped only for short-range fighting."[214]

I took it up. "It's like this, Potan: if he could get you to land unsuspectingly near the mouth of his cavern...."

I pictured how Grantline might have figured on a sudden surprise attack upon the ship. It was his only chance to catch it unprepared.

We were all three in friendly, intimate mood now. Potan said, "We'll land down there right enough! But I need a few hours for my assembling."

"He will not dare advance," I said. "For one thing, he can't leave the treasure."

"He knows we have unmasked his lure," Anita put in smilingly. "Haljan and I joining you—that silenced him. His light went out very promptly, didn't it?"

She flashed me a side-gaze. Were we acting convincingly? But if Miko started up his signals again, they might so quickly betray us! Anita's thoughts were upon that, for she added:

"Grantline will not dare show his light! If he does, Set Potan, we can blast him with a ray from here! Can't we?"

"Yes," Potan agreed. "If he comes within ten miles, I have one powerful enough. We are assembling it now."

"And we have thirty men?" Anita persisted. "When we sail down to attack him it should not be very difficult to kill all the Grantline party. Thirty of us—that's enough to share in this treasure. I'm glad Miko is dead."

"By Heaven, Haljan, this girl of yours is small, but very blood-thirsty!"

"That accursed Miko murdered her brother," I explained.

---

cting! And never once did we dare relax! If only Miko's signals would hold off and give us time!

We may have talked for half an hour. We were in a small, steel-lined cubby, located in the forward deck-space of the ship. The dome was over it. I could see from where I sat at the table that there was a forward observatory tower under the dome quite near here. The ship was laid out in rather similar fashion to the *Planetara*, though considerably smaller.

Potan had dismissed his men from his cubby so as to be alone with us. Out on the deck I could see them dragging apparatus about— bringing the mechanisms of giant projectors up from below, beginning to assemble them. Occasionally some of the men would come to our cubby windows to peer in at us curiously.

My mind was roaming as I talked. For all my manner of casualness, I knew that haste was necessary. Whatever Anita and I were to do must be quickly done. But to win this fellow's utter confidence first was necessary, so that we might have the freedom of the ship, might move about unnoticed, unwatched.

I was horribly tense inside. Through the dome windows across the deck from the cubby the rocks of the Lunar landscape were visible. I could see the brink of this ledge upon which the ship lay, the descending crags down the precipitous wall of Archimedes to the Earthlit plains far below. Miko, Moa, and a few of the *Planetara's* crew were down there somewhere.

nita and I had a fairly definite plan. We were now in Potan's confidence. With this interview at an end, I felt that our status among the brigands would be established. We would be free to move about the ship, join in its activities. It ought to be possible to locate the signal-room, get friendly with the operator there.

Perhaps we would find a secret opportunity to flash a signal to Earth. This ship, I was confident, would have the power for a long-range signal, if not of too sustained a length. It was a desperate thing to attempt but our whole procedure was desperate! And I felt—if Anita perhaps could cajole the guard or the duty-man from the signal-room—I might send a single flash or two that would reach the Earth. Just a distress call, signed "Grantline." If I could do that and not get caught.[215]

Anita was engaging Potan in talking of his plans. The brigand leader was boasting of his well-equipped ship, the daring of his men, and questioning her about the size of the treasure. My thoughts were free to roam.

A signal to Earth. And while we were making friends with these brigands, the longest range electronic projector was being assembled. Miko then could flash his signal and be damned to him! I would be on the deck with that projector. Its operator, and I would turn it upon Miko—one flash of it and he and his little band would be wiped out.

But there was our escape to be thought of. We could not remain very long with these brigands. We could tell them that the Grantline camp was on the Mare Imbrium. It would delay them for a time, but our lie would soon be discovered. We must escape from them, get away and back to Grantline. With Miko dead—a distress signal to Earth— and Potan in ignorance of Grantline's location, the treasure would be safe until help arrived from Earth.

It all fitted together so nicely! It seemed possible of success.

Our futile plans! Star-crossed always, doomed, fated always to be upset by such unforeseen evil chances!

"By the infernal, little Anita, you look like a dove, but you're a tigress! A comrade after my own heart—blood-thirsty as a fire-worshipper!"

H

er laugh rang out to mingle with his. "Oh no, Set Potan! I am treasure-thirsty."

"We'll get the treasure, never fear, little Anita."

"With you to lead us, Potan, I'm sure we will."

A man entered the cubby. Potan looked frowningly around. "What is it, Argle?"

The fellow answered in Martian, leered at Anita and withdrew.

Potan stood up. I noticed that he was unsteady with the drink.

"They want me with the work at the projectors."

"Go ahead," I said.

He nodded. We were comrades now.

"Amuse yourself, Haljan. Or come out on deck if you wish. I will tell my men you are one of us."

"And tell them to keep their hands off Miss Prince."

He stared at me. "I had not thought of that—a woman among so many men."

His own gaze at Anita was as leeringly offensive as any of his men could have given. He said, "Have no fear, little tigress."

Anita laughed. "I am afraid of nothing."

But when he had lurched from the cabin she touched me. Smiled with her mannish swagger, for fear we were still observed, and murmured:

"Oh, Gregg, I am afraid!"

We stayed in the cubby a few moments, whispering—trying to plan.

"You think the signal room is in the tower, Gregg? This tower outside our window here?"

"Yes, I think so."

"Shall we go out and see?"

"Yes. Keep near me always."

"Oh, Gregg. I will!"

We deposited our Erentz suits carefully in a corner of the cubby. We might need them so suddenly! Then we swaggered out to join the brigands working on the deck.

CHAPTER XXX

Desperate Plans

The deck glowed lurid in the queer blue-greenish glare of Martian electro-fuse lights. It was in a bustle of ordered activity. Some twenty of the crew were scattered about, working in little groups. Apparatus was being brought up from below to be assembled. There was a pile of Erentz suits and helmets, of Martian pattern, but still very similar to those with which Grantline's expedition was equipped. There were giant projectors of several kinds, some familiar to me, others of[216] a fashion I had never seen before. It seemed there were six or eight of them, still dismantled, with a litter of their attendant batteries and coils and tube-amplifiers. They were to be mounted here on the deck, I surmised; I saw in the dome-side one or two of them already rolled into position at the necessary pressure portes.

Anita and I stood outside Potan's cubby, gazing around us curiously. The men looked at us, but none of them spoke.

"Let's watch from here a moment," I whispered. She nodded, standing with her hand on my arm. I felt that we were very small, here in the midst of these seven-foot Martian men. I was all in white, the costume used in the warm interior of the Grantline camp. Bareheaded, white silk *Planetara* uniform jacket, broad belt and tight-laced trousers. Anita was a slim black figure beside me, somber as Hamlet, with her pale boyish face and wavy black hair.

The gravity being maintained here on the ship we had found to be stronger than that of the Moon—rather more like Mars.

"There are the heat-rays, Gregg."

A

pile of them was visible down the deck-length. And I saw caskets of fragile glass globes, bombs of different styles; hand-projectors of the paralyzing ray; search-beams of several varieties; the Benson curve-light, and a few side-arms of ancient Earth-design—swords and dirks, and small bullet projectors.

There seemed to be some mining equipment also. Far along the deck, beyond the central cabin in the open space of the stern, steel rails were stacked; half a dozen small-wheeled ore-carts; a tiny motor engine for hauling them—and what looked as though it might be the dismembered sections of an ore-shute.

The whole deck was presently strewn with this mass of equipment.

Potan moved about, directing the different groups of workers. The news had spread that we knew the location of the treasure. The brigands were jubilant. In a few hours the ship's armament would be ready, and it would advance to attack Grantline.

I saw many glances being cast out the dome side-windows toward the distant, far-down plains of the Mare Imbrium. The brigands believed that the Grantline camp lay in that direction.

Anita whispered, "Which is their giant electronic projector, Gregg?"

I could see it amidships of the deck. It was already in place. Potan was there now, superintending the men who were connecting it. The most powerful weapon on the ship, it had, Potan said, an effective range of some ten miles. I wondered what it would do to a Grantline building! The Erentz double walls would withstand it for a time, I was sure. But it would blast an Erentz fabric-suit, no doubt of that.

Like a lightning bolt, it would kill—its flashing free-stream of electrons shocking the heart, bringing instant death.

I whispered, "We must smash that before we leave! But first turn it on Miko, if he signals now."

I was tensely watchful for that signal. The electronic projector obviously was not yet ready. But when it was connected, I must be near it, to persuade its duty-man to fire it on Miko. With this done we would have more time to plan our other tasks. I did not think Potan would be ready for his attack before another time of sleep here in the ship's routine. Things would be quieter then—I would watch my chance to send a signal to Earth, and then we would escape.

With my thoughts roving, we had been standing quietly at the cubby door-oval for perhaps fifteen minutes. My hand in my side pouch clutched the little bullet projector. The brigands had taken it from me and given it to Potan. He had placed it on the settle with my Erentz suit; and when[217] we gained his confidence he had forgotten it and left it there. I had it now, and the feel of its cool sleek handle gave me a measure of comfort. Things could go wrong so easily—but if they did, I was determined to sell my life as dearly as possible. And a vague thought was in my mind: I must not use the last bullet. That would be for Anita.

I shook myself free from such sinister fancy.

"That electronic projector is remote-controlled. Look, Anita—that's the signal room over us. The giant projector will be aimed and fired from up there."

It seemed so. A thirty-foot skeleton tower stood on the deck near us, with a spiral ladder leading up to a small square steel cubby at the top. Through the cubby window-ovals I could see instrument panels. A single Martian was up there; he had called down to Potan concerning the electronic projector.

————————————————

T

he roof of this little tower room was close under the dome—a space of no more than four feet. A pressure lock-exit in the dome was up there, with a few steps leading up to it from the roof of the tower signal-room. We could escape that way, perhaps. In the event of dire necessity it might be possible. But only as a desperate resort, for it would put us on the top of the glassite dome, with a sheer hundred feet or more down its sleek bulging exterior side, and down the outside bulge of the ship's hull, to the rocks below. There might be a spider ladder outside leading downward, but I saw no evidence of it. If Anita and I were forced to escape that way, I wondered how we could manage a hundred foot jump to the rocks and land safely. Even with the slight gravity of the Moon it would be a dangerous fall.

"You are Gregg Haljan?"

I started as one of the brigands, coming up behind us, addressed me.

"Yes."

"Commander Potan tells me you were chief navigator of the *Planetara*?"

"Yes."

"You shall pilot us when we advance upon the Grantline camp. I am control-commander here—Brotow, my name."

He smiled. A giant fellow, but spindly. He spoke good English. He seemed anxious to be friendly.

"We are glad to have you and George Prince's sister with us." He shot Anita an admiring glance. "I will show you our controls, Haljan."

"All right," I said. "Whatever I can do to help...."

"But not now. It will be some hours before we are ready."

I nodded, and he wandered away. Anita whispered:

"Did he mean that signal room up here in the tower? Oh, Gregg, maybe it's only the ship's control room!"

"I don't know. But the projector range-finders are up there, and I think it's the signal room."

"Suppose we go up and see? Gregg, Miko's signals might start any minute."

A

nd the electronic projector now seemed about ready. It was time for me to act. But a reluctant instinct was upon me. Our Erentz suits were here close behind us in Potan's cubby. I hated to leave them: if anything happened and we had to make a sudden dash, there would be no time to garb ourselves in the suits. To adjust the helmets was bad enough.

I whispered swiftly, "We must get into our suits—find some pretext." I drew her back through the cubby doorway where we would be more secluded.

"Anita, listen: I've been a fool not to plan our escape more carefully! We're in too great a danger here."

It seemed to me suddenly that we were in desperate plight. Was it premonition?

"Anita, listen: if anything happens and we have to make a dash—"

"Up through that dome-lock, Gregg?[218] It's a manual control; you can see the levers."

"Yes. It's a manual. But up there—how would we get down?"

She was far calmer than I. "There may be an outside ladder, Gregg."

"I don't think so. I haven't seen it."

"Then we can get out the way they brought us in. The hull-porte—it's a manual, too."

"Yes, I think I can find our way down through the hull corridors. I mean, for a quick run. If we have to run, you stay close behind me. I've this bullet projector, and evidently there aren't many men in the lower corridors."

"There are guards outside on the rocks."

We had seen them through the dome windows. But there were not many—only two or three. A surprise rush at them would turn the trick.

---

e donned our Erentz suits.

"What will we do with the helmets?" Anita demanded. "Leave them here?"

"No—take them with us. I'm not going to get separated from them; it's too dangerous."

"We'll look strange going up to that signal room equipped like this," she commented.

"I can't help it. We'll figure out something to explain it."

She stood before me, a queer-looking little figure in the now deflated, bagging suit with her slim neck and head protruding above the metal circle of its collar.

"Carry your helmet, Anita. I'll take mine."

We could adjust the helmets and start the Erentz motors all within a few seconds.

"I'm ready, Gregg."

"Come on, then. Let me go first."

I had the bullet projector in an outer pouch of the suit where I could instantly reach it. This was more rational: we had a fighting chance now. The fear which had swept me so suddenly began to recede. I was calm.

"We'll climb the tower to the signal room," I whispered. "Do it boldly."

We stepped from the cubby. Potan was not in sight; he was on the further deck beyond the central cabin structure perhaps, or had gone below.

On the deck, we were immediately accosted. This was different— our appearance in the Erentz suits!

"Where are you going?"

This fellow spoke in Martian. I answered in English.

"Up there."

e stood before us, towering over me. I saw a group of nearby workers stop to regard us. In a moment we would be causing a commotion, and it was the last thing I desired.

I said in Martian, "Commander Potan told me, what I wish I can do. From the dome we look around—see where is the Grantline camp— I am pilot of this ship to go there."

The man who had called himself Brotow passed near us. I appealed to him.

"We put on our suits. I thought we might go up on the dome for a minute and look around. If I'm to pilot the ship...."

He hesitated, his glance sweeping the deck as though to ask Potan. Someone said in Martian:

"The commander is down in the stern storeroom."

It decided Brotow. He waved away the Martian who had stopped me.

"Let them alone."

Anita and I gave him our most friendly smiles.

"Thanks."

He bowed to Anita with a sweeping gesture. "I will show you over the control room presently."

His gaze went to the peak of the bow. The little hooded cubby there was the control room. Satisfaction swept me. Then this, above us in the tower, must surely be the signal room. Would Brotow follow us up? I hoped not. I wanted to be alone with the[219] duty-man up there, giving me a chance to get at the projector controls if Miko's signal should come.

I drew Anita past Brotow, who had stood aside. "Thanks," I repeated. "We won't be long."

We mounted the little ladder.

CHAPTER XXXI

In the Tower Cubby

"H urry, Anita!"

I feared that Potan might come up from the hull at any moment and stop us. The duty-man over us gazed down, his huge head and shoulders blocking the small signal room window. Brotow called up in Martian, telling him to let us come. He scowled, but when we reached the trap in the room floor-grid, we found him standing aside to admit us.

I flung a swift glance around. It was a metallic cubby, not much over fifteen feet square, with an eight-foot arched ceiling. There were instrument panels. The range-finder for the giant projector was here; its little telescope with the trajectory apparatus and the firing switch were unmistakable. And the signalling apparatus was here! Not a Martian set, but a fully powerful Botz ultra-violet helio sender with its attendant receiving mirrors. The *Planetara* had used the Botz system, so I was thoroughly familiar with it. I saw, too, what seemed to be weapons: a row of small fragile glass globes, hanging on clips along the wall—bombs, each the size of a man's fist. And a broad belt with bombs in its padded compartments.

My heart was pounding as my first quick glance took in these details. I saw also that the room had four small oval window openings. They were breast-high above the floor; from the deck below I knew that the angle of vision was such that the men down there could not see into this room except to glimpse its upper portion near the ceiling. And the helio set was banked on a low table near the floor.

In a corner of the room a small ladder led through a ceiling trap to the cubby roof. This upper trap was open. Four feet above the room-roof was the arch of the dome, with the entrance to the upper exit-lock directly above us. The weapons and the belt of bombs were near this ascending ladder, evidently placed here as equipment for use from the top of the dome.

———————————

I

turned to the solitary duty-man. I must gain his confidence at once. Anita had laid her helmet aside. She spoke first.

"We were with Set Miko," she said smilingly, "in the wreck of the *Planetara*. You heard of it? We know where the treasure is."

This duty-man was a full seven feet tall, and the most heavy-set Martian I had ever seen. A tremendous, beetling-browed, scowling fellow. He stood with hands on his hips, his leather-garbed legs spread wide; and as I fronted him I felt like a child. He was silent, glaring down at me as I drew his attention from Anita.

"You speak English? We are not skilled with Martian."

I wondered if at the next time of sleep this fellow would be on duty here. I hoped not; it would not be easy to trick him and find an opportunity to flash a signal. But that task was some hours away as yet; I would worry about it when the time came. Just now I was concerned with Miko and his little band, who at any moment might arrive in sight. If we could persuade this scowling duty-man to turn the projector on them....

He answered me in ready English:

"You are the man Gregg Haljan? And this is the sister of George Prince—what do you want up here?"

"I am a navigator. Brotow wants me to pilot the ship when we advance to attack Grantline."

"This is not the control room."

"No, I know it isn't."

I put my helmet carefully on the floor-grid beside Anita's. I straight[220]ened to find the brigand gazing at her. He did not speak; he was still scowling. But in the dim blue glow of the cubby I caught the look in his eyes.

I

said hastily, "Grantline knows your ship has landed here on Archimedes. His camp is off there on the Mare Imbrium. He sent up a signal—you saw it, didn't you?—just before Miss Prince and I came aboard. He was trying to pretend that he was your Earth-party, Miko and Coniston."

"Why?"

The fellow turned his scowl on me, but Anita brought his gaze back to her. She put in quickly:

"Grantline, as Brother always said, has no great cunning. I believe he's planning now to creep up on us, catch us unaware by pretending that he is Miko."

"If he does that," I said, "we will turn this electronic projector on him and annihilate him. You have its firing mechanism here."

"Who told you so?" he shot at me.

I gestured. "I see it here. It's obvious. I'm skilled at trajectory-firing. If Grantline appears down there now, I'll help you——"

"Is it connected?" Anita demanded boldly.

"Yes," he said. "You have on your Erentz suits: are you going to the dome-roof? Then go."

But that was what we did not want to do. Anita's glance seemed to tell me to let her handle this. I turned toward one of the cubby windows; she said sweetly:

"Are you in charge of this room? Show me how that projector is operated; it will be invincible against the Grantline camp."

"Yes."

I

had my back to them for a moment. Through the breast-high oval I could see down across the deck-space and out through the side dome windows. And my heart suddenly leaped into my throat. It seemed that down there in the Earthlit shadows, where the spreading base of the giant crater joined the plains, a light was bobbing. I gazed, stricken. Miko's lights? Was he advancing, preparing to signal? I tried to gauge the distance; it was not over two miles from here.

Or was it not a light at all? With the naked eye, I could not be sure. Perhaps there was a telescopic finder here in the cubby....

I was subconsciously aware of the voices of Anita and the duty-man behind me. Then abruptly I heard Anita's low cry. I whirled around.

The giant Martian had gathered her into his huge arms, his heavy-jowled gray face with a leering grin close to hers!

He saw me coming. He held her with one arm: his other flung at me, caught me, knocked me backward. He rasped:

"Get out of here! Go up to the dome, leave us."

Anita was silently struggling with her little hands at his thick throat. His blow flung me against a settle. But I held my feet. I was partly behind him. I leaped again, and as he tried to disengage himself from Anita to front me, her clutching fingers impeded him.

My bullet projector was in my hand. But in that second as I leaped, I had the sense to realize I should not fire it and with its noise alarm the ship. I grasped its barrel, reached upward and struck with its heavy metal butt. The blow caught the Martian on the skull, and simultaneously my body struck him.

We went down together, falling partly upon Anita. But the giant had not cried out, and as I gripped him now, I felt his body limp. I lay panting. Anita squirmed silently from under us. Blood from the giant's head was welling out, hot and sticky against my face as I lay sprawled on him.

I

cast him off. He was dead, his fragile Martian skull split open by my blow.[221]

There had been no alarm. The slight noise we made had not been heard down on the busy deck. Anita and I crouched by the floor. From the deck all this part of the room could not be seen.

"Dead!"

"Oh, Gregg—"

It forced our hand. I could not wait now for Miko to come. But I could flash the Earth signal now, and then we would have to make our run to escape.

Abruptly I remembered that light down at the crater-base! I kept Anita out of sight on the floor and went cautiously to a window. The deck was in turmoil with brigands moving about excitedly. Not because of what had happened in our tower signal room; they were unaware of that.

Miko's signals were showing! I could see them now plainly, down at the crater-base. A group of hand-lights and a small waving helio-beam.

And they were being answered from the ship! Potan was on the deck—a babble of voices, above which his rose with roars of command. At one of the dome windows a brigand with a hand search-beam was sending its answering light. And I saw that Potan was working over a deck telescope-finder.

It had all come so suddenly that I was stunned. But I did not wait to read the signals. I swung back at Anita.

"It's Miko! And they are answering him! Get your helmet; I'll try firing the projector."

Or would I instead try to send a brief flash-signal to Earth? There would be no time to do both: we must escape out of here. The route up through the dome was the only feasible one now.

This range mechanism of the projector was reasonably familiar, and I felt that I could operate it. The range-finder and switch were on a ledge at one of the windows. I rushed to it. As I swung the little telescope, training it down on Miko's lights, I could see the huge projector on the deck swinging similarly. Its movement surprised the men who were attending it. One of them called up to me, but I ignored him.

T

hen Potan looked up and saw me. He shouted in Martian at the duty-man, whom he doubtless thought was behind me: "Be ready! We may fire on them, whoever they are. I'll give you the word."

The signals were proceeding. It had only been a moment. I caught something like, "*Haljan is impostor.*"

I was aiming the projector. I was aware of Anita at my elbow. I pushed her back.

"Put on your helmet!"

I had the range. I flung the firing switch.

At the deck window the giant projector spat its deadly electronic stream. The men down there leaped away from it with surprise. I heard Potan's voice, his shout of protest and anger.

But down in the Earthglow at the crater-base, Miko's lights had not vanished! I had missed! An error in the range? Abruptly I knew it was not that. Miko's lights were still there. His signals still coming. And I remarked now a faint distortion about them, the glow of his little group of hand-lights faintly distorted and vaguely shot with a greenish cast. Benson curve-lights! I realized it.

My thoughts whirled in the few seconds while I stood there at the tower window. Miko had feared he might summarily be fired upon. He had gone back to his camp, equipped all his lights with the Benson curve. He was somewhere at the crater-base now. But not where I thought I saw him! The Benson curve-light changed the path of the light-rays traveling from him to me—I could not even approximate his true position!

Anita was plucking at me. "Gregg, come."

"I can't hit him!" I gasped.

Should I try the flash-signal to Earth? Did we dare linger here? I[222] stood another few seconds fascinated at the window. I saw Potan down in the confusion of the deck, training a telescope. He had shouted up violently at his duty-man here not to fire again.

And now he suddenly let out a roar. "I can see them! It's Miko! By the Almighty—his giant stature—Brotow, look! That's not an Earthman!"

He flung aside his little telescope finder. "Disconnect that projector! It's Miko down there! This Haljan is a trickster! Where is he? Braile—Braile, you accursed fool! Are Haljan and the girl up there with you?"

But the duty-man lay weltering in his blood at our feet.

I had dropped back from the window. Anita and I crouched for an instant in confusion, fumbling with our helmets.

The ship rang with the alarm. And amid the turmoil we could hear the shouts of the infuriated brigands swarming up the tower ladder after us!

CHAPTER XXXII

A Speck Amid the Stars

I was only inactive a moment. I had thought Anita would have on her helmet. But she was reluctant, or confused.

"Gregg."

"We've got to get out of here! Up through the overhead locks to the dome."

"Yes—" She fumbled with the helmet. Under the floor-grid the climbing men on the ladder were audible. They were already nearing the top. The trap door was closed: Anita and I were crouching on it. There was a thick metal bar set in a depressed groove of the grid. I slid it in place—it would seal the trap for a time, at any rate.

A degree of confidence came to me. We had a few moments before there could be any hand-to-hand conflict. That giant electronic projector would eventually be used against Grantline: it was the brigands' most powerful weapon. Its controls were here—by Heaven, I would smash them! That at least I could do!

I jumped for the window. Miko's signals had stopped, but I caught a glimpse of his distant moving curve-lights.

A flash came up at me, as in the window I became visible to the brigands on the ship's deck. It was a small hand-projector, hastily fired, for it went wide of the window. It was followed by a rain of small beams, but I was warned and I dropped my head beneath the high sill. The rays flashed diagonally upward through the oval opening, hissed against our vaulted roof. The air snapped and tingled with a shower of blue-red sparks, and the acrid odor of the released gases settled down upon me.

The trajectory controls of the projector were beside me. I seized them, ripped and tore at them. There was a roar down on the deck. The projector had exploded. A man's agonized scream split the confusion of sounds.

It silenced the brigands on the deck. Under our floor-grid those on the ladder had been pounding at the trap-door. They stopped, evidently to see what had happened. The bombardment of our windows ceased momentarily.

I cautiously peered out the window again. In the wreck of the projector three men were lying. One of them was screaming horribly. The dome-side was damaged. Potan and other men were frantically investigating to see if the ship's air were hissing out.

A triumph swept me. They had not found me so meek and inoffensive as they might have thought!

Anita clutched at me. She still had not donned her helmet.

"Put it on!"

"But Gregg—"

"Put it on!"

"I—I don't want to put it on until you put yours on."

"I've smashed the projector! We've stopped them coming up for a while."[223]

But they were still on the ladder under our floor. They heard our voices; they began thumping again. Then pounding. They seemed now to have some heavy implement. They rammed with it against the trap.

But the floor seemed holding. The square of metal grid trembled, yielded a little. But it was good for a few minutes longer.

I called down, "The first one who comes through will be shot." My words mingled with their oaths. There was a moment's pause, then the ramming went on. The dying man on the deck was still screaming.

I

whispered, "I'll try an Earth-signal."

She nodded. Pale, tense, but calm. "Yes, Gregg. And I was thinking—"

"It won't take a minute. Have your helmet ready."

"I was thinking—"

She hurried across the room. I swung on the Botz signaling apparatus. It was connected. Within a moment I had it humming. The fluorescent tubes lighted with their lurid glare; they painted purple the body of the giant duty-man who lay sprawled at my feet. I drew on all the ship's power. The tube-lights in the room quivered and went dim.

I would have to hurry. Potan could shut this off from the main hull control room. I could see, through the room's upper trap, the primary sending mirror mounted in the peak of the dome. It was quivering, radiant with its light-energy. I sent the flash.

The flattened, past-full Earth was up there. I knew that the western hemisphere faced the Moon at this hour. I flashed in English, with the open Universal Earth-code:

"*Help! Grantline.*"

And again: "*Send help! Archimedes region near Apennines. Attacked by brigands. Send help at once! Grantline!*"

If only it would be received! I flung off the current. Anita stood watching me intently. "Gregg, look!"

She had taken some of the glass globe-bombs which lay by the foot of the ascending ladder. She held some of them now.

"Gregg. I threw some."

t the window we gazed down. The globes she flung had shattered on the deck. They were occulting darkness bombs.[5]

[5] Filled with an odorless, harmless gas, these bombs were used in warfare, taking the place of the old-fashioned smoke screens. The diffusing gas was of such a nature that, when released, it absorbed within itself all the color inherent to the light-rays striking it, thus creating a temporary darkness.

Through the blackness of the deck, the shouts of the brigands came up. They were stumbling about. But the ramming of our trap went on, and I saw that it was beginning to yield. One corner of it was bent up.

"We've got to go, Anita!"

"Yes."

From out of the darkness which hung like a shroud over the deck an occasional flash came up, unaimed—wide of our windows. But the darkness was dissipating. I could see now the dim glow of the deck lights, blurred as through a heavy fog.

I dropped another of the bombs.

"Put on your helmet."

"Yes—yes, I will. You put on yours."

We had them adjusted in a moment. Our Erentz motors were pumping.

I gripped her. "Put out your helmet-light."

She extinguished it. I handed her my bullet projector.

"Hold it a moment. I'm going to take that belt of bombs."

The trap-door was all but broken under the ramming blows of the men on the ladder. I leaped over the body of the duty-man, seized the belt of bombs and strapped it about my waist.

Anita stood with me.

"Give me the projector."

She handed it to me. The trap-door burst upward! A man's head and [224]shoulders appeared. I fired a bullet into him—the little leaden pellet singing down through the yellow powder-flash that spat from the projector's muzzle.

T

he brigand screamed, and dropped back out of sight. There was confusion at the ladder-top. I flung a bomb at the broken trap. A tiny heat-ray came wavering up through the opening, but went wide of us.

The instrument room was in darkness. I clung to Anita.

"Hold on to me! You go first—here is the ladder."

We found it in the blackness, mounted it and went through the cubby's roof-trap.

I took a hasty look and dropped another bomb beside us. The four-foot space up here between the cubby roof and the overhead dome went black. We were momentarily concealed.

Anita located the manual levers of the lock-entrance.

"Here, Gregg."

I shoved at them. Fear leaped in me that they would not operate. But they swung. The tiny porte opened wide to receive us. We clambered into the small air-chamber; the door slid closed, just as a flash from below struck at it. The brigands had seen our little cloud of darkness and were firing up through it.

We were through the locks in a moment, out on the open dome-top. A sleek, rounded spread of glassite, with broad aluminite girders. There were cross-ribs which gave us footing, and occasional projections—streamline fin-tips, the casings of the upper rudder shafts, and the upstanding stubby funnels into which the helicopters were folded.

We moved along the central footpath and crouched by a six-foot casing. The stars and the glowing Earth were over us. The curving dome-top—a hundred feet or so in length, and bulging thirty feet wide beneath us—glistened in the Earthlight. It was a sheer drop down these curving sides past the ship's hull, a hundred feet to the rocks on which the vessel rested. The towering wall of Archimedes was beside us; and beyond the brink of the ledge the thousands of feet down to the plains.

I

saw the lights of Miko's band down there. He had stopped signaling. His little lights were spread out, bobbing as he and his men advanced up the crater's foothills, coming to join their ship.

I had an instant's glimpse. Anita and I could not stay here. The brigands would follow us up in a moment. I saw no exterior ladder. We would have to take our chances and jump.

There were brigands down there on the rocks. I saw three or four skulking helmeted figures, and they saw us! A bullet whizzed by us, and then came the flash of a hand-ray.

I touched Anita. "Can you make the leap? Anita, dear...."

Again it seemed that this must be farewell.

"Gregg, dear one—oh, we've got to do it!"

Those waiting figures would pounce on us.

"Anita, lie here a moment."

I jumped up and ran twenty feet toward the bow; then back, toward the stern, flinging down the last of my bombs. The darkness was like a cloud down there, enveloping the outer brigands. But up here we were above it, etched by the starlight and Earthglow.

I came back to Anita.

"We'll have to chance it now."

"Gregg...."

"Good-by, dear. I'll jump first, down this side—you follow."

To leap into that black patch, with the rocks under it....

"Gregg—"

She was trying to tell me to look overhead. She gestured. "Gregg, see!"

I saw it out over the plains—a little speck amid the stars. A moving speck, coming toward us!

"Gregg, what is it?"[225]

gazed, held my breath. A moving speck out there. A blob now.

CHAPTER XXXIII

Besieged!

ake up, Gregg! They're coming!"

I forced myself to consciousness. "Coming—"

"Yes. Wake up!"

I leaped from my bunk, followed Snap with a rush into the corridor. We had returned safely to the Grantline Camp. Anita and I found ourselves exhausted from lack of sleep, our arduous climb of Archimedes and that tense time on the brigand ship. On the flight back Snap had explained how the landing of the ship on Archimedes was observed through the Grantline telescope, using but little of its power for this local range. They had read with amazement my signals to the brigands. Snap[226] had rushed to completion the first of our contemplated flying platforms. Then he had seen Miko's signals from the crater-base, seen the lights of the fight to capture Anita and me in the cubby, and had come to rescue us.

Back at the camp we were given food, and Grantline forced me to try and sleep.

"They'll be on us in a few hours, Gregg. Miko will have joined them by now. He'll lead them to us. You must rest, for we need everyone at his best."

And surprisingly, in the midst of the camp's turmoil of last minute activities, I slept soundly, until Snap called me that the ship was coming.

The corridor echoed with the tramp of Grantline's busy crew. But there was no confusion now; a grim calmness had settled upon everyone.

Anita and Venza rushed up to join us. "It's in sight!"

T

here was no need of going to the instrument room. From the windows fronting the brink of the cliff the brigand ship was plainly visible. It came sailing from Archimedes, a dark shape blurring the stars. All its lights were extinguished save a single white search-beam in the bow-peak, slanting diagonally down.

The beam presently caught our little group of buildings; its glare shone in the windows as it clung for a moment. I could envisage the triumphant curiosity, of Potan and his fellows up there, gazing along the beam.

Then it swung away. The ship was at an altitude of no more than three thousand feet when I first saw it, coming upon a level keel. Would it circle over us, firing at us? Or sail past, after inspecting us? Or land, perhaps, boldly crowded upon our little ledge?

We were ready—as ready as we could be with our meager equipment. The camp was in a state of siege. The cliff-lights were extinguished: the interior lights were dim, save in the workshops of the main building, where the final assembling of Snap's other flying platforms and their insulated protective shields was still in progress.

We had dimmed the lights to conserve our power, and to enable the Erentz motors to run at full capacity. Our buildings would have to withstand the brigand rays which soon would be upon us.

Outside on our dim, Earthlit cliff, the tiny lights showed where our few guards were lurking. As I stood at the window watching the oncoming ship, Grantline's voice sounded:

"Call in those men! Ring the call-lights, Franck!"

The siren buzzed over the camp's interior; the warning call-lights on the roof brought in the outer guards. They came running to the admission portes, which had been repaired after Miko disabled them.

T

he guards came in. We dimmed our lights further. The treasure sheds were black against the cliff behind us. No need for guards there— the bulk of the ore was such that we reasoned the brigands would not attempt to move it until our buildings were captured. But, if they should try it, we were prepared to sally out with our hand-weapons and defend it.

In the dim lights we crouched. A silence was upon us, save for the clanging in the workshop down the corridor. Most of us wore our Erentz suits, with helmets ready, though I am sure there was not a man of us but who prayed he might not have to go out. At many of the windows—our weakest points to withstand the rays—insulated fabric shields were hung like curtains.

The brigand ship slowly advanced. It was soon over the opposite rim of our little crater. Its search-beam swung about the rim and down into the valley.

My thoughts ran like a turgid stream as I stood tensely watching.

Four hours ago I had sent that flash-signal to Earth. If it were received, a patrol-ship could come to our rescue and arrive here in another eight hours—or perhaps even less.[227]

Ah, that "if!" *If* the signal were received! *If* the patrol-ship were immediately available! *If* it started at once....

Eight hours at the very least. I tried to assure myself that we could hold out that long....

The brigand ship crossed the opposite crater-rim. It dropped lower. It seemed poised over the crater-valley, almost at our own level and less than two miles from us. Its search-beam vanished. For a moment it hung, a sleek, cylindrical silver shape, gleaming in the Earthlight.

Snap looked at me and murmured, "It's descending."

It slowly settled, cautiously picked its landing-place amid the crags and pits of the tumbled scarred valley floor. It came to rest, a vague silver menacing shape lurking in the lower shadows, close at the foot of the inner opposite crater-wall.

A few moments of tense waiting passed. Soon tiny lights were moving down there, some out on the rocks near the ship, others up under its deck-dome.

A stab of searchlight shot across the valley, swung along our ledge and clung with its glaring ten-foot circle to the front of our main building. Then a ray flashed.

The assault had begun!

(To be concluded)

[228]

The object shot forth another tentacle.

The Jovian Jest

By Lilith Lorraine

There came to our pigmy planet a radiant wanderer with a message—and a jest—from the vasty universe.

C

onsternation reigned in Elsnore village when the Nameless Thing was discovered in Farmer Burns' corn-patch. When the rumor began to gain credence that it was some sort of meteor from inter-stellar space, reporters, scientists and college professors flocked to the scene, desirous of prying off particles for analysis. But they soon discovered that the Thing was no ordinary meteor, for it glowed at night with a peculiar luminescence. They also observed that it was practically weightless, since it had embedded itself in the soft sand scarcely more than a few inches.

By the time the first group of newspapermen and scientists had reached the farm, another phenomenon was plainly observable. The Thing was growing!

Farmer Burns, with an eye to profit, had already built a picket fence around his starry visitor and was charging admission. He also flatly refused to permit the chipping off of specimens or even the touching of the object. His attitude was severely criticized, but he stubbornly clung to the[229] theory that possession is nine points in law.

I

t was Professor Ralston of Princewell who, on the third day after the fall of the meteor, remarked upon its growth. His colleagues crowded around him as he pointed out this peculiarity, and soon they discovered another factor—pulsation!

Larger than a small balloon, and gradually, almost imperceptibly expanding, with its viscid transparency shot through with opalescent lights, the Thing lay there in the deepening twilight and palpably shivered. As darkness descended, a sort of hellish radiance began to ooze from it. I say hellish, because there is no other word to describe that spectral, sulphurous emanation.

As the hangers-on around the pickets shudderingly shrank away from the weird light that was streaming out to them and tinting their faces with a ghastly, greenish pallor, Farmer Burns' small boy, moved by some imp of perversity, did a characteristically childish thing. He picked up a good-sized stone and flung it straight at the nameless mass!

I

nstead of veering off and falling to the ground as from an impact with metal, the stone sank right through the surface of the Thing as into a pool of protoplastic slime. When it reached the central core of the object, a more abundant life suddenly leaped and pulsed from center to circumference. Visible waves of sentient color circled round the solid stone. Stabbing swords of light leaped forth from them, piercing the stone, crumbling it, absorbing it. When it was gone, only a red spot, like a bloodshot eye, throbbed eerily where it had been.

Before the now thoroughly mystified crowd had time to remark upon this inexplicable disintegration, a more horrible manifestation occurred. The Thing, as though thoroughly awakened and vitalized by its unusual fare, was putting forth a tentacle. Right from the top of the shivering globe it pushed, sluggishly weaving and prescient of doom. Wavering, it hung for a moment, turning, twisting, groping. Finally it shot straight outward swift as a rattler's strike!

Before the closely packed crowd could give room for escape, it had circled the neck of the nearest bystander, Bill Jones, a cattleman, and jerked him, writhing and screaming, into the reddish core. Stupefied with soul-chilling terror, with their mass-consciousness practically annihilated before a deed with which their minds could make no association, the crowd could only gasp in sobbing unison and await the outcome.

T

he absorption of the stone had taught them what to expect, and for a moment it seemed that their worst anticipations were to be realised. The sluggish currents circled through the Thing, swirling the victim's body to the center. The giant tentacle drew back into the globe and became itself a current. The concentric circles merged—tightened—became one gleaming cord that encircled the helpless prey. From the inner circumference of this cord shot forth, not the swords of light that had powdered the stone to atoms, but myriads of radiant tentacles that gripped and cupped the body in a thousand places.

Suddenly the tentacles withdrew themselves, all save the ones that grasped the head. These seemed to tighten their pressure—to swell and pulse with a grayish substance that was flowing from the cups into the cord and from the cord into the body of the mass. Yes, it was a grayish something, a smokelike Essence that was being drawn from the cranial cavity. Bill Jones was no longer screaming and gibbering, but was stiff with the rigidity of stone. Notwithstanding, there was no visible mark upon his body; his flesh seemed unharmed.

Swiftly came the awful climax. The[230] waving tentacles withdrew themselves, the body of Bill Jones lost its rigidity, a heaving motion from the center of the Thing propelled its cargo to the surface—and Bill Jones stepped out!

Yes, he stepped out and stood for a moment staring straight ahead, staring at nothing, glassily. Every person in the shivering, paralysed group knew instinctively that something unthinkable had happened to him. Something had transpired, something hitherto possible only in the abysmal spaces of the Other Side of Things. Finally he turned and faced the nameless object, raising his arm stiffly, automatically, as in a military salute. Then he turned and walked jerkily, mindlessly, round and round the globe like a wooden soldier marching. Meanwhile the Thing lay quiescent—gorged!

---

rofessor Ralston was the first to find his voice. In fact, Professor Ralston was always finding his voice in the most unexpected places. But this time it had caught a chill. It was trembling.

"Gentlemen," he began, looking down academically upon the motley crowd as though doubting the aptitude of his salutation. "Fellow-citizens," he corrected, "the phenomenon we have just witnessed is, to the lay mind, inexplicable. To me—and to my honorable colleagues (added as an afterthought) it is quite clear. Quite clear, indeed. We have before us a specimen, a perfect specimen, I might say, of a—of a—"

He stammered in the presence of the unnamable. His hesitancy caused the rapt attention of the throng that was waiting breathlessly for an explanation, to flicker back to the inexplicable. In the fraction of a second that their gaze had been diverted from the Thing to the professor, the object had shot forth another tentacle, gripping him round the neck and choking off his sentence with a horrid rasp that sounded like a death rattle.

Needless to say, the revolting process that had turned Bill Jones from a human being into a mindless automaton was repeated with Professor Ralston. It happened as before, too rapidly for intervention, too suddenly for the minds of the onlookers to shake off the paralysis of an unprecedented nightmare. But when the victim was thrown to the surface, when he stepped out, drained of the grayish smokelike essence, a tentacle still gripped his neck and another rested directly on top of his head. This latter tentacle, instead of absorbing *from* him, visibly poured into him what resembled a threadlike stream of violet light.

acing the cowering audience with eyes staring glassily, still in the grip of the unknowable, Professor Ralston did an unbelievable thing. He resumed his lecture at the exact point of interruption! But he spoke with the tonelessness of a machine, a machine that pulsed to the will of a dictator, inhuman and inexorable!

"What you see before you," the Voice continued—the Voice that no longer echoed the thoughts of the professor—"is what you would call an amoeba, a giant amoeba. It is I—this amoeba, who am addressing you—children of an alien universe. It is I, who through this captured instrument of expression, whose queer language you can understand, am explaining my presence on your planet. I pour my thoughts into this specialised brain-box which I have previously drained of its meager thought-content." (Here the "honorable colleagues" nudged each other gleefully.) "I have so drained it for the purpose of analysis and that the flow of my own ideas may pass from my mind to yours unimpeded by any distortion that might otherwise be caused by their conflict with the thoughts of this individual.

"First I absorbed the brain-content of this being whom you call Bill Jones, but I found his mental instrument unavailable. It was technically untrained in the use of your words that would[231] best convey my meaning. He possesses more of what you would call 'innate intelligence,' but he has not perfected the mechanical brain through whose operation this innate intelligence can be transmitted to others and, applied for practical advantage.

"N

ow this creature that I am using is, as you might say, full of sound without meaning. His brain is a lumber-room in which he has hoarded a conglomeration of clever and appropriate word-forms with which to disguise the paucity of his ideas, with which to express nothing! Yet the very abundance of the material in his storeroom furnishes a discriminating mind with excellent tools for the transportation of its ideas into other minds.

"Know, then, that I am not here by accident. I am a Space Wanderer, an explorer from a super-universe whose evolution has proceeded without variation along the line of your amoeba. Your evolution, as I perceive from an analysis of the brain-content of your professor, *began* its unfoldment in somewhat the same manner as our own. But in your smaller system, less perfectly adjusted than our own to the cosmic mechanism, a series of cataclysms occurred. In fact, your planetary system was itself the result of a catastrophe, or of what might have been a catastrophe, had the two great suns collided whose near approach caused the wrenching off of your planets. From this colossal accident, rare, indeed, in the annals of the stars, an endless chain of accidents was born, a chain of which this specimen, this professor, and the species that he represents, is one of the weakest links.

"Your infinite variety of species is directly due to the variety of adaptations necessitated by this train of accidents. In the super-universe from which I come, such derangements of the celestial machinery simply do not happen. For this reason, our evolution has unfolded harmoniously along one line of development, whereas yours has branched out into diversified and grotesque expressions of the Life-Principle. Your so-called highest manifestation of this principle, namely, your own species, is characterized by a great number of specialized organs. Through this very specialization of functions, however, you have forfeited your individual immortality, and it has come about that only your life-stream is immortal. The primal cell is inherently immortal, but death follows in the wake of specialization.

e, the beings of this amoeba universe, are individually immortal. We have no highly specialized organs to break down under the stress of environment. When we want an organ, we create it. When it has served its purpose, we withdraw it into ourselves. We reach out our tentacles and draw to ourselves whatsoever we desire. Should a tentacle be destroyed, we can put forth another.

"Our universe is beautiful beyond the dreams of your most inspired poets. Whereas your landscapes, though lovely, are stationary, unchangeable except through herculean efforts, ours are Protean, eternally changing. With our own substance, we build our minarets of light, piercing the aura of infinity. At the bidding of our wills we create, preserve, destroy—only to build again more gloriously.

"We draw our sustenance from the primates, as do your plants, and we constantly replace the electronic base of these primates with our own emanations, in much the same manner as your nitrogenous plants revitalize your soil.

"While we create and withdraw organs at will, we have nothing to correspond to your five senses. We derive knowledge through one sense only, or, shall I say, a super-sense? We see and hear and touch and taste and smell and feel and know, not through any one organ, but through our whole structure. The homogeneous force of our omni-substance subjects the plural world to the processing of a powerful unity.[232]

e can dissolve our bodies at will, retaining only the permanent atom of our being, the seed of life dropped on the soil of our planet by Infinite Intelligence. We can propel this indestructible seed on light rays through the depths of space. We can visit the farthest universe with the velocity of light, since light is our conveyance. In reaching your little world, I have consumed a million years, for my world is a million light-years distant: yet to my race a million years is as one of your days.

"On arrival at any given destination, we can build our bodies from the elements of the foreign planet. We attain our knowledge of conditions on any given planet by absorbing the thought-content of the brains of a few representative members of its dominant race. Every well-balanced mind contains the experience of the race, the essence of the wisdom that the race-soul has gained during its residence in matter. We make this knowledge a part of our own thought-content, and thus the Universe lies like an open book before us.

"At the end of a given experiment in thought absorption, we return the borrowed mind-stuff to the brain of its possessor. We reward our subject for his momentary discomfiture by pouring into his body our splendid vitality. This lengthens his life expectancy immeasurably, by literally burning from his system the germs of actual or incipient ills that contaminate the blood-stream.

---

his, I believe, will conclude my explanation, an explanation to which you, as a race in whom intelligence is beginning to dawn, are entitled. But you have a long road to travel yet. Your thought-channels are pitifully blocked and criss-crossed with nonsensical and inhibitory complexes that stand in the way of true progress. But you will work this out, for the Divine Spark that pulses through us of the Larger Universe, pulses also through you. That spark, once lighted, can never be extinguished, can never be swallowed up again in the primeval slime.

"There is nothing more that I can learn from you—nothing that I can teach you at this stage of your evolution. I have but one message to give you, one thought to leave with you—forge on! You are on the path, the stars are over you, their light is flashing into your souls the slogan of the Federated Suns beyond the frontiers of your little warring worlds. Forge on!"

The Voice died out like the chiming of a great bell receding into immeasurable distance. The supercilious tones of the professor had yielded to the sweetness and the light of the Greater Mind whose instrument he had momentarily become. It was charged at the last with a golden resonance that seemed to echo down vast spaceless corridors beyond the furthermost outposts of time.

s the Voice faded out into a sacramental silence, the strangely assorted throng, moved by a common impulse, lowered their heads as though in prayer. The great globe pulsed and shimmered throughout its sentient depths like a sea of liquid jewels. Then the tentacle that grasped the professor drew him back toward the scintillating nucleus. Simultaneously another arm reached out and grasped Bill Jones, who, during the strange lecture, had ceased his wooden soldier marching and had stood stiffly at attention.

The bodies of both men within the nucleus were encircled once more by the single current. From it again put forth the tentacles, cupping their heads, but the smokelike essence flowed back to them this time, and with it flowed a tiny threadlike stream of violet light. Then came the heaving motion when the shimmering currents caught the two men and tossed them forth unharmed but visibly dowered with the radiance of more abundant life. Their faces were positively glowing and their eyes were illuminated by[233] a light that was surely not of earth.

Then, before the very eyes of the marveling people, the great globe began to dwindle. The jeweled lights intensified, concentrated, merged, until at last remained only a single spot no larger than a pin-head, but whose radiance was, notwithstanding, searing, excruciating. Then the spot leaped up—up into the heavens, whirling, dipping and circling as in a gesture of farewell, and finally soaring into invisibility with the blinding speed of light.

T

he whole wildly improbable occurrence might have been dismissed as a queer case of mass delusion, for such cases are not unknown to history, had it not been followed by a convincing aftermath.

The culmination of a series of startling coincidences, both ridiculous and tragic, at last brought men face to face with an incontestable fact: namely, that Bill Jones had emerged from his fiery baptism endowed with the thought-expressing facilities of Professor Ralston, while the professor was forced to struggle along with the meager educational appliances of Bill Jones!

In this ironic manner the Space-Wanderer had left unquestionable proof of his visit by rendering a tribute to "innate intelligence" and playing a Jovian Jest upon an educated fool—a neat transposition.

A Columbus from a vaster, kindlier universe had paused for a moment to learn the story of our pigmy system. He had brought us a message from the outermost citadels of life and had flashed out again on his aeonic voyage from everlasting unto everlasting.

FOR VACATION ADVENTURERS

Truth is stranger than fiction. Ask the Regular Army man who has soldiered in the far-off corners of the earth, gone "over the top" in action, and has experienced the thrill of service in the tropics or the sub-arctic.

Better yet, get an earful of real Astounding Stories yourself, at first hand this summer, as one of the thirty thousand young men between the ages of seventeen and twenty-four enjoying those thirty glorious days and nights as a student-camper at one of Uncle Sam's Citizens' Military Training Camps.

All of these Camps are pitched at Regular Army posts, and it is the custom for grizzled old-timers who have followed the Flag for many long years to drift down to "the boys" around campfire time each night and regale the student campers with thrilling, real life yarns of action and adventure in many strange and unusual circumstances.

It is not necessary for one to be a rich man's son in order to enjoy the manifold benefits of their Camps. Uncle Sam pays all the necessary bills including transportation, the best of food, bedding, laundry service and medical treatment if needed. And there is no obligation for future military service entailed by attendance at any of these Nation-wide CMT camps. Their primary mission is the upbuilding of American youth in health and good citizenship.

Detailed information, together with illustrated literature about the Citizens' Military Training Camp, may be obtained by addressing the CMTC Officer at the U.S. Army post nearest your home.

ASTOUNDING STORIES

Appears on Newsstands

THE FIRST THURSDAY IN EACH MONTH

---

[234]

It was sublime and terrible, and on the result of that conflict depended—what?

The Atom-Smasher

By Victor Rousseau

CHAPTER I

The "Vanishing Place"

"Look at that plane! That fellow's crazy! Took off with the wind behind him! He'll nose dive before he clears the clubhouse! He'll crash into those trees along the edge of the golf course!"

> Four destinies rocket through the strange Time-Space of the Fourth Dimension in Tode's marvelous Atom-Smasher.

The group on the field at Westbury, Long Island, held their breaths as they watched James Dent take off in the wildest, most erratic flight that they had ever seen. Under lowering storm clouds, with the wind roaring half a hurricane behind him, Dent spiraled upward as if unconscious of the laws of Earthly gravity.

"I told you so! You ought to have stopped him, even if it is his private plane! A feller's got no business trying to break his neck! Look there! He's cleared those trees after all!"

James Dent had cleared them, and the clubhouse too, and was already disappearing across the Hempstead Plains, looking like a leaf whirling up in a winter storm. At a height of five hundred feet he sped eastward.

"Didn't tell you where he was going?"

"Nope, acted like a crazy man. Something on his mind sure. Wherever he's bound for, he'll never get there!"[235]

B

ut James Dent was already out of sight, and the little group dispersed. And Dent, winging his way due east, over the oak barrens of central Long Island, was conscious neither of the storm that howled about him nor of the excitement that his rash take-off had occasioned.

The rain lashed him in the open cockpit, the ground fog swirled about him, and, though it was still afternoon, there brooded a somber twilight over the wastes. But in his mind Dent was already anticipating his descent at the "Vanishing Place," as the natives called it near Peconic Bay.

The "Vanishing Place" was so called because of the terrible and inexplicable catastrophe that had occurred there five years previously. In the two-century-old farmhouse, Miles Parrish, the world's greatest authority on physical chemistry, had been conducting investigations into the structure of the atom.

James Dent and Lucius Tode had been associated with old Parrish in this work, which, carried to a successful issue, would revolutionize the social organization of the world. The energy locked up in the atom is so stupendous that, as Eddington indicated, a thimbleful of coal, disintegrated, would carry the *Mauretania* from England to America and back again. To unlock this energy would be to set man free from bondage, to restore the pristine leisure and happiness of Eden.

nd because the three men were playing with deadly forces, of incalculable power, this deserted spot had been selected for the carrying on[236] of the investigations. The old farmhouse had been converted into a laboratory. For days together the three had bent over their tubes and laboratory apparatus, hardly eating or sleeping. And the day had come when success had seemed almost within their grasp.

Dent had received six months' leave of absence from his duties at Columbia University in order to prosecute the experiments. As the weeks went by, and the blind track that the three were following opened into a clear road, a sort of madness settled upon every one of them.

The Planck-Bohr quantum theory that the energy of a body cannot vary continuously, but only by a certain finite amount, or exact multiples of this amount, had been the key that unlocked the door. But always it had been Lucius Tode who led the way. Tode was a graduate of the University of Virginia, and accounted one of the most brilliant minds of his generation. At thirty, he stood head and shoulders above his contemporaries.

Dark, handsome, fearless, with a will power that nothing seemed able to subdue, he had taken the leadership away from old Miles Parrish, who eagerly and without thought of his own reputation followed in his assistant's footsteps.

There were the three men—and there was the girl, Lucille Parrish, the child of Miles's old age. Seventeen, when the catastrophe occurred, she had come out to the deserted spot sometimes of a Sunday from her boarding school at Garden City.

And Tode had found time to make love to her when he rushed her back to her school in his high-powered foreign car!

Jim Dent had known nothing of that until after the catastrophe. Lucille had been afraid of him, afraid to open her mouth upon the subject even to her father. And she had been fascinated too, as a young girl may well be, when a fascinating man of thirty uses his arts to win her.

I

t was only by chance that Jim had failed to be involved in the hideous catastrophe that had stamped the old farmhouse with the name of "Vanishing Place" whenever the natives spoke of it.

"Two Killed in Laboratory Explosion!" was the heading in the next morning's paper which gave Jim his first intimation of the accident. He had been to Columbia overnight to look up a new publication that contained an article on the hydrogen spectrum.

It was only a long paragraph, and the names of Parrish and Tode meant nothing to the man who had written it. But Jim had taken train to Hempstead, taxied to the flying fields, and essayed his first plane ride to Peconic Bay, in the charge of a pilot.

A group of natives, three newspaper men and a Suffolk County policeman were near the spot where the farmhouse had been—near the spot, not on it.

For where the farmhouse had been was a great pool of stagnant water, black as ink, covering an expanse of perhaps three-quarters of an acre.

"No, sir, there was no explosion," said the officer. "At least, none of these fellows heard anything. Just a—you tell the Professor, Mr. Lumm."

"It was about half-past eight last night, Mr. Dent," said Andrew Lumm, who kept the village store a mile away. "Ground seemed to rock. Earthquake, I says to myself, holdin' on to the door. But it wasn't no earthquake. Too gentle for that. Nothin' broke, not even a plate. Then I says to Mrs. Lumm, 'They're gone, poor fellers, and I allus knowed it would be that way. It's lucky young Mr. Dent went out last night on the 7.15.'

"We hurried here, but there wasn't no sign of the place, jest a hole on the ground with a sort of sticky mud in it. Water's been fillin' in since then, but I guess it's reached its level now. They jest blowed themselves to bits, Mr. Dent."

"Tell him about the vi'let light, Andy," put in one of the bystanders.[237]

"Yeah, like a pillar of vi'let fire that were, Mr. Dent. We seed it through the trees, but by the time we got here it was 'most gone. Gosh, that throwed a scare into some of us!"

"It was Mr. Tode's soul a-burnin'," squeaked Granpop Dawes. "I allus said that feller'd come to no good end."

The group shook their heads and remained silent. It was clear that, if they did not share Granpop Dawes's opinion, at least they considered it not without the bounds of plausibility. Lucius Tode had created a bad impression among the natives.

J

im Dent stooped and picked up something lying imbedded in the mud at the edge of the black pool, and slipped it into his pocket. He had been present at the inquest and had gone back to Columbia. That had been five years before.

Professor McDowd, the palaeontologist, had identified the object Jim had found as the milk molar of *merychippus insignis*, the miocene representative of the modern horse. And that had made Jim Dent think furiously.

The catastrophe must have been a gigantic one to h fossil tooth from strata far beneath the level of the ing up that More, there were even traces of archaean deposits surface. borders of the pool, whose depth, in the center, was asc nd the be 164 feet. ned to

Black, silent, uninhabited, unstirred save by a passing breeze, e pool had remained those five years past. The spot was shunned a haunted or accursed by the superstitious country folks. Dense underbrush had grown up around it.

Periodically, Jim had gone out to visit it. That was how he had come to invest in a private plane. It was only an hour to the flying-fields, and less than an hour from there to Peconic Bay. What he expected to achieve he did not know. In the back of his mind was the belief that some day he would light upon some clue that would tell something of the unusual catastrophe.

And then that afternoon he had been shaken to the depths when a message came to him in Lucille's voice over the telephone:

"I've heard from dad!"

---

inging his way eastward through the storm, Jim Dent was mentally reconstructing all that had led up to the present moment.

Lucille had finished her high school course and gone into business life. Jim had found a position for her as secretary to a small group of physicists, who were conducting private investigations, a position r training well fitted her. She had done well. He had for which with her. kept in

Six ths before, their relations had altered. They had realized that the ere in love with each other. In the months that followed they he discovered all sorts of things about each other that neither had spected, which might be summed up by saying that they had become all in all to each other.

It was so amazing, this transformation of ordinary friendship into radiant love, that they were still bewildered over it. They were to be married at the end of the year.

It was then that Lucille had first told Jim about Lucius's wooing, and her fear of the man. Apart from that, both had refrained, by tacit agreement, from making reference to the past.

And then, that afternoon, there sounded Lucille's voice over the telephone, "I've heard from dad!"

"From—your father? You're mistaken, dear!"

"No, Jim, I'm not mistaken. He called me on the 'phone two hours ago. I couldn't mistake his voice, and, besides, he called me "Lucy," like he used to do. He told me to come at once to the Vanishing Place, but not to tell a soul unless I wished to do him a great evil. Then he rang off."

"Where are you now?" asked Jim.

"I'm 'phoning from Amityville. I[238] took the train immediately, but I was so frightened, and—and at last I decide I must tell you. I didn't think dad would have minded my telling you. So I got out. There's another train in a few minutes, and I shall go on to Hampton Bays and walk the two miles to the Vanishing Place. I—I'll meet you there."

"Lucille, wait! Can't you meet me somewhere else, and we'll go on together. I'll get my plane and—"

"Oh, I just can't wait, Jim! I'm in such terror that I won't find dad when I get there. And he told me to tell nobody. I—I'll meet you at the Vanishing Place, Jim."

And so great had been her agitation that with that arrangement Jim had had to rest content. He had taken a taxi out to the flying fields at once.

I

n half an hour he would know what had happened. And he was obsessed by the terror that he would not find Lucille or anything except the lonely pool.

That was why he opened the throttle and drove on wildly through the scurrying wraiths of mist, pierced by the tops of trees that at times rose dangerously near the spreading wings.

That gap in the trees was Lake Ronkokoma. Not far now! Jim would know soon. But as he flew, vague fears that had beset his mind since he had received Lucille's message began to crystallize into the single fear of Tode. If Parrish was really alive—why not Tode too?

Beneath the polish and the surface comradeship, Jim had always been conscious of some *diablerie* about the man, of some inner life of which he knew nothing. Something unscrupulous and relentless, something infinitely cruel—as when he had tested the Atom Smasher on a stray cur that had run into the laboratory, not for experimentation, but in mere ruthless savagery, converting the living beast instantly into a shapeless mass of flesh and bone.

And Tode had known more about the Atom Smasher—as they affectionately called the mechanism for releasing atomic energy—than old Parrish and he together. Suppose Lucille's story were true! Suppose old Parrish were actually alive, suppose Tode were responsible for some designed scheme which would, in the end place Lucille in his power!

Wild thoughts and fears—but Jim would soon know. And with throttle stretched to the limit he went roaring over the scrub oak toward Peconic Bay.

I

t was beginning to grow dark, almost too dark for landing. But now Jim could feel the tang of the salt wind upon his face. He slowed down. The fog was as thick as ever, but the scrub oak had given place to more open country. In a minute or two he ought to sight some landmark. Yes, he had overshot his mark, for suddenly, through a gap in the mists, he saw the line of breakers forming a white ridge upon the sand.

A mile southward! Jim knew where he was now, for he knew every curve of that shore. He banked and turned. And then he saw something that for an instant chilled his blood.

Not far away, and not far beneath him, a ghostly violet haze was spreading through the fog, and the fog itself was coiling back from it until it formed a dense white wall.

For a moment Jim's hand was paralysed upon the stick. The next, his decision was made. He closed his throttle and went down in a slow descent right toward the heart of that column of lavender smoke that seemed to be springing straight up out of the ground. "A pillar of violet fire!" It could not have been described better.

The plane dived through the dense wall of fog, which for a moment shut out the violet fire completely. Then Jim was through, and almost immediately beneath him lay the black and glassy surface of the pool. Out of the very heart of it rose the fire, burning[239] like some infernal flame that consumed nothing, and between it and the fog was a space of almost translucent air, extending to the borders of the pool.

Jim began to circle the pool to find a landing-place. But as he looked down, the surface of the pool began to change its aspect.

I

n place of the unruffled calm, it began to work with some devil's yeast all around the central pillar of flame, until its depths seemed to be churned up in frothy masses and the movement extended almost to the circumference. Then the whole surface of the water began to tilt and sway with a slow, shimmering, undulatory movement, as if it was a giant roulette wheel in rotation.

And something was materializing out of the heart of the violet flame itself.

It was a face—a human face, with bestial features, distorted and enormously magnified through the substance in which it was. Such a face as might look back upon an observer out of one of those distorting mirrors at Coney Island, or some other place of popular amusement, but twisted and enlarged beyond conception, so that it covered half the area of a city block.

Curiously blurred, too, as if each atom of that face was in isolated motion on its own account. And beneath the face appeared the vague outlines of a hand, apparently manipulating some sort of infernal mechanism.

And that face, enlarged as it was out of all proportion, filled Jim's heart with greater horror than any face he had ever known.

For it was the visage of Lucius Tode, and on those huge and distorted features was something that looked like a diabolical smile.

E

verything vanished. Jim was back in the surrounding wall of fog. Instinctively he banked again. He strove to drive the horror from his brain. He must circle, circle incessantly, in the hope of finding Lucille. She must have already arrived. But if she had not fallen into Tode's power, she would hear the roaring of the plane and manage to signal him.

He circled back into the clear space between the white and the violet, and now he saw that the effect upon the pool was still more pronounced. The waters were rising up in a rim all around, and yet not overflowing. They were standing up like a bowl of clay upon the potter's wheel, and down in the depths Jim could see the head and shoulders of Tode, much less magnified, more natural in appearance, and less blurred. And Tode was looking up at him and pointing that infernal mechanism at him—something that looked like the tube of a telescope.

Suddenly the plane shivered and stood still. The motor died abruptly. The stick went dead. And yet the plane did not fall. As if upheld by the same repulsive force that drove back the white fog, it simply hung suspended three hundred feet above the heart of the violet flame.

Then—there was no longer any plane. The stick had melted in Jim's hand, the wings dissolved like wreaths of mist. The entire body had disintegrated into nothingness. Jim sat suspended in the void, and felt himself very slowly descending into the violet column.

Down into the vortex of that bubbling pool, which rimmed him on all sides ... down into the central aperture out of which emerged the leering face of Tode! And as he dropped Jim heard, thin, faint, and very far away, the despairing cry of Lucille....

CHAPTER II

Old Friends—and Foes

Jim must have lapsed into unconsciousness, for when he opened his eyes there was a gap in his consciousness of the passage of time, though none in his memory. He opened his eyes, and instantly he remembered everything.[240]

Only a brief interval could have elapsed, for it was not quite dark. The fog and the violet flame had cleared away. Overhead a few stars twinkled. Jim was lying on his side, half-buried in the black, slimy mud of the dried up pool.

There was nothing but the smooth, shelving mud basin, with the scrub oak surrounding it. Tode and the machine had vanished.

Jim pulled himself with an effort out of the sucking mud, and, heavily clogged with it, began to make his way toward the margin.

Stumbling, struggling through the viscid ooze, he shouted Lucille's name despairingly. But no answer came, and his cries only made the utter silence all about him seem more fearsome.

Exhausted by his efforts, he gained the edge of the pool at last, and stopped, trying to orientate himself. As he did so, he saw a human face peering at him out of a clump of scrub oak.

It was the face of an aged man, with a long white beard and rags of clothes that were festooned about him. Jim took a step toward it, shouting a challenge. Next moment it had hurled itself out of its shelter toward him, and two skeletonlike arms were twined about his shoulders, while the fingers worked upward toward his throat.

The face was that of a madman, crazed by fear. And Jim recognized it. It was the face of Professor Parrish.

Parrish, the trim, immaculate, clean-shaven, urbane old man, whose lectures, imbued with wit and scholarship, had always been the delight of his classes—Parrish reduced to this gibbering maniac! And yet Parrish himself, returned to the site of their experiments after five years!

S

o fierce was the old man's onset, so desperate his clutch, that for a half-minute or more Jim was reduced to fighting for his life. The clawing fingers, armed with long nails, furrowed Jim's throat, there was a terrific strength in the body, wasted though it was almost to a skeleton.

But it was only for a half-minute that old Parrish's endurance lasted. Suddenly the old man went limp and tottered forward, dropped upon the ground. Jim bent over him.

"Parrish, you know me! I'm Jim Dent!" he cried. "I came here to save you."

Parrish was muttering something. Jim caught the words "Tode," and "God help Lucille!"

"Parrish, I'm Jim Dent!" Jim cried again, and the old man, shuddering, opened his eyes and recognized him.

"Jim!" he muttered. "Jim Dent! Then where is she? I got away from that devil, found farmhouse empty, got telephone book, found her and 'phoned her. Told her to come. Save—Lucille!"

He fell back, his eyes closed. Jim crouched over the unconscious old man. He was in a state of utter perplexity. He could not quite gather what Parrish had been trying to tell him, and it was with difficulty that he could focus his mind upon the situation, so great had been the shock of finding his former chief in that condition.

What had become of his plane, and where was Lucille? Jim was positive that he had heard her cry for help out of the vortex in the water.

But there was no water, only the circle of black mud extended in the starlight.

Again and again Jim shouted Lucille's name, and his cries went echoing away through the scrub without result.

Jim looked down at the unconscious old man beside him. He must get Parrish away, get him to Andy Lumm's. He bent over him again and raised him in his arms.

S

uddenly he heard two familiar sounds behind him, two dull thumps that sounded less like explosions than echoes, long drawn out, and receding into infinity. There was no other sound quite like them that he had ever heard.[241]

They were the snap of the electrical discharge as the Atom Smasher began to operate, and why the snap had sounded like a heavy body falling a long distance away, was not known.

Tode had said one day, with what Jim had taken for sarcasm, that they represented the wave series of a single sound extended in time to make four-dimensional action, but Jim had never considered the explanation seriously.

That sound, bringing back all Jim's memories of their experiments, brought him to his feet sharply. He swung around. The surface of the pool was a bubbling, seething mass of mud and water. And over its surface that faint violet haze was beginning to spread.

In the center where the light was thickest, something like a gyroscope appeared to be revolving. Out of the gyroscope something was beginning to project—that infernal tube of Lucius Tode. And Jim knew that in the heart of the flame that enormous, distorted face of Lucius Tode would again be visible.

The human nervous system can only endure a certain amount of impact. The sight of that ghastly flame, already condensing into a violet pillar, was more than Jim could stand. He dragged old Parrish to his feet and started off with him into the thickest part of the undergrowth.

A fearful scream behind him stopped him at the very edge of the scrub. He looked back, still supporting the half-conscious old man in his arms. The violet flame was shooting up in a straight pillar, the whole central portion of the pool was dry, and the waters were heaped up all around it.

From the slightly elevated spot where Jim stood, he could see Tode holding Lucille in his arms in the very heart of the fire, which threw a pale, fluorescent light over their faces. Tode was wearing a spotted skin, like that of a leopard, and Lucille was in the blue frock that she had worn when Jim and she had dinner together two evenings before.

Jim dropped old Parrish, shouted in answer, and dashed back like a madman down the slope into the solid wall of water.

H

e fought his way desperately through that wall, which seemed of the consistency of soft rubber or treacle, as if some subtle change had taken place in its molecular isomers. It adhered to him without wetting him, and he plunged through it, hearing Lucille cry out again, and yet again.

And now he was through, and once more struggling over the viscid surface of the pond. Behind him he heard old Parrish blundering, and screeching at the top of his voice, but he paid no attention to him.

He could see Lucille more clearly, and the large, hazy outlines of Tode's features were beginning to assume the proper proportions. There was a diabolical leer upon Tode's face, unchanged during the five years since Jim had seen him last, except that it had become more evil, more powerful. The enormous and distorted face that Jim had seen had been simply due to the presence of some refracting medium.

The pillar of violet light was thinning, spreading out over the pool, but Jim could now see the scene more clearly than before, even as he rushed onward.

The machine was inside what looked like a flat boat, but more circular than a boat, and apparently was made of some metal resembling aluminum. Either from the metal hull or from the mechanism inside it there was emitted a pungent odor resembling chlorine.

The mechanism itself bore some resemblance to the old Atom Smasher of five years before, but it appeared to be immensely more complicated. Wheels of various sizes were set at every conceivable angle around the central tube, from which the violet light was emanating, and all were rotating and gyrating so fast that they looked like discs of light. The boat itself was trembling, and this movement appeared to be com[242]municated to the boiling mud in the central part of the pool.

---

s Jim tried to leap down through the sucking mud to snatch Lucille from Tode, the latter stopped, straightened himself, and pointed a short tube at Jim's heart.

Jim felt as if an enormous, invisible force had struck him in the chest. It was apparently the same repulsive force that had driven back the waters. The shock was not a violent one. It did not throw him off his feet. It merely pushed him slowly and irresistibly backward.

And the whole picture was beginning to fade. Etched sharply in the violet light one moment, it now looked like a drawing that had been covered with tissue paper.

The outlines were dissolving into a haze—or, rather, each line seemed reproduced an infinite number of times, as the edge of a vibrating saw shows an infinitude of edges. The violet fire was becoming still more diffused. It hovered over the waters, a pale, flickering glow. And simultaneously the walls of water began to break and come surging forward.

Jim saw Lucille stretching out her arms toward him, and tried to struggle forward, but in vain. She cried out his name, and he put all his strength into that desperate futile struggle to reach her. But he was being borne backward by the invisible power in the tube. The rushing torrent was surging about his knees; grew waist deep: in another moment Jim was swimming for his life against the furious flood.

Suddenly, however, the tremendous pressure on his chest was relaxed. Tode had turned the tube away from him. He was leaning forward out of the boat and grasped old Parrish, who had been flung violently against it by the dissolving waters.

The same flood carried Jim to the boat's side. Here, however, the flood was only knee deep, owing to the repulsion still being exercised by the violet light, which was glimmering feebly. Jim found his feet and leaped into the craft. He grasped Lucille in his arms.

H

e turned to confront Tode, who had just dragged old Parrish over the side. The three men confronted one another.

"Turn that tube on me, and I'll jump into your damn machinery and bust it!" Jim shouted.

An ironical expression came on Tode's face. It was clear that he still considered himself master of the situation. "At the immediate moment, Dent, the lives of all of us depend upon your keeping absolutely still," he answered. "Take my advice and sit down!"

Jim saw Lucille's face, ghastly in the faint violet light that played about it. The girl had fainted. She was lying unconscious, her feet against the circular metal plate that protected the machinery, her head upon the rail that ran around the boat's upper edge. Tode, without waiting for Jim's answer, stepped over the plate and took his seat at a sort of instrument board with control levers and thumb screws that apparently controlled the needles on four dials. He touched a button, and instantly the violet light disappeared.

With its vanishing, the waves came surging forward, and lapped violently against the hull, as if about to overwhelm the vessel, which, however, seemed immovable. It simply rose higher in the water.

Jim understood the cause of this. Those gyroscopes would retain the hull in the same position against anything but a mechanical force strong enough to ruin it. He watched Tode as he sat at the instrument board, which was illuminated by two tiny lights of what looked like mercury-vapor. His face, handsome and cruel as ever, was tense as he manipulated the thumb screws. Beside him lay Parrish, faintly whimpering. The old man had evidently abandoned all hope of effecting his escape, or of rescuing his daughter.

It was unbearable to have to sit there,[243] knowing that the three of them were absolutely at Tode's mercy, and yet there was nothing else to do.

T

ode looked up with a saturnine smile. "It's a delicate operation to blur the present without shooting out a hundred years or so in time," he said, "but my micrometer's pretty accurate, Dent. Don't move, I caution you!" He smiled again. "Yes, Dent, time is something like the fourth dimension of space, as we believed in the old days, and I've proved it."

Jim saw Tode touch the screw that controlled the fourth dial, and instantly it was borne in on him that each of the dials controlled one spatial dimension. This fourth, then, was the time dimension!

Could it be true that Tode had solved the practical problem of traveling in time, theoretically implied since the discoveries of Einstein?

He had known in the old days that the Atom Smasher might be adapted to this purpose, but neither Parrish nor he had dreamed of turning aside from their endeavor to utilize it for the purpose of releasing atomic energy.

Thump! Thump! The familiar old sound, rushing back into memory after all those years, the release of the electrical discharge, echoing through infinity! The scrub around the pool blurred and was gone. A vast gray panorama extended itself on either side of them.

They were travelling—in space—and time too. Jim no longer doubted. And, chilled with horror, he sat there, his arm about Lucille's unconscious form.

CHAPTER III

Into the Infinite

ow long he sat there he did not know. Minutes or hours seemed all the same to him. Nothing but that gray monochrome, of neither light nor darkness, that endless panorama of miles and years, blended together into this chaos!

But suddenly there came a shout from Tode. The blur ceased, the lights flickered. Again there sounded the two thumps of the electrical discharge. The vibrating mechanism grew steady. Above them, out of the grayness, a moon disclosed itself, then the pin-points of stars. All about them was an immense, sandy waste.

"Know where we are, Dent?" came Tode's chuckle.

Jim was not sufficiently master of himself to attempt to answer.

"We are on what will be the Russian steppes some fifty thousand years ahead of us in time," grinned Tode. "This is an interlude between two ice ages. Observe how pleasantly warm the climate is, for Russia. Unfortunately the receding glaciers carried off the top-soil, which accounts for the barrenness of the district, but in another century this country will be overgrown with ferns, and inhabited by the mastodon and wild horse, and a few enterprising palaeolithic hunters, who will come in to track them down and destroy them with their stone axes."

"I think you're the same sort of damn liar you always were, Tode," answered Jim—but without conviction. There was something terrific about that desolation. Nothing within a thousand miles of Long Island corresponded to it.

"You'll be convinced pretty quickly, when you see my specimen," answered Tode. "I let him off here on the way to the pool. He's not exactly presentable, and when I got the idea of picking up Lucille and taking her back with me, I thought it best not to let her see him. He didn't want to be let off. Was afraid I wouldn't pick him up again, and I'll admit it was a matter of pretty careful reckoning. But this is the place, almost to the yard.

"Yes, I've done some close reckoning, Dent, but the cleverest part of the business was letting old Parrish think he'd got away from me. I knew he'd telephone Lucille. You know, I always[244] had the brains of the outfit, Dent," he continued, with a smirk of self-satisfaction.

He looked out of the boat. "And here, if I'm not mistaken, comes my specimen," he added.

Something was running across the steppes toward them. It came nearer, took human form. It was human! A man—but such a man as

Jim had never seen before outside the covers of a book. And he recognised the race immediately.

It was a Neanderthal man, one of the race that co-existed with the highly developed Cro-Magnons some thirty thousand years ago. Man and not ape, though the face was bestial, and there were huge ridges above the eyebrows.

And if Jim had needed conviction, the sight of this gibbering creature, now climbing into the boat and fawning upon Tode, convinced him. For the Neanderthal man vanished from the scene long before the beginning of recorded history.

For a few moments a deathly faintness overcame him ... his eyes closed, he felt unconsciousness rushing in upon him like a black cloud.

"It's all right, Dent—don't look so scared!" came Tode's mocking voice.

Jim opened his eyes, shook off that cloud of darkness with an immense effort. The boat was throbbing violently as the wheels gyrated, the violet light had become a pillar as thick as a man, and shot straight up to a height of fifty feet, before it rolled away. Lucille was lying where she had been, her eyes still staring up unseeing at the stars. Old Parrish was whining and whimpering as he crouched in his place.

And at Tode's feet crouched the Neanderthal man, repulsive, bestial, even though hardly formidable, and filling the last vacant spot inside the boat. He was gibbering and mouthing as he fawned upon Tode and pressed his hand to his hairy face. He continued to crouch and looked up at his master with doglike eyes.

R

epulsive, and yet man, not ape. Distinctly human, perhaps a little lower than the Australian aborigine, the Neanderthal showed by his reverence that the human faculty of worship existed in him.

"Meet Cain, one of my Drilgoes," said Tode, with a grin. "A faithful servant. I left him here to wait for me on the return journey. Cain's just my pet name for him because he subsists on the fruits of the earth, don't you, Cain?"

The Drilgo grunted, and pressed Tode's hand to his repulsive lips, which were fringed with a reddish beard. Suddenly Tode began to laugh uproariously. "Feel anything wrong with your head, Dent?" he asked.

Dent put up his hand and pulled away a quantity of charred hair. His forehead began to itch, and, rubbing his finger across it, he realized that his eyebrows were gone. Tode laughed still louder.

"You've kept your teeth by about two seconds' grace, Dent, but I shouldn't be surprised if you needed dental attention shortly," he said. "What a pity dentists won't be invented for another forty or fifty thousand years."

"You're a devil!" cried Jim.

"You see, the human body is very resistant to the Ray," Tode went on. "It almost seems as if there is an organizing principle within it. Even the animal tissues are resistant, though not to the same extent as the human ones. It takes about twenty seconds for the organized human form to be disintegrated. But hair and beaks and claws, being superficial matter, vanish almost as soon as the Ray is turned on them. Ten seconds more, and you'd have been obliterated, Dent, just as your plane was.

"Yes, rub your head. Your hair will probably grow again—if I decide to let you live. It rather depends upon what impression you make upon Lucille as a bald-headed hero. After all, I didn't invite you to accompany us. It's your own lookout."[245]

J

im could find nothing to say to that. He was discovering more and more that they were all helpless in Tode's hands.

"Sit back!" snarled Tode suddenly. He gave the Drilgo a push that sent him sprawling into the bottom of the boat. "Dent, your life depends upon your absolute acquiescence to my proposals. I didn't like you particularly in the old days, any more than you liked me. I thought you were a fool. On the other hand, I've no active reason to hate you, at present. It may be that I can use you.

"Meanwhile we've got a longish journey before us, ten thousand years more, multiplied by the fourth power of two thousand miles. Seems simple? Well, I had to invent the mathematical process for it. Reckon in the gravitational attraction of the planets, and you'll begin to get an idea of the complexity of it. So, in vulgar parlance, we're not likely to arrive till morning."

He glanced at Lucille, who was still lying unconscious with Jim's arm about her. Then his eyes rose to meet Jim's, and a sneering smile played about his lips. That smile was the acknowledgment of their rivalry for the girl's affections. And it was more—it was a challenge.

Tode welcomed that rivalry because, Jim could see, he meant to keep him alive under conditions of servitude, to demonstrate to Lucille his superiority.

Tode turned his thumbscrews, and the two thuds resounded. The violet column sank down, the boat vibrated, the level stretch of land became a blur again. The moon and stars vanished. Once more the four were off on that terrific journey.

t first they seemed to be traversing space that was shot through by alternate light and darkness, so that at times Jim could see the other occupants of the boat clearly, while at other times there was only Tode visible at the instrument board, with the dark outlines of the Drilgo, Cain, sprawled at his feet. But soon these streaks seemed to come closer and closer together, until the duration of each was only a fraction of a second. And closer, until light and darkness blended into a universal gray. These, Jim knew, were the alternations of night and day.

They were traveling—incredible as it was—in time as well as space, though whether backward or forward Jim could not know. From the presence of the Neanderthal man, however, Jim was convinced that Tode was taking them back more thousands of years, into the beginnings of humanity.

A fearful journey! A madder journey than Jim could have conceived of, had he not been a participant in it. He was losing all sense of reality. He was hardly convinced that he would not awaken in New York, to discover that the whole episode had been a dream.

Was this Lucille, the girl he loved ... with whom he had dined in New York only a day or two before ... this unconscious form, stretched out on the deck of the weird ship that was rushing through eternity? Or, rather, it was they who were rushing through space and time upon a stationary ship! What was reality, and what was dream, then?

Tode called "Come over here, Dent! I want to talk to you!"

J

im picked his way over the metal floor of the round boat, came up to Tode, and sat down beside him above the sprawling form of the Drilgo, Cain.

"You were a fool to come here, Dent." Tode turned with a malicious smile from his seat at the instrument board. "You didn't have to come. I take it that you are in love with Lucille, you poor imbecile, and still cherish dreams of winning her. We'll take up that matter in due course.

"Do you think I've been idle during these five years of my exile? I've been too busy even to come back for the woman I was in love with. And do you know what I've been doing during all this hellish period? Charting[246] courses, Dent! Mapping out all the planetary movements back for uncounted ages—roughly, crudely, of course, but the best I was able to. These are difficult seas to navigate, though they may not seem so. You fool," he added savagely, "why didn't you come in with me in the old days? I told you that the Atom Smasher could be used to travel through time, and you mocked at me as a dreamer.

"I chose my hour. When everything was ready, I set forth on the most desperate journey ever attempted by man. Talk of Columbus!—he had nothing on me. I tell you, Dent, I've been back to the Archaean Age, back to the time when nothing but crawling worms moved on the face of the earth. And I've been forward to the time when an errant planet will disrupt the earth into a shower of lava—and I nearly wrecked the boat. Dent.

"I've won, Dent! I've won! I've solved the problem that gives man immortality! All the epochs that have existed since God first formed the world are mine to play with! I have seen myself as a puling infant, and as a greybeard. I have made myself immortal, because, with this machine, I can set back the clock of time. I have found a land where I am worshipped as a god."

T

ode's eyes glittered with maniacal fires. He went on in a voice of indescribable triumph:

"I'm a god there, Dent. Do you want to know where that land is? It is Atlantis, sunk beneath the waves nine thousand years before recorded history opened. It is Atlantis, from which the Cro-Magnons fled in their ships, to land on the coasts of Spain and France, and become the ancestors of modern man.

"In old Atlantis, still not wholly submerged, I have made myself a god. I have mastered the savage Drilgoes whom the Atlanteans oppressed. All the spoils of their ruined cities are at my disposal. And I came back to get Lucille, whom I had never ceased to love. Together Lucille and I will rule like god and goddess.

"Join me, Dent. I'm a god in Atlantis—a god, I tell you. The lesser races fear me as a supernatural being. Only the city remains uncaptured, but it is mine whenever I choose to take it. A god—a god—a god!"

Jim saw now what he had not realized before, that Tode was insane. It would, indeed, have been a miracle if he had been able to retain his sanity under such circumstances as he had described. His voice rose into a wild scream. Yes, Tode was mad—just such a madman as any of the old Roman emperors, drunk with power, each in his turn the sole ruler of the world.

"The Earth is mine!" Tode screamed. "Before the modern world was dreamed of, before the nations were created, Atlantis was the sole power that held dominion over the scattered tribes of mankind. And she is in my hand whenever I strike.

"Wealth incalculable, treasures such as man has never since seen, marvels of scientific discovery, flying machines that would make ours look foolish, paintings grander than have since been executed—all these things exist in the proud city that will shortly be at my command. And I have my Drilgoes, the inferior race, to serve me. They worship me because they know I am a god. Join me, Dent, and taste the joys of being one of the supreme rulers of the world."

I

n spite of his undoubted madness, there was such power in Tode's voice that Jim could not help believe what he had said.

"Well," snarled Tode. "You hesitate to give me your answer, Dent?"

"Lucille and I are engaged to be married," answered Jim, and the words were drawn from his lips almost against his will. "We love each other. I am not going to lie to you and then betray you, Tode."

The expression on Tode's face was[247] demoniacal. He snatched up the deadly tube that contained the violet fire and turned it upon Jim. Again Jim felt that repulsive force pushing him back. He gasped for breath, and tensed his whole body in supreme resistance, while he tried to grapple with Tode in vain.

But suddenly Tode dropped the tube, and a roar of laughter broke from his lips.

"You fool!" he shouted. "I tell you I am a god, the one god, supreme above all. Do you think to match your puny will against my own? I tell you Lucille is mine. And for ever, Dent. Whenever we two have reached old age, all that will be necessary for us to do will be to turn this screw a hair's breadth back into the past, and we are both young again. By holding this vessel steady in four-dimensional space, I can achieve immortality."

"Yes, Tode," answered Jim, "but, you see, that's the one thing that you haven't been able to work out yet."

The words seemed to come automatically from Jim's lips. It was only after he had spoken them that he realized they were true. For a moment Tode glared at him; then suddenly, with a shriek of insane rage, he leaped from the instrument board and swung the ray tube with all his might.

Jim felt the blow descend with stunning force upon his head. He reeled, flung out his arms, and toppled forward, unconscious....

CHAPTER IV

Escape

n intolerably bright light that seemed to sear his eyeballs was the first thing of which Jim was conscious. Then he became aware of his aching head, of a sense of utter lassitude, as if he had been bruised all over in some machine that had caught him up and held him in its grip for endless aeons.

At last, despite the pain in his eyes, he managed to get his eyelids open. He tried to struggle to his feet, only to discover that he was firmly bound with what appeared to be tough creepers, pliant as ropes.

After the lapse of a few minutes, during which he struggled with the receding waves of unconsciousness, he came to a realization of his surroundings. That light that had so distressed him—though the effects were now beginning to pass off—was a pillar of smoke and flame, shooting out of the crater of a volcano about a mile away, across a valley.

He was lying in the entrance to a cave, pegged out on his back, and bound by the tough creepers to the stakes driven into the ground. Up to the mouth of the cave grew huge tree-ferns, cattails, cycads, and such growths as existed in earlier ages in the warm, moist regions of the world.

Beneath the level of the cave a heavy white fog completely shrouded the valley, extending up to within a short distance of the volcano opposite. But on the upper slopes of the volcano the sunlight played, making its crater a sheen of glassy lava, intolerably bright.

Beyond the volcano Jim could see what looked like an expanse of ocean.

H

e groaned, and at the sound a creature came shambling forward, carrying what looked like a huge melon in either hand. Jim recognized the Drilgo, Cain.

Chattering and mumbling, Cain placed one of the fruits to Jim's mouth. It was a sort of bread-fruit, but he was too nauseated to eat, and rejected it with disgust. Cain offered him the second fruit.

It was a hollow gourd, the interior filled with a clear fluid. Jim drank greedily as the Drilgo put it to his lips. The contents were like water, but slightly acid. Jim felt refreshed. He looked about him.

The Drilgo uttered a chattering call, and immediately a host of the savages swarmed into the cave. Men—undoubtedly men, in spite of the brow ridges[248] and the receding foreheads, carrying long spears, consisting of chipped and pointed heads of stone, with holes bored in them, through which long bands of creepers passed, fastening them firmly to the shaft.

Chattering and gesticulating, the Drilgoes surrounded Jim as he lay helpless on the ground. Their savage faces, their rolling eyes, the threatening gestures that they made with their spears, convinced Jim that his end was a foregone conclusion.

But suddenly a distant rumbling sound was heard, increasing rapidly in volume. The floor of the cave vibrated; masses of rock dropped from the walls. The light of the volcano across the valley was suddenly obscured in an immense cloud of black smoke. The twilight within the cave was succeeded by almost impenetrable darkness.

Shrieking in terror, the Drilgoes bolted, while Jim lay straining at his ropes, expecting each moment to be crushed by the masses of rock that were falling all about him.

Suddenly a soft whisper came to Jim through the darkness: "Jim! Are you safe! Where are you? I can't see you! Speak to me!"

It was Lucille's voice, and Jim called back, husky and tremulous in the sheer joy that had succeeded his anticipation of instant death.

T

hen he felt the girl kneeling at his side, and heard her hacking at his bonds. A whole minute passed before the stone knife was able to sever the last of the stout withes, however.

Then Jim was swaying on his feet, and Lucille's arms were about him, and for a few moments their fears were forgotten in the renewal of their love.

"I heard what that devil said to you last night," the girl said. "He means to kill you with awful tortures. He is away now, on some task or other, but he'll be back at any moment. We must get away at once—we three. Dad's in another cave not far away, and his guards bolted after the earthquake."

The earth was still rumbling, and the cavern still vibrating, but it was clear that there was no time to lose. As soon as the quake subsided the Drilgoes would return. Guided by Lucille, Jim groped his way through the cavern. The girl called softly at intervals, and presently Jim heard old Parrish's answering call. Then the old man's form appeared in silhouette against the dark.

"I've got Jim," Lucille whispered. "Are you ready, dad?"

"Yes, yes, I'm ready," chattered the old man. "Now's our chance. I know a place where we can hide in the thick forests, where the Ray of the Atlanteans cannot penetrate the mists. Let's go! Let's go!"

Gripping hands, the three started back toward the point where a faint patch of darkness showed out the entrance to the cavern. They were nearing it when another and more violent shock flung them upon their faces.

Huge masses of rock came hurtling down from the roof and sides of the cavern, and again the three seemed to escape by a miracle.

S

uddenly a huge shaft of fire shot from the crater opposite, evolving into an inverted cone that made the whole land dazzlingly bright. It pierced the mists in the valley underneath, and by that light Jim could see a great wave of lava streaming down the mountain sides, like soup spilled out of a bowl.

A gush of black smoke followed, and the light went out.

"Now!" gasped Parrish, and, clinging to one another, the three darted out of the cavern's entrance. Another terrific shock sent them stumbling and reeling and sprawling down the side of the mountain.

Jim heard old Parrish wailing, and, as the shock subsided, groped his way to his side.

"You hurt?" he shouted.

"Lucille, Lucille," moaned the old man. "She's dead! A big rock crushed her. I wish I was dead too."

Jim called Lucille's name frantically,[249] and to his immense relief heard her crying faintly out of the darkness. He rushed to her side and held her in his arms.

"Where are you hit, darling?"

"I'm—all right," she panted. "I was stunned for a moment. I—can—go on now."

But she went limp in Jim's arms, and Jim picked her up and stood irresolute, until he heard Parrish shambling toward him over the heaving ground.

"She's not hurt, I think, only fainted," said Jim. "Which way, Parrish? You lead us."

"Down the slope," panted Parrish. "We'll be in the ferns in a minute. We can hide there for a while, till she's able to walk. God help us all! And I was once Professor of Physical Chemistry at Columbia!"

The outcry might have seemed comical under other circumstances; as it was, Jim heartily re-echoed old Parrish's sentiments in his heart.

The last shock was subsiding in faint earth tremors. The two men plunged down into the heavy fog, which quickly covered them, Jim carrying Lucille in his arms. He felt the ferny undergrowth all about him, the thick boles of tree-ferns emerged out of the mist.

"We can stop here for a while," panted Parrish. "Crouch down! They'll never find us in this fog, and in a few minutes, when Lucille's better, we can go on."

ou must tell me where we are and what our chances are," said Jim, after again ascertaining that Lucille was unharmed.

"I'll tell you, Dent, as quick as I can. It's the place where I've spent five years of hell as the slave of that devil, Tode. I never dreamed, when we were working on the old Atom Smasher, that he had adapted it to travel in the fourth dimension. He's taken us back twelve thousand years or so to the island of Atlantis. History hasn't begun yet. Atlantis is the only civilization in the world. The rest are Drilgoes, Neanderthal men, wandering in the forests, and still in their stone age.

"It's true, Dent, what old Plato learned from the Egyptian priests. Atlantis has been slowly sinking for thousands of years, and all that's left now is the one great island that we're on. Nearly all the Atlanteans, the Cro-Magnon men, have perished, except for a few who have crossed in ships to the coasts of France and Spain. They'll be the founders of modern Europe—Basques and Iberians, and Bretons and Welshmen. Our ancestors! It makes my brain reel to think of it!"

"Go on! Go on!" said Jim.

"There's a great city on the island, known as Atlantis too. As big as London or New York. With flying-machines and temples and art galleries and big ships that they're building to carry them away when the next subsidence comes. They know they're doomed, for every few days there's an eruption now.

"Tode means to make himself master of Atlantis, and transport it into another epoch by means of the Atom Smasher. But he's never managed to enter. He's made himself a god in the eyes of the Drilgoes, the savages who inhabit these forests. He's planning to lead them against the city, and he's got an army of thousands from all parts of the interior, who worship him as divine.

"T

he Atlanteans are unwarlike. They've forgotten how to fight in their thousands of years of peace. But they've got a Ray ten times as strong as Tode's, that brings instant death to everything it touches. It shrivels it up. It's a different principle. I don't understand it, but it's this Ray that keeps the Drilgoes from capturing the city.

"Tode's got a laboratory inside the cave, fitted up with apparatus that he brought from Chicago, the world capital of the year 3000 A. D., after disintegrating the atoms and recombining them. But he hasn't succeeded alto[250]gether. He hasn't learned everything. The future isn't quite clear, like the past. There's a dark cloud moves across the spectral lines and blurs them. I think it's the element of free will— or God!"

"I know," Jim answered. "He can't hold that boat steady in four-dimensional space, as he pretends he can. If he could, it would mean that man was wholly master of his destiny. He can't and he never will.

"There's an unknown quantity comes in, Parrish. It is God, and that's what's going to beat him in the end."

"I've not been as idle as Tode thinks," said Parrish, with a senile leer. "I know more about the Atom Smasher than he dreams of. He thinks me just an old fool, the remnants of whose brains are useful to him in his laboratory. That's why he's kept me alive so far. He'll find out his mistake," he chuckled. "I have something Tode doesn't dream of."

Suddenly Parrish's air of intense seriousness vanished. He chuckled and fumbled in his rags. Jim felt a small object like a lever pressed into his hand and then withdrawn.

"It's death, Dent," chuckled old Parrish. "The concentrated essence of the destructive principle. It's a lever I fitted into a concealed groove in the Atom Smasher unknown to Tode. This lever has a universal joint and connects with a hidden chamber, and when pulled will catapult the annihilated components of a small quantity of uranium in any direction we desire. The release of the slumbering energy of this uranium will produce an explosion of proportions beyond the wildest dreams of engineers—perhaps, one great enough to throw the Earth out of its orbit!"

"Uranium!... Breaking up its components!" gasped Jim. "You mean you can actually do that?"

"Yes!" chuckled Parrish. "I'm keeping it for the day when Tode becomes a god. When he's steadied the boat in time-space and halted the march of the past, and when he's got Lucille—then, Dent, I shall so pull the lever that it will release the energy straight at Tode—and destroy the Atom-Smasher, ourselves, and even, perhaps, the whole Earth!"

And he burst into a peal of such wild laughter that Jim realized the old man's wits were gone.

W

as it true, that amazing story? It was difficult to know, and yet anything seemed possible in this amazing world into which Jim had suddenly been thrown.

The vast pall of smoke cast out by the volcano was beginning to subside. Slowly a spectral light began to filter through the valley. Through the fog Jim could see glimpses of the ferny undergrowth, the giant tree-ferns and cycads that towered aloft. It was like a picture of the earth when the mastodons, the grass-eaters and the meat-eaters disputed for its supremacy.

Jim bent over Lucille. He saw her stir, he heard her murmur his name. Suddenly she sat up, fixed her eyes on his, and shuddered.

"I'm all right, Jim. Let's go," she said. "I can walk now."

She staggered to her feet. Jim put out his hand to support her, but she shook her head. Jim touched old Parrish on the arm. He started and uttered a wild screech; then seemed to come to himself and rose.

But that screech of his was re-echoed from the mountainside above. Other voices took up the echoes. Lucille clutched at Jim in a frenzy of fear.

"The Drilgoes!" she whispered. "They're on our trail!"

Seizing old Parrish by the arm, Jim started to drag him into the recesses of the fern forest. Suddenly the bestial face of a Drilgo appeared.

A yell broke from the man's throat. The hairy arm shot back. Jim saw the stone tip of the long spear poised overhead. He leaped forward, delivering a blow in the man's midriff with all the strength of his right arm.[251]

T

he Drilgo grunted and doubled forward, the spear falling from his hand. The heavy head of stone embedded itself in the soft ground, so that the spear remained upright. As the man collapsed he yelled at the top of his voice.

"This way! This way!" gibbered old Parrish, suddenly alert.

But now the undergrowth all about them was alive with Drilgoes. The three dodged and doubled like hunted hares. High overhead something began to clack with a sound like that made by a woodpecker drilling a tree, but infinitely louder.

And out of the void above came Tode's voice, shouting commands to the Drilgoes in their own language.

Suddenly a column of fire shot up from the volcano, infusing the white mists with a reddish glare. Overhead the three could see Tode. He was flying with a pair of mechanical wings strapped to his shoulders, not more than two hundred feet above them. With a shout of triumph he swooped down. In his hand was a small cylinder, about the mouth of which a phosphorescent violet light was beginning to play.

"I've got you, Dent," he screamed in triumph, hovering above the three, while the wings drummed and vibrated till they seemed the mere play of light and shadow about Tode's shoulders. "Halt, or I'll blast your body and soul to hell! Halt, or I'll kill *her*!"

The deadly tube was pointing steadily at Lucille's body as Tode hovered ten feet overhead, perfectly still save for the whirring wings. The three stopped dead, and Tode, with a shout of triumph, began calling the Drilgoes, who swarmed forward out of the undergrowth.

Huge brown bodies, nude save for their skins of jungle-cat or serpent, they emerged, quickly forming a ring about the three prisoners. Tode fluttered to the ground.

"Fools, did you think you could escape that way?" he asked. "As for you, Dent. I'm going to convince you of the reality of four-dimensional space as you would not be convinced in the old days. Do you know what I'm going to do with you? I'm going to strip the skin from you with the ray, and take you into the anatomical room at Columbia University and leave you there as an exhibit, Dent!"

Tode grinned like a madman. But Jim was looking past him, at something that had suddenly appeared upon the far horizon.

I

t was a round disc of bluish white, a disc like the moon, but slightly smaller, a disc that flickered as if it had an eyelid that was being winked repeatedly. Simultaneously screams broke from the throats of all the Drilgoes. They stampeded.

Tode whirled about and saw. With a curse he leaped into the air and whirred away.

Out of that disc a slender, blue-white beam shot suddenly, driving a pathway through the fog, and disclosing the dark depths of the valley.

"The Eye! The Eye!" screeched Parrish. "Down on the ground! Down! Down!"

He dropped, and Jim caught Lucille and flung himself headlong with her. To and fro overhead, but only a few feet above them, moved the searchlight. Shrieks broke from the Drilgoes' throats as they scattered through the jungle.

Everywhere that ray moved, trees and undergrowth simply disappeared. A bunch of Drilgoes, caught by it, were obliterated in an instant. Great gaps were left through the undergrowth as the ray passed.

It faded as quickly as it had come, and instantly old Parrish was on his feet, dragging at his daughter.

"Now! Now!" he babbled, heading along one of the burned tracks through the undergrowth.

Jim seized Lucille and the two raced in the wake of old Parrish. Behind them they could hear the Drilgoes[252] shouting, but a dense, impenetrable darkness was already beginning to settle down over the valley. They lost the track and went crashing through the ferns, on and on until all was silence about them.

Suddenly Parrish went down like a log. He lay breathing heavily, completely exhausted. When Jim spoke to him a feeble muttering was the only answer. Jim and Lucille dropped to the ground exhausted beside him.

CHAPTER V

The Eye of Atlantis

For perhaps half an hour the three lay there, hearing nothing. It seemed to be night, for the darkness was impenetrable, save for the lurid flashes of fire from the volcano. Parrish, who was slowly recovering his strength, was mumbling incessantly. It was with difficulty that Jim recalled him to a realization of his surroundings.

"Where is the city of Atlantis?" he asked him.

"Over there," mumbled Parrish. "Behind the volcano. Why do you ask me?"

"I'm thinking of going there."

"Eh? Going there? You're mad. The Eye will see you, the Eye that can see for a hundred miles. They'll turn the Ray on you. Nothing is too small for the Eye. And they watch night and day."

"The Eye is off now."

"It's never off. The Eye is dark. It grows white only when they are about to use the Ray. Perhaps the Eye is watching us now."

"Nevertheless," said Jim, "I think we would do well to try to enter the city. We can't live here in the jungle at the mercy of these Drilgoes."

"It is impossible to enter. All strangers are killed by the Atlanteans."

"Dad," interposed Lucille, "I think we'd better do what Jim suggests. One of us must decide."

"My idea is that you take us to some place where we can get a view of the city," said Jim. "Then we can make up our minds what to do. We've got to get somewhere out of this jungle."

P

arrish rose to his feet, mumbling. "If we go round the base of the volcano we can see Atlantis," he said. "It's always light there. In the daytime they drive away the fogs by some means they've got, and at night they have an artificial sun. But we'll be killed, we'll all be killed."

Mumbling and muttering, he began groping his way through the undergrowth in the direction of the volcano, whose flashes were again becoming more frequent, affording a means of directing their route. Obscure rumblings were again beginning to shake the earth. For an hour the three picked their way steadily upward through the ferns, until the ground became more open.

They were approaching the base of the volcano, whose side now towered above them, the upper part glassy with vitreous lava.

Suddenly Parrish, who was still leading, stopped and began to tremble with fear. Stepping to his side, Jim heard the low muttering of voices not far away.

Very cautiously he moved forward through the thin fern scrub, until the glow of burning embers caught his sight. He stopped, hearing the voices more distinctly, and again moved forward.

Three Drilgoes, huge, bestial men, and evidently an outpost, were squatting around the ashes, devouring something with noisy gusto.

Softly as Jim had moved, their acute ears had caught the sound of his footsteps. They rose, still holding what they were eating in their hands, and, grasping their stone spears, moved in three separate ways toward the edge of the clearing.

The man nearest Jim uttered a guttural exclamation and, after sniffing a moment, began to lope in his direction.[253] Suddenly he stopped short, petrified with astonishment and fear at the sight of a man who, instinct told him, was neither Atlantean nor of his own kind.

J

im leaped, tackling him about the knees, and brought him heavily to the ground. As the Drilgo fell, the spear clattered from his hand, but from his snakeskin girdle he pulled a long, curved knife of chipped obsidian, sharp as a razor.

Jim grasped the Drilgo's wrist, but in a moment he saw that he was no match for the creature in strength. He drew back his right arm and delivered a punch to the solar plexus with all his strength.

As the Drilgo's hand grew limp he snatched away the knife. There was no helping what he did for the two others were close upon him.

A thrust, a slashing blow, and the Drilgo was weltering in his life-blood. A backward leap, and Jim evaded the flung spear by a hair's breadth.

Knife in hand he leaped forward, and, dodging in beneath the long shaft of the weapon, got in a slash that almost cut the Drilgo's body in two.

The third Drilgo, seeing his two companions in their death-throes, flung away his spear and fled with loud howls into the jungle.

Jim stepped back. Lucille and her father were already almost at his heels. "It's all right," he called. "Come this way!" He led them through the ferny growth in such a manner that they should not see the two dead bodies. Nevertheless, he felt that Lucille knew.

"Let's see what they were cooking," he said.

But again he turned quickly. He could not know for sure what flesh that was, roasting and scorching on the embers, and he had no desire to know. It might have been monkey, but ... he turned away, and as he did so, Parrish picked up several round objects that were lying a little distance away.

"These are good to eat," he said. "A sort of bread-fruit. I've lived on it for five years," he added with a sort of grotesque pathos.

They munched the fruit as they proceeded up the mountain, and found it satisfying. Parrish seemed more himself again, though he still muttered at intervals. Lucille clung closely to Jim as they proceeded.

T

hey were treading on lava now, vitreous, and smooth as glass. It was impossible to proceed further in that direction. They turned their steps around the base in the direction of the sea.

After another hour, during which their way was lit by almost continuous lurid flashes from the crater, a patch of illumination, apparently out at sea, began to become visible. A half hour more, and they were rounding the volcano's base, and suddenly it burst upon them, a stupendous spectacle that drew an exclamation of amazement from Jim's lips.

That low, flat background was the sea, the sound of whose breakers was faintly audible. Between sea and land ran a narrow, slender causeway, perhaps a mile in length. And beyond that, set on a small island, was the most splendid city that Jim could have imagined.

Like New York—very like New York, with its mighty towers, but more symmetrical, sloping upward from the sea toward a towering rampart at the heart of it, crowned with huge domes and minarets and serpentine ramps and mighty blocks of stone that must have sheltered as many occupants as New York's highest skyscrapers.

The whole was snow-white, and gleamed softly in an artificial light dispensed from an enormous artificial planet that seemed to hover above the ramparts.

"God!" whispered Jim in awe as he gazed at the great city.

"You cannot cross that causeway," whimpered old Parrish. "It's death to try. One sweep of the Ray will blot out every living thing."[254]

"Hush! Listen!" came from Lucille's lips. "Something's moving down there!"

he distant murmur of voices, the indescribable "feel" of the proximity of other human beings told Jim that they were in imminent danger. He glanced about him. A little overhead was an outcrop of enormous boulders, standing up like a little fortress above the smooth lava.

"Get behind there!" Jim whispered.

They turned and ran, slipping and stumbling up the smooth slope. Reaching the boulders, they ensconced themselves hastily behind them. Jim peered out through a crevice between two of the largest stones. The sound of moving things became more audible.

Then, as a flash of flame shot from the crater overhead, Jim saw a black human horde creeping like an array of ants around the base of the mountain not far beneath.

Just like an army of warrior ants it seemed to flow onward, in perfect order. And in the midst of it a faint violet light began to be visible.

Parrish seized Jim's arm, shaking with terror. "You know what that is, Dent?" he whimpered.

"It's Tode's Drilgoes, moving for a night attack upon Atlantis," answered Jim. "And that thing in the middle is the Atom Smasher."

I

t seemed hours before the last of the serried ranks of Drilgoes had passed. By the light of a lurid flash from the volcano Jim could see the column winding toward the causeway. Then all was shrouded in impenetrable darkness, save for the snow-soft city upon the island.

"What are we going to do?" chattered old Parrish. "I wish I was back in Tode's cave. He gave me food and let me help with his work sometimes. I'll die here. We'll never get away. We'll never get anywhere."

"We're safer here than anywhere else," answered Jim. "We'll have to stay till morning, or—God, look at that!"

Out of the ramparts of the city the round, blue-white disc of the Eye had suddenly disclosed itself. And simultaneously a violet flare shot up above the moving hosts of the Drilgoes in the middle of the causeway.

Out of the center of the Eye that blinding searchlight streamed. And the pillar of violet fire rose up to counter it, clove it in two, as a man cuts off the tentacle of a cuttlefish, and left it groping helplessly above the heads of the Drilgoes.

T

o and fro wavered the blue-white beam, and like a protective wall the violet column spread and extended, till the air was interlaced with the play of the two colors. Streaks of white shot through streaks of purple and black neutral clouds twirled, swirling in ghostlike forms. It was a scene inconceivably beautiful, and it was impossible to realize what must be happening out there.

Men must be dying, withering like stubble in the blue-white flames, whenever they caught them. And yet, under that play of colors, Jim could see the vast host crawling forward to the assault.

H

e held his breath. It was sublime and terrible, and on the result of that conflict depended—what? What difference, when all this was forgotten history, antedating the written records of the human race?

Then of a sudden the blue-white rays were seen to win. They were beating down the violet light. Like living fingers they pierced that protective wall, flinging it back, until only the tall central pillar remained. And then for the first time the sound of combat became audible.

A groan of despair, of defeat, of hopelessness. The black stream was recoiling, turning upon itself. In the vivid glare of the white light it could be seen dissolving, breaking into a[255] thousand pieces, streaming back toward the land. And, as it broke, the blue-white light pursued, eating its way and blasting all it met. Atlantis had triumphed.

Another sound was audible. From the city it came, a whirring as of innumerable grasshoppers, increasing till it sounded once more like the tapping of innumerable woodpeckers. Suddenly the night broke into whirling balls of fire.

Lucille cried out. Jim leaped to his feet to see more clearly.

"It's men with wings," he cried. "Scores of them. They're hurling something at the Drilgoes!"

T

he clacking of the wing mechanism filled the air. Now the fugitives from the Drilgo host were streaming along the base of the mountain underneath, seeking the safety of the jungles, and over them, riding them, harrying them, flew the Atlantean birdmen, hurling their fiery balls. And where the balls fell, conflagrations of cold fire seemed to start and run like mercury, and shrivel up everything they touched.

But the birdmen were not without casualties of their own. Here and there one could be seen to drop, and then the massed Drilgoes would turn savagely upon him with their stone-pointed spears. The fight was coming very close now. The savage cries of the Drilgoes filled the night.

A ball of fire broke hardly fifty yards away from where the three were crouching. A birdman fluttered down like a wounded hawk and lay a-sprawl just underneath the rampart of boulders. Jim surmounted them, ran down the slope of the mountainside, and bent over the dying man. He was hideously wounded by the thrust of a Drilgo spear—whether because the mechanism had failed, or because he had swooped too low, Jim could not determine. As Jim bent over him he looked up at him.

A youth in his teens, with the face and build of a Greek warrior, a worthy ancestor of European man. Jim looked at him and shuddered. "My grandfather four hundred generations removed," he thought.

Seeing that this was no Drilgo, with eyes widened by the anticipation of death, the Atlantean smiled, and died.

Jim detached the straps that held the wings to his shoulders and examined them. They were multi-hinged, built of innumerable layers of laminated wood, which seemed to have been subjected to some special treatment. In the base of each, just where it fitted to the curve of the shoulder-blade, a tiny light was burning.

J

im looped the straps about his arms and walked back to the rampart. Old Parrish saw him and screamed. Lucille cried out.

"I'm going to try to get the Atom Smasher," said Jim, pointing to the thin spire of violet flame that was still visible in the center of the causeway. "It's our only chance. You must stay here. If I live, I'll return. If I don't return—"

But he knew that he must return. Nothing could kill him, because Lucille would be waiting for him behind that rampart of stones upon the bare, vitreous mountainside.

"I'm going to get the Atom Smasher," Jim repeated. "In these wings I'll be taken for Atlantean. I'll—bring it back." He spoke with faltering conviction. And yet there was nothing else to do. Everything depended upon his being able to bring back the Atom Smasher and take Lucille and her father away.

"I think you're right, Jim," answered Lucille. "We'll—wait here till you—come—back."

Her voice died away in a sob. Jim bent and kissed her. Then he began examining the mechanism of the wings. It did not appear difficult. A leather strap fastened around the body. Through this strap ran cords operated by levers upon the breast, and there[256] was a knob in a groove that looked as if it controlled the starting of the mechanism.

"I'll be back," said Jim.

And suddenly the Eye appeared again, and with it there sounded once more the whir of wings.

"Down!" shouted Jim.

H

e was too late. A score of birdmen shot out of the dark and hovered over them. Next moment they had descended to the ground. Lucille and Parrish were seized, and Jim, struggling furiously, quickly found himself equally helpless in their grasp.

The accents of the Atlanteans as they spoke to one another were soft and liquid, their faces were refined and gentle, but their strength was that of athletes. Jim saw Lucille and Parrish lifted into the air; next moment he himself was raised in the arms of one of the birdmen, who shot upward like an arrow and headed a course back toward the city, carrying Jim as if he had been as light as a child.

CHAPTER VI

Human Sacrifice

In a great open space, flanked by temples and colonnades, the flight had come to rest. There, under the soft artificial light that made the whole city as bright as day, Jim, Lucille, and her father were set down before a sort of rostrum, on which were gathered the dignitaries of the city.

Jim's hopes were rising fast, for between the Atlanteans and the savage Drilgoes there was as much difference as between a modern American and a blackfellow from the Australian bush. These men were civilized to a degree that even modern America has not attained.

Nowhere was there a speck of dirt to be seen. Vehicles moved soundlessly along the wide streets on either side of this central meeting-place, and the whole city was roofed with glass, through which could be seen the brilliant moon and stars—invisible from the mist-filled valley without.

Soft garments of white wool clothed men and women alike, fashioned something like togas, but cut short at the knee, leaving the lower part of the leg bare and disclosing the sandaled feet. The hair was long and flowed about the shoulders. But what struck Jim most forcibly was the look of utter gentleness and benignity upon these faces.

"I guess we've fallen into pretty good hands after all," he whispered to Parrish.

But one of the dignitaries upon the platform, an elderly man with a face reminiscent of William Jennings Bryan in his inspired moments, was leaning forward out of his curved chair and addressing the old man, and, to Jim's astonishment, Parrish was answering.

But these were not the liquid accents of the Atlanteans. The words resembled the barking of a dog, and across Jim's brain there suddenly flashed the explanation. The dignitary was speaking in the tongue of the Drilgoes, which Parrish, of course, would have learned in his five years of captivity.

Suddenly Parrish turned to Jim. "He wants to know where we come from," he said. "I've told him from a far country. He thinks we're ambassadors from some of the parts of Europe that the Atlanteans who sailed away some years ago landed at. It's no use trying to explain—they don't seem to have succeeded in inventing an Atom Smasher for themselves."

Jim nodded, and the colloquy went on and on, while the Atlanteans listened with languid interest, their kind and smiling faces seeming to exude benignity. At length the session seemed to have ended.

Parrish wore a wide grin. "Everything's coming right, dear," he told Lucille. "The old chap says we are to be the guests of the city either for a night or for a week. It's something to[257] do with the moon, and there seems to be a full moon to-night. Some quaint superstition or other. And then I guess we'll have a chance to get away in the Atom Smasher. I've learned something of the mechanism, and it won't be hard to operate it. We've fallen into good hands."

A

squad of four soldiers or policemen, with shorter robes and what looked like truncheons in their hands, made signs to the three to accompany them. Amid mutual bows, the city's guests filled into a small court-way, closed at the further end, on which a number of Atlanteans were standing.

While Jim was wondering what the next move was to be, to his astonishment the whole courtyard began to rise slowly up the walls of the tall buildings on either side.

"An elevator!" gasped Lucille. "Now I do feel that everything is coming out all right, Jim, dear."

Jim did not question the psychology of this. He pressed her hand tenderly. Already Tode and the past were becoming a bad dream.

"Did you say anything about the Atom Smasher, Parrish?" he asked.

"No, I thought it better not to," replied the old scientist. "You see, they know it only as a force that neutralizes the blue-white ray. Best not to let them know we're sailing for home in it."

"I think that was wise," answered Jim, and just then the rising court-way came to a stop level with the top story of the great building at one side.

Smiling courteously, the guards invited the three to precede them inside an enormous hall, supported on pillars of gleaming stone resembling alabaster. In the center was a small, low table, triangular in shape, with three of the low, curved chairs. The guards invited the three to be seated.

Almost immediately smiling servitors brought in fruits on platters of porcelain, dishes of cooked vegetables, somewhat like the modern ones, but seasoned and flavored with delicious herbs. The staple dish was something like an oval banana, but infinitely more succulent. The three fell to and made a hearty meal, which was washed down with fine wines.

"We've certainly fallen into good hands," said Jim. "All we've got to do is to lie low, and look pleasant, and it won't be long before we get an opportunity to get hold of the Atom Smasher."

T

he guards, seeing that they had finished their meal, smilingly invited them to accompany them through a huge bronze door at one end of the hall. It swung back, disclosing complete darkness.

Jim felt Lucille's hand upon his arm. The girl was hesitating, and for a moment Jim hesitated too, half afraid of a fall into emptiness. Then he heard the footsteps of the guards ahead, and went on.

It was eery, moving there with the sound of feet in front of them, and, apart from that, utter silence. Then Lucille uttered a little cry.

"Jim, do you feel something pushing you?" she asked.

"There is something—" Jim swung around, but some invisible force continued to propel him forward. He moved sidewise, and the force gently corrected him. The sound of footsteps had ceased.

"What is it, Jim?" cried the girl. "Help me! Something's got hold of me!"

Old Parrish was struggling close beside them. Jim panted as he wrestled with the force, but his efforts were absolutely futile. Slowly, as if slid on wires, he was propelled forward, until a cushion of air seemed to block his further progress.

Dark as it was, and silent, Jim had the consciousness of other human beings about him, of a vast, unseen multitude that was watching him.

Suddenly the droning of a chant began to fill the place, as if a priest were[258] intoning hymns. As that chant rose and fell, voices all about took up the echoing refrain. Jim tried to reach Lucille, but he could move his arm only a few inches against that resilient force pressing in on all sides of him.

Then, in an instant, a blinding, stabbing light shot through his eyeballs. He heard Lucille scream, old Parrish yelp, and, with eyelids screwed tight against the intolerable glare, fought once more desperately and ineffectively to reach Lucille's side.

***

S

lowly Jim managed to unscrew his eyes. He began to realize that he was standing in what appeared to be an enormous amphitheatre. But high up, upon a narrow tongue of flooring that ran like a bridge from one end to the other, with Lucille on his right and Parrish on his left. Nothing visible seemed to be restraining them, and yet they were as securely held as if fastened with tight chains.

Jim's brain reeled as he looked down. Imagine a bridge about half-way up an amphitheatre of a hundred stories, the ground beneath packed with human beings no larger than ants, the whole of the vast interior lined with them, tier above tier, faces and forms increasing from pismire size below to the dimensions of the human form upon a level, and, again, fading almost to pin-points at the summit of the vast building, where the soft glow of the artificial light filtered through the glass of the roof.

He clutched at the air, felt the soft pressure of the force that was restraining him, looked at Lucille, and saw her half-unconscious with fear, leaning against it, leaning against that soft, resilient, cushionlike, invisible substance; looked at Parrish, whom the shock had thrown into a sort of semi-catalepsy—Parrish, mouthing and staring!

He looked forward to where the tongue of flooring ended. Here, upon a stage, flanked with huge carven figures, a group was gathered. At first he was unable to discern what was being enacted there, so brilliant was the light that glared overhead.

It was the Eye, a round disc perhaps ten feet in diameter, that all-seeing Eye of Atlantis that guarded the great city, but how it worked Jim was totally unable to discover. He saw, however, that it was blinking rapidly, the alternations being so swift that it was only just possible to be conscious of them. Perhaps the Eye was opening and closing ten times a second.

Jim strained his eyes to see what was taking place on the stage at the end of the tongue on which he stood. What was it? What were they doing there? And was that the captured Atom Smasher standing between what looked like grinning idols? A group of captured Drilgoes near it?

A shrill scream from Lucille echoed through the vast amphitheatre. Her eye had seen what Jim's had not yet seen—something that had shocked her into complete unconsciousness.

A marble figure, she stood leaning against the invisible force that kept her on her feet, and in those open, staring eyes was a look of ineffable horror.

J

im could see clearly now, for the light from the Eye was slowly diminishing in brilliancy, or else his own eyes were growing more accustomed to it. Those carven figures, forming a semi-circle upon the platform were figures of gods, squat, huge forms seeming to emerge out of the blocks of rock from which they had been fashioned.

Hideous, gruesome carvings they were, resembling some futuristic sculpture of to-day, for the artist who had fashioned them had given hardly more than a hint of the finished representation. It was rather as if the masses of rock that had been transported there had become vitalized, foreshadowing the dim yet awful beings that were some day to emerge from them.

Only the arms were clearly sculptured, and each of the half-dozen fig[259]ures squatting upon its haunches in that semi-circle had four of them. Arms that protruded so as to form an interlacing network, and the fingers were long claws fashioned of some metal. Over the arms the shapeless heads beat down with a leering look, and from each mouth protruded a curved tongue.

A masterpiece of horror, that group, like the great stone figures of the Aztecs, or some of the hideous Indian gods. Seen under the glare of the Eye, they formed a background of horrible omen. In a flash it dawned upon Jim that these hideous figures might be gods of bloody sacrifice.

"That's why these people seem so gentle," he heard himself saying. "It's the—the contrast."

He pulled himself together. Again he tried to move towards Lucille, and again that invisible force restrained him.

Yes, it was the captured Atom Smasher upon the platform, and those forms grouped in front of the dignitaries were captured Drilgoes, a dozen or so of them. And the concealed priest was droning a chant again. Every other sound was hushed, but from each square foot of the great amphitheatre a pair of eyes was watching.

A myriad of eyes turned upon the platform! What was going to happen next?

S

uddenly the priest's voice died away, and simultaneously the three dignitaries, who seemed to be officiating priests, from their solemn gestures, stepped backward, passing beneath the protruding arms of the idols. There sounded the deep whir of some mechanism somewhere, and the same invisible force that had Jim and his two companions in its control suddenly began to agitate the captive Drilgoes.

It was shuffling them! It was forcing them into line, pushing here and pulling there, in spite of the Drilgoes' terrified struggles. They writhed and twisted, groaning and clicking in abject terror as they wrestled with that unseen power, and all in vain. Slowly the foremost of the Drilgoes was propelled forward, inch by inch, until he stood immediately beneath the interlacing arms.

And what happened next filled Jim with sick horror and loathing. For of a sudden the arms began to move, the iron claws cut through the air—a shriek of terror and anguish broke from the Drilgo's mouth ... and he was no longer a man, but a clawed and pulped mass of human flesh!

"Aiah! Aiah! Aiah!" broke from the throats of the assembled multitude.

The weaving arms had stopped. From behind them an attendant was gathering up what had been the Drilgo in a basket. Then the mechanism had begun again, and again that shrill cry of the spectators was ringing in Jim's ears.

Louder still rose the shriek of old Parrish as he understood. Jim put forth all his strength in a mad effort to break free. A child would have had more chance in the grip of a giant. And each time the arms of the gods revolved, the unseen force pushed Jim, Lucille, and Parrish nearer the platform.

Now Jim understood. This horrible sacrifice was a part of the religion of the Atlanteans, and he, Lucille, and Parrish, were being reserved for the final spectacle.

And at the sight of Lucille beside him, stonily unconscious, and yet standing, and moving like a mechanical doll, in little forward jerks—at the sight of the girl, hardly six feet distant, and yet utterly beyond the touch of his finger-tips, Jim went mad. He would not shout; he closed his lips in pride of race, pride of that civilization that he had left twelve thousand years ahead of him. Not like the shrieking Drilgoes on the platform, howling as each of them in turn was forced into that maze of revolving knives. But he fought as a madman[260] fights. He hammered at the resilient air, while the sweat ran down his face, he braced his feet upon the wooden tongue, and sought to stay his forward progress. And all the while that infernal force moved him steadily onward.

H

e was on the platform now. He was traveling the same route that the Drilgoes had taken. The unseen force was shuffling him, Lucille, and Parrish, pushing and pulling them. And, despite Jim's efforts, it was Lucille who was first of the three ... and Jim second ... and old Parrish third....

Jim heard Parrish's hoarse whisper behind him, "Death! Death! The uranium!" He was fumbling at his breast, but the significance of the words and gestures escaped him. He was staring ahead. Only three living Drilgoes of the whole number of prisoners remained alive, and suddenly it was borne in upon Jim that he knew the last of the three.

It was the Drilgo, Cain, who had been their companion in the Atom Smasher—there, not a dozen feet distant. Cain, his bestial face, with the ridged eyebrows and great jaws convulsed with terror and dripping sweat. Cain, immediately in front of Lucille.

"God, let her not wake! Let her never know!" Jim breathed. The agony would be but momentary. And there was nothing a man could not endure if he must. He could even endure to see Lucille become— what the Drilgoes had become. It would soon be over now.

The Eye was blinking overhead. The hideous stone faces of the Atlantean gods looked down in leering mockery. Another of the Drilgoes had gone the same route as the others. Cain was the second now, Lucille the third victim, and he, Jim, would be the fourth.

Gritting his teeth, Jim saw the next Drilgo propelled forward into the whirling knives. He saw the man fling up his arms, as if to shield his head—and then he was a man no longer, and the horrible knives revolved, and "Aiah! Aiah! Aiah!" cried the multitude.

Once more the mechanism whirred.... Once more the arms revolved. A howl of terror broke from Cain's lips as he was propelled onward....

Then suddenly the whirring stopped. The arms of the stone gods, with their hooked, razorlike claws, to which clung particles of flesh, were arrested in mid-air. Cain, unharmed, was leaning backward, his features set in a mask of awful fear.

Simultaneously Jim knew that the force which had held him in thrall was gone. He flung his arms out. He was free. He grasped Lucille, held her tightly against his breast, stood there drawing great, labored breaths, waiting—for what?

---

film was creeping over his eyes, but he was aware that the Eye had suddenly gone out. And out of the dark the priest was chanting.

Then came a deep-drawn sigh from the spectators, followed by a ringing shout. In place of the Eye the full moon appeared, sailing overhead. And, holding off that deathly weakness, Jim understood. The sacrifice had ended; a new month had begun....

CHAPTER VII

Back to Long Island

J

im, seated beside Lucille, was listening to Cain's gruntings and chucklings as he expounded the situation to old Parrish.

It was the day following the scene in the amphitheatre. The four had been escorted back along the tongue of flooring into a hall with walls of fretted stone and sumptuous colorings. The floor was strewn with rich rugs woven of some vegetable fibre. There were divans and low chairs. At brief intervals, servitors, always smiling, passed carrying trays with wines and foods. And in the corridors were always glimpses of the guards.[261]

"It was the rising of the full moon saved our lives, Dent," Parrish explained. "It appears they have this sacrifice at each of the moon's phases. The victims, captives or criminals, are eaten by the priests. We've got a week's respite, Dent, and then—God help us."

Jim's arm tightened about Lucille, but the girl turned and smiled into his face. There was no longer any fear there. And Jim swore to himself that he would yet find some way of outwitting their devilish captors.

"What the devil are we supposed to be, criminals or what?" he asked her father. "Why do they smile at us all the time in that confounded way?"

Parrish questioned the Drilgo, but apparently he was unable to explain himself to him. "Maybe they think it an honor for us, Dent," he answered, "or maybe it's their idea of etiquette. Anyway, we four are to head the list when the moon's at the three-quarters. God, if only we could reach the Atom Smasher, I'm certain I could find out how it works!"

J

im had tried more than once to reach it. Through the colonnades at the end of the hall he could see the mechanism standing on the platform, always being inspected by half a dozen or so of the dignitaries of Atlantis. But all his attempts to cross that tongue of flooring had been vetoed by the guards.

They had presented their hands to him, palms outward, and on the palms were fine steel points, about two inches long, set into leather gauntlets. It had been impossible to try conclusions with them.

Two days went by. Once a group of dignitaries had entered the hall and, with smiles and profuse bows, inspected the prisoners. Then they had departed. And Jim had paced the floor, to and fro, thinking desperately.

There was no sort of weapon with which to hazard an attack. Jim knew that they were under the closest observation. He could only wait and hope. And if all else failed, he meant to hurl himself, with Lucille in his arms, off the tongue of floor into the depths below when their time came.

On the third morning, after a troubled sleep induced by very weariness, Jim was awakened by one of the guards, and started up to see one of the bowing dignitaries before him, and Parrish and Lucille sitting up among their rugs.

Bowing repeatedly, the smiling old man addressed some words to Jim, and then turned to Parrish.

"He says he wants you to show him the way the Atom Smasher works," said Parrish. "Now's our chance, Dent. He thinks it's simply an apparatus for neutralizing the blue-white ray. Don't let him guess—"

"I won't let him guess," Jim answered. "Tell him we'll go and show him—"

"I've told him, and he says only you are to go. He's suspicious. Say something quickly, Dent."

"Tell him," said Jim, "that I must have my two assistants and the lady. Tell him I may also need the help of some of his people. It requires many men to operate the machine."

P

arrish translated, speaking in the Drilgo tongue, which was their only means of communication. The Atlantean considered. Then he spoke again.

"He says that we three men may go, but Lucille must be left behind," groaned Parrish.

"The answer is no," said Jim.

The old dignitary, who seemed somewhat crestfallen, departed with an expressive gesture. Jim and Parrish looked at each other.

"That's our end," groaned Parrish.

"No, he'll bite," answered Jim, with the first grin that had appeared on his countenance since their arrival. "Let's make our plans quickly. We must contrive to get Lucille inside the machine, under the pretense of assisting with[262] the mechanism. And Cain, of course," he added, glancing at the goggly-eyed Drilgo. "You do your best to locate the starting mechanism, Parrish, and signal me the moment you're ready. We'll both leap in, and the four of us will sail—God, I don't care where we sail to, so long as we get away from here! Into eternity, if need be. But I hope it's Long Island!"

Back came the dignitary with two of the guards. Smiling at Jim, he indicated by signs that the three others might accompany him. The Atlanteans had bitten, as Jim had forecast.

The four proceeded along the hall and over the tongue of flooring. This time the force that had previously controlled their movements was not in action. At the farther end of the bridge they saw the group of dignitaries gathered about the Atom Smasher, examining it curiously. Over their heads the hooked arms of the hideous gods were raised. The Eye was darkened, as if with a curtain, and through the glass roof, high overhead, the sunlight streamed down upon the empty amphitheatre.

I

n spite of their smiles, the dignitaries of Atlantis were very much on the alert, as their tense attitudes denoted. Two more guards had appeared, and Jim saw that they were uncovering some apparatus at the base of the Eye. They were swinging a camera-like object toward him, its lens focused upon the Atom Smasher. It was not difficult to understand what was in the minds of the Atlanteans. The dignitaries were uneasy and mistrustful, and at the first suspicion of treachery they meant to loose the blue-white Ray contained in the apparatus, and blow the Atom Smasher and the group about it to destruction.

Jim intercepted a sign from Parrish, indicating that he was to make pretense of assisting him. He bent over the machine, Lucille beside him. Parrish was busily examining the wheels and levers. He was adjusting the thumbscrews, moving the needles along the dials.

One of the Atlanteans spoke, and Cain translated into "Drilgo" for Parrish's benefit. Parrish answered. Then, without raising his head, the old man said quietly, "I've located the starting lever, Dent. You and Lucille get inside quickly and pretend you're doing something to the machinery."

They stepped over the bow of the boat and stood beside Parrish, who continued examining the wheels. "We mustn't forget Cain," whispered the girl to her father. "Oh, I hope he understands!"

But there was no direct evidence that Cain did understand, and Parrish dared not warn him in "Drilgo," for fear one of the Atlanteans might understand the language. Cain was standing close beside the boat. But he was not in the boat.

Again one of the Atlanteans shot a question at Parrish. Parrish beckoned to Cain, and awaited the translation. He answered.

Each moment was growing tenser. It was impossible that the Atlanteans could fail to understand what was being planned. The only saving chance was that they did not realize the possibilities of escape that the vessel offered. A full minute went by.

S

uddenly Parrish raised his head. "I've got it fixed, I think, Dent," he said. "I'm going to count. When I reach 'three,' seize Cain and pull him aboard."

Jim nodded. The uneasiness was increasing. The guards at the camera-like object were each holding some sort of mechanical accessory in their hands. It looked like a small sphere of glass, and it connected with the apparatus by means of a hollow tube of fibre. Jim guessed that in an instant the Ray could be made to dart out of the lens. It would be quick work—as nearly as possible instantaneous work.

"Ready, Dent?" asked Parrish in an even voice. In this crisis the old man[263] had become astonishingly calm. He seemed the calmest of the lot. "One!"

Jim beckoned to Cain, who came toward him, his eyes goggling in inquiry.

"Two!"

Jim reached out and took Cain by the arm. There was a sharp question from the Atlantean who had spoken before.

"Three!"

With all his force Jim yanked Cain over the edge of the boat. The Drilgo stumbled and fell headlong with a howl of terror. But headlong—inside.

What happened was practically instantaneous. A sudden whir of the mechanism, a violet glow from the funnel, the smell of chlorine—a flash of blinding blue-white light. The Atlantean guards had fired—a quarter-second too late!

The thump, thump of the electrical discharge died away. The four were in the boat, whirling away through space. Cain was rising to his knees, a woe-begone expression on his face. And there was a clean cut, with charred, black edges along one side of the boat, showing how near the Atlanteans had come to success.

T

he relief, after the hideous suspense of the past days, was almost too much for the three white people. "We're free, we're going back home!" cried Jim exultantly, as he caught Lucille in his arms. And she surrendered her lips to his, while the tears streamed down her checks. Old Parrish, at the instrument board, looked up, smiling and chuckling. Even Cain, understanding that they were not to be hacked to bits with knives, gurgled and grinned all over his black face.

"How long will it take us to get back?" Jim asked Parrish after a while.

"I—I'm not quite sure, my boy," the old man replied. "You see—I haven't quite familiarized myself with the machine as yet."

"But we'll get back all right?" asked Jim.

"Well, we—we're headed in the right direction," answered Parrish. "You see, my boy, it's rather an intricate table of logarithmic calculations that that scoundrel has pasted on this board. The great danger appears to be that of coming within the orbit of the giant planet Jupiter. Of course, I'm trying to keep within the orbit of the Earth, but there is a danger of being deflected onto Pallas, Ceres, or one of the smaller asteroids, and finding ourselves upon a rock in space."

Jim and Lucille looked at Parrish in consternation. "But you don't have to leave the Earth, do you?" Jim asked.

"Unfortunately, it's pretty hard sticking to the Earth, my lad," said Parrish. "You see, Earth has moved a good many million miles through space since the time of Atlantis."

But both Jim and Lucille noticed that Parrish was already speaking of Atlantis as if it was in the past. They drew a hopeful augury from that. And then there was nothing to do but resign themselves to that universal greyness—and to hope.

T

hey noticed that Cain seemed to be watching Parrish's movements with unusual interest. The Neanderthal man seemed fascinated by the play of the dials, the whir of the wheels and gyroscopes.

"Are you setting a course, dad?" asked Lucille presently. "I mean, do you know just where we are?"

"To tell you the truth, my dear," answered her father, "I don't. I'm relying on some markings that Tode made on the chart—certain combinations of figures. God only knows where they'll take us to. But I'm hoping that by following them we shall find ourselves back on Long Island in the year 1930.

"No, that rascal could hardly have written down those figures to no purpose. They seem to me to comprise a course, both going and returning. But the calculations are very intricate, especially in the *time* dimension. I've nearly reached the last row now. Then, we shall have arrived, or—we sha'n't."[264]

Jim and Lucille sat down again. There was nothing that they could do. But somehow their hopes of reaching Long Island in the year of grace 1930 had grown exceedingly slim. Everything depended upon whether or not Tode had meant those figures to represent the course back to the starting point or not.

A desperate hope—that was all that remained to them. They watched Parrish as his eyes wandered along the rows of figures, while his fingers moved the micrometer screws. And then he looked up.

"We're reaching the end of our course," he said. "We're going to land somewhere. God knows where it will be. We must hope—that's all that's left us."

His hands dropped from the dials. He pressed a lever. The blur of nights and days began to slow. A column of vivid violet light shot from the funnel.

"Grip tight!" shouted Parrish.

Thump, thump! The Atom Smasher was vibrating violently. A jar threw Jim against Lucille. It was coming to a standstill. Trees appeared. Jim uttered a shout. He stepped across to Parrish and wrung his hand. He put his arms about Lucille and kissed her.

They were back at the Vanishing Place, and all their sufferings seemed to be of the past....

CHAPTER VIII

A Fruitless Journey

"Why don't you stop the boat, Parrish?"

"I'm trying to, lad!"

The Atom Smasher was still vibrating, even more violently than before. A column of violet light was pouring from her funnel. The pool, the mud, the walls of heaped up water were discernible, but all quivering and reproduced, line after line, to infinity. It was like looking into the rear-view mirror of a car that is vibrating rapidly. It was like one of those Cubist paintings of a woman descending the stairs, where one had to puzzle out which is the woman and which is the stairs.

A dreadful thought shot through Jim's mind. He remembered what he had said to Tode: "You can't hold the boat still in four-dimensional space."

This was not quite the same. By stopping the infernal mechanism, one re-entered three-dimensional space, and landed. Certainly the Atom Smasher could land. They were not like the motorcyclist who got on a machine for the first time, and rode to the admiration of all who saw him, except that he couldn't find out how to stop.

Yet there was Parrish still fumbling with the controls, and the boat was still vibrating at a terrific rate of speed. It is impossible to dream of leaping out, for there was no solidity, no continuity in the scenery outside.

It was not like attempting to leap from a moving train, for instance. In that case one knows that there is solid earth beneath, however hard one lands. Here everything was distorted, a sort of mirror reflection. And Jim noticed a strange thing that had never occurred to him before. Everything was reversed, as in a mirror picture. That clump of trees, for instance, which should have been on the right, was on the left.

Parrish looked up. "There's some means of stopping her, of course," he said. "There must be a lever—but I don't know where to look for it in all this mess." He pointed to the revolving wheels. No, it might be a matter of days of experimenting in order to discover the elusive switch.

"It may be a combination of switches," said Parrish. "I don't know what we're going to do."

"Suppose I jumped and chanced it," Jim suggested.

Lucille caught his arm with a little cry. Parrish shook his head.

"That devil—Listen: there was a Drilgo he disliked. He threw him out of the boat just before she landed at the cave. Everything was in plain[265] sight, plainer than things are here. But he was never seen again. For God's sake, lad, sit still. I'll try—"

H

ours later Parrish was still trying. And gradually Jim and Lucille had ceased to hope.

Side by side they had sat, watching that glimmering scene about them. Sometimes everything receded into a blur, across which sunlight and shadow, and then moonlight raced, at others the surroundings were so clear that it almost seemed as if, by steadying the boat, they could leap ashore. And once there happened something that sent a thrill of cold fear through both of them.

For where the pool had been there appeared suddenly a hut—and Tode, standing in the doorway, looking about him, a malicious sneer curving his lips.

Jim leaped to his feet, and old Parrish, who had seen Tode too, sprang up in wild excitement.

"Sit down, lad," he shouted. "It's nothing. I—I turned the micrometer screw a trifle hard. I got us back to five years ago, when we were living here with Tode. That's just a picture—out of the past, Jim!"

Jim understood, but he sank down again with cold sweat bathing his forehead. The terrific powers of the Atom Smasher were unveiling themselves more and more each moment. Jim felt Lucille's hand on his arm. He looked into her face.

"Jim, darling, what's going to happen to us if dad can't find how to work the machine?"

"I don't know, dear. I've thought that we might all jump out and chance it. If we held each other tight, we'd probably land in the same place—"

ld Parrish stood up. "I can't work it, Jim," he said. "Tode's got us beat. There's only one thing for us to do. You can guess what it is."

"I think I can," said Jim, glancing askance at Lucille. Yes, he knew, but he lacked the heart to tell her. "If we were all to jump out, tied together—don't you think we might land—somewhere near where we want to land?" he asked.

"Jim, do you realize what each vibration of this boat means?" asked Parrish. "There's a table on the instrument-board. It's a wave length of four thousand miles in space and nineteen years in time."

"You mean we're moving to London or San Francisco and back—"

"Further than that, every infinite fraction of a second," answered Parrish. "No, Jim, we—we wouldn't land. So we must just go back to where we came from, and—"

He had been speaking in a low voice, calculated not to reach Lucille's ears. The girl had been leaning back, her eyes closed, as if half asleep. Now she rose and stepped up to her father and lover. "You can tell me the truth," she said. "I'm not afraid."

"We've got to go back, Lucille," answered her father. "It's our only chance. By following the course in reverse we can expect to make Atlantis again—"

"Back to that horrible place?"

"No, my dear. The chart will lead us, obviously, back to the cave where Tode has his headquarters. We must try to surprise him, and force him to bring us back to Long Island."

"And then?" asked Lucille.

Parrish shrugged his shoulders. "We'll face that problem when we come to it," he answered.

"But how do you expect to be able to land at the other end any more than this?" asked Jim. "Suppose the machine continues to vibrate instead of coming to a standstill?"

"I think," said Parrish, "that we'll be able to strike a bargain with Tode. Obviously he will be willing to bring the machine to a standstill in order to parley with us. We'll make terms—the best we can. After all, he can't afford to remain marooned on the isle of Atlantis without the Atom Smasher."[266]

"I hate the idea of bargaining with that wretch," said Lucille.

"So do we all, dear," answered Jim. "But there's nothing else that we can do. It's just a matter of give and take. And I'd be glad to consent to any terms that would bring us three safe back to earth, with all this business behind us."

"I'll start back, then," said Parrish, turning back to the instrument board.

And, to the familiar thump, thump of the electrical discharge, the Atom Smasher took up its backward journey once more.

long time passed. With her head resting against Jim's breast, Lucille rested. Jim bent over her, trying to discover whether she was asleep or not. Her eyes were closed, her breathing so soft that she hardly seemed alive. An infinite pity for the girl filled Jim's heart, and, mingled with it, the intense determination to overcome the madman who had subjected her to these perils. He glanced across at Parrish, fingering his screws. Old Parrish looked up and nodded. There was a new determination in the old man's face that made him a different person from the crazed old man whom Jim had encountered at the Vanishing Place.

"We can beat him, Parrish!" Jim called, and Parrish looked back and nodded again. "We're nearly back to the top of the column," he answered.

Not long afterward Parrish looked up once more. "Stand by, Jim!" he called. "And be ready. Tode will be aware of our approach by means of the sensitive instruments he keeps in his laboratory. But don't harm him. We want him aboard, and we want him badly. He won't be able to play any more tricks with us. I've learned too much about the Atom Smasher."

He pressed a lever, and the greyness dissolved into its component parts of light and darkness. A jar. Thump, thump! The violet light! Lucille looked up, raised herself, uttered a low cry and caught at Jim's arm, trembling.

They had run their course truly. The Atom Smasher was vibrating outside the entrance to Tode's cave. And that was Tode, standing there, watching them, that devilish grin of his accentuated to the utmost. A blurred figure that appeared and vanished, and a surrounding crowd of Drilgoes—how many it was impossible to guess, for they looked like a crowd of apes in motion.

Suddenly Tode disappeared, and a moment later Lucille uttered a terrified cry as his voice spoke in her ear:

"I thought you'd be back. I knew you'd got away from Atlantis when my recorder showed the waves of electrical energy proceeding from the city. You were clever, Dent, but you see, you had to come back to me to get my help."

"Don't be afraid, dear," said Jim, trying to soothe the girl. "That's a wireless receiving apparatus." He pointed to a sort of cabinet enclosed among the rotating wheels, and then it was evident that Tode's voice was proceeding from it.

T

ode's figure appeared again, dancing through a haze of lines and patches. He was holding something in his hand which Jim made out to be the mouthpiece of a microphone. The voice inside the Atom Smasher spoke again:

"Turn all the micrometer screws until the needles register zero, Parrish. Then turn Dial D to point 3, Dial C to 5, Dial B to 1, and Dial A to 2. I'll repeat.... Now press the starting lever, Parrish, and you'll find yourself on firm ground again."

A few moments later the Atom Smasher was pouring out an immense column of the violet light, and slowly the vibration ceased. The blurred forms of Tode, of the Drilgoes grew clear. They had arrived.

Tode stepped over the rail. "And now, my friends, we'll have a talk," he said.[267]

"No tricks, Tode," Jim warned him, "You've probably got a number of deviltries up your sleeve—"

"One or two, Dent," grinned Tode.

"We're willing to negotiate."

"Of course you are. You see, I hold the trumps, Dent. Those dial deflections, which are inevitable in the construction of any piece of mechanism, are not the same for Earth in 1920. Don't think you can use the same figures to land with. You must remember that there has been a precession of the equinoxes since the time of Atlantis, with a consequent shift in the earth's axis. No, Dent, I've got you very much where I want you. But I'm willing to discuss terms with you. First of all, let's get rid of this useless cargo. I don't believe in overburdening a ship," he grinned.

He picked up Cain bodily and heaved the astonished Drilgo over the side before he knew what was happening to him. Cain picked himself up and rubbed his sides, whimpering mournfully. The Drilgoes crowded closer, their faces agape with astonishment. Tode spoke a command sharply, and they scattered.

"**B**efore we come to terms, Dent, I'll give you a piece of news that may interest you," said Tode. "Much has happened during the time you've been away. Ambassadors have been out to see me from Atlantis. With the aid of a Drilgo interpreter, they conveyed to me that they had been greatly impressed by the disappearance of the Atom Smasher. They have nothing like it, of course, and they think I'm a Number One magician.

"The upshot is, they want me to accept the supreme rule of the city, and use my arts to restore the lost territory that has sunk beneath the waves. They swore on an image of their god, Cruk, that they were sincere. I told them that I'd sent the Atom Smasher away on a journey, but that it would be back shortly, and that I'd then give them their answer.

"Now, Dent"—Tode's face took on that look of fanaticism that Jim had seen on it before—"I'm going to repeat the proposition I made to you before. Join me. I'll make you my chief subordinate, and I'll load you and Parrish down with honors. Everything that a human being can desire shall be yours. And in a year or two, when we're tired of being gods, we'll take the Atom Smasher back to Earth and destroy it, and with our wealth we'll become the supreme rulers of Earth too. I need you, Dent. You don't realize how lonely life can be when one is worshiped as a god. As for Lucille, there are a thousand maidens more beautiful than she is, in Atlantis. Come, Dent, your answer! Your last chance, Dent! Don't throw it away!"

He read the answer before Jim could speak it. Jim saw Tode's face flicker, and hurled himself upon him. Lucille screamed. The two men wrestled together in the narrow confines of the circular boat. Jim struck Tode a blow that sent him reeling against the rail. Then he felt himself seized from behind. A giant Drilgo had him in his arms. He lifted him over the side and flung him to the earth. In an instant the chattering Drilgoes were crowding down upon him.

Struggling madly, Jim saw Tode fell old Parrish with a blow, push back Lucille as she sprang at him, and quickly press the starting lever. The column of violet fire faded, there came the whir of the mechanism—the Atom Smasher vanished....

CHAPTER IX

The Blinded Eye

J

im fought with all his strength; he managed to shake off his assailants and regain his feet. Then one of the Drilgoes poised his stone-tipped spear, ready to hurl it through his body.

But the spear never left the Drilgo's hand in Jim's direction. Like a great black ape, Cain leaped upon the fellow and bore him to the ground, his[268] feet twined around his shoulders, his hands gripping his throat. Not until the Drilgo had been reduced to a heaving, half-strangled hulk did Cain leave him.

Then Cain, bending until his stomach almost touched the ground, came worming toward Jim, making signs of obeisance.

What had happened that Jim had won the Drilgo's faith? Why did Cain now look upon him, apparently, as his master? It was impossible to gauge the processes of the black man's mind, and at the moment Jim was in no mood to wonder. The stunning disaster that had overtaken him monopolized his thoughts.

Lucille and Parrish were once more in Tode's power. That was the dominating fact. The only gleam of comfort in the situation was that Tode had given him the clue to his movements.

Beyond a doubt Tode had taken his captives into Atlantis with him. It was impossible to disbelieve Tode's statement that he had been offered the supreme power in the city. Tode's egotism would have compelled him to blurt out that fact. Besides, Tode had certainly not gone back to earth.

Jim must force his way into Atlantis. He would find and rescue the two prisoners or die there.

He turned away from the groveling Cain and the chattering Drilgoes, who, inspired by Cain's example, now seemed animated by the same instinct to obey him, and went into the cave. But at the entrance he turned for a moment and looked back.

———————————

I

t was night. The valley was swathed in mists, the volcano opposite was spouting a shaft of lurid fire. On the water was a path of moonlight, where the clouds had been dispersed by the Atlanteans. Jim took in the scene, he raised one arm and shook his fist. Then, without a word, he passed inside.

There was a soft light in the cave, streaming out from an inner chamber, access to which was through a narrow orifice in the rock. Jim passed through, and found himself in Tode's laboratory.

He was astonished at its completeness, still more so at the existence of numerous pieces of apparatus whose purpose it was difficult to understand. There was a radio transmitter and receiver, but improved out of all recognition from those in use in the prosaic year 1930. Three or four tiny dynamos, little more than toys in appearance, were generating as much voltage, from the indicators, as a modern power station. And overhead was a dial, with two series of figures in black and red, and two needles, both of which were swinging briskly, indicating that there was an intense electrical disturbance in the vicinity.

The Atom Smasher! Jim took heart. Tode could not be far away! He looked about him, subconsciously trying to discover some implement that would prove of service to him, but there was nothing that he could see, not even one of the ray tubes. He looked about uneasily.

Then his eyes fell upon something so singularly out of place that it looked, for the moment, like some pre-historic weapon. It was the last thing Jim would have expected to find there—nothing more nor less than a sporting rifle!

Deer shooting had been one of Tode's pastimes in the old days, and more than one fat buck had been surreptitiously shot for the benefit of the larder at the Vanishing Place. There was something almost pathetic in the sight of that rifle and the fifty cartridges in their cardboard carton. Perhaps Tode had pictured himself shooting big game in Atlantis at some period or other. It was a human weakness that for an instant lessened Jim's hate and horror of the man. It brought him to a saner view of the situation. Jim had been on the point of losing his powers of reason. The sight of the rifle restored them.[269]

H

e turned sharply as he heard a sound in the entrance. Cain was coming toward him, with many genuflexions, and much stomach wriggling. He stopped, straightened himself. There was a look of singular intelligence on the Drilgo's face.

He began chattering, pointing in the direction of Atlantis. Jim could make nothing of what he was trying to convey.

"Yes, they're there," he said bitterly, "but I don't see how that's going to help me."

"Oh my poor Lucille!" said Cain unexpectedly.

The words were like a parrot's speech, the intonation so remarkable a copy of old Parrish's that Jim was flabbergasted. Nevertheless it was evident that Cain knew he was referring to Lucille.

With a strange, slinking motion he crossed the laboratory and bent beneath a huge slab of stone, resting on two great hewn rocks. He emerged, holding in his arms two curious contrivances. He laid them at Jim's feet.

Jim stared at them, and suddenly understood what they were. They were two pairs of wings, of the kind the Atlanteans had used when they made their aerial sortie against the Drilgoes.

Cain picked up one pair and began adjusting it about his body. He made fluttering movements with his arms.

"You mean that you've learned how to fly, you black imp of Satan?" shouted Jim.

And Cain, as if understanding, nodded and beamed all over his black face.

With that Jim's idea was born. If the Drilgoes would follow him, he would lead them against Atlantis. And, before the assault began, he would fly to the great Eye that guarded it, and blind it.

H

e thought afterward that it was like a supernatural revelation, this scheme, that leaped full-fledged into his brain. And Cain had developed extraordinary executive ability. Outside the cave, through rifts in the swirls of fog, Jim could see innumerable Drilgoes massing in the valley, as if they understood Jim's purpose. From Cain's gesticulations, and the number of times he rubbed his stomach, it was evident that he counted upon sacking Atlantis and was imagining innumerable meals of fat captives.

Each flash of lurid light from the volcano disclosed further masses of Drilgoes, armed with their stone spears, apparently assembling for the attack. Whether Tode had summoned them before the Atlanteans offered him the rulership of the city, or whether Jim's own plan had been communicated to them by some telepathic process, it was impossible to guess, but there was not the least doubt but that they were prepared to follow him.

Cain nudged Jim and began strapping the other pair of wings about his body. Jim saw that the energy was supplied by two tiny, lights burning in the base, cold fire, stored energy whose strength he did not guess. For, when Cain took him by the hand, and motioned to him to slide the knob in the groove, he was hurled skyward like a rocket.

There followed a delirious hour. Tossing and tumbling like a pigeon in a gale, Jim by degrees acquired mastery over the apparatus. At the end of the hour he could fly almost as well as Cain, who, like a black guardian angel kept beside him, reaching out a hand when he overbalanced, and pulling him out of aerial side-slips.

S

uddenly Cain motioned toward the volcano, and started toward it in a rocketlike swoop. Jim understood. The Drilgoes were ready for the attack upon Atlantis.

Jim dropped to earth, ran back into the cave, and picked up the rifle and the carton of ammunition. He filled the magazine, and, with the rifle on his arm, rose into the air again. Cain was circling back, uttering weird cries of[270] distress at finding his master absent.

"It's all right, Cain," said Jim. "I'm here."

Side by side they flew steadily toward the base of the great cone, which was pouring out a fan-shaped stream of fire. Rumblings shook the earth; it was evident that another upheaval was in course of preparation. The long column of the Drilgoes could be seen, extending around the flank of the mountain.

Then of a sudden the Eye opened. And across the causeway came the blue-white Ray, carrying death and destruction.

The Drilgoes, who had learned wisdom, remained concealed out of the Ray's path, and escaped, but a great dinosaur, fifty or sixty feet in length, startled by the light, came blundering out of the ferns, uttered a bellow, and melted into an amorphous mass. Birds dropped from their roosting places with a sound like that of falling hail. Black paths were cloven through the midst of the jungle.

Rifle in hand, Jim soared into the air, and shot forward, high above the causeway toward the glowing Eye.

He had noticed that the blue-white ray appeared in cycles of about two minutes, and had made his plans accordingly. Two minutes in which to accomplish his task, or take the chance of a hideous death. Some thirty seconds carried him right into the glowing heart of the winking Eye: he hovered and raised his rifle.

Underneath him the breakers thundered: round the Eye a myriad sea-birds fluttered, dashing themselves against it, falling into the waves. Huge and high the great city towered into the skies, lit by its soft incandescence. Jim could see the throngs in the streets, the traffic. But what was happening in the other side of the Eye?

S

uddenly he saw the moon in her third quarter sailing through the skies, and a hideous fear overcame him. Suppose Tode had met with treachery; suppose that this very night Lucille were doomed to be sacrificed to the terrible god Cruk!

Suppose that even at that moment her tender flesh were being sacrificed by the awful hooks!

He drew a bead upon the Eye and fired—and missed. The bullet went wide. But even if it struck, what guarantee had he that it would shatter the glass, or whatever substance it was that covered the orb?

He lost position, and knew that the two-minute interval was drawing to a close. He soared and fired again. The Eye still glowed.

Then of a sudden a blinding ray shot forth from it, so dazzling that it seemed to sear Jim's eyeballs. The interval was ended.

It shot beneath him, but no more than a few feet, and turning his eyes shoreward, Jim saw it sweep along the causeway and tear a black path through the forest. Frantically he soared, and circled around the temple.

The ray went out. Two minutes more. And now the temporary panic had passed; Jim's nerves grew steady as a rock. He eased the controls and floated in toward the glowing orb. Sea-mews, screaming, dashed themselves against it and fell, wounded and broken, into the breaking seas below. They fluttered past Jim's face, one impacted against his chest with a thud that rocked him where he hovered.

But Jim knew that he could not fail. At a distance of fifty feet he drew a bead upon the centre of the Eye and pressed the trigger.

And instantly the light went out....

CHAPTER X

The Fight in the Dark

H

e dropped down softly to the causeway. Within the city he heard a sound such as he had never heard before, as if some ancient prophecy of doom had been fulfilled, a wailing "Aiah! Aiah! Aiah!" that was caught up from throat to throat and[271] rose upon the wind in a clamor wild and mournful as that of the sea-birds around the broken Eye. It was the death-keening of proud Atlantis, Queen of the Atlantic for fifty thousand years. She was dying in darkness.

For, with the blinding of the Eye, all the soft lights within the city had gone out. Dense, utter, impenetrable darkness reigned, and even the gibbous moon, floating overhead, seemed to give no light.

Jim dropped to the causeway and began running in the direction of the city. But, feeling the drag of his wings, he unbuckled the strap and flung them away. He might need them, but his one thought was to get to Lucille, if she were still alive. And he felt that each moment lost might mean that he would be too late.

Through the blackness he raced forward, hearing that sobbing ululation within the walls. But behind him he heard another sound, and shuddered at it, all his hopes suddenly reversed. For that sound was the shouting of the Drilgoes as they rushed forward to conquest. And now it seemed a monstrous thing that proud Atlantis should be at the mercy of these hordes. He had let loose destruction upon the world. But it was to save Lucille.

That was his consolation. Yet he hardly checked the racing thoughts within his mind even for a moment, to meditate on what he had done. Those thoughts were all of Lucille. He must get to her before the Drilgoes entered. And he ran faster, panting, gasping, till of a sudden the portals loomed before him, and he saw a crowd of frenzied Atlanteans struggling to pass through, and a file of soldiers struggling to keep them back.

H

e could distinguish nothing more than the confused struggle. He hurled himself into the midst of the crowd and swept it back. He was within the walls now, and struggling to pass through the mob of people that was swarming like homeless bees.

He fought them with flailing fists, he clove a pathway through them, until he found himself in a great shadowy space that he recognized as the central assembly of the city. More by instinct than design he hit upon the narrow court that was the elevator. But the court was filled with another mob of struggling people, and in the darkness there was no possibility of discovering the secret of raising it.

He blundered about, raging, forcing a path now here, now there. He ran into blind alleys, into small threading streets about the court, which led him back into the central place of assembly. It was like a nightmare, that blind search under the pale three-quarter moon and the black, star-blotched sky.

Suddenly Jim found himself wedged by the pressure of the crowd into a sort of recess leading off the elevator court. So strong was the pressure here that he was unable to move an inch. Wedged bolt upright, he could only wait and let the frenzied mob stream past him. And louder above the sound of wailing came the roars of the Drilgoes swarming along the causeway.

Suddenly something gave behind him—a door, as it seemed, broken off its hinges by the mob pressure. Jim was hurled backward, and fell heavily down a flight of stone stairs, bringing up against a stone balustrade. He got up, unconscious of his bruises, ran to the top of the flight, and saw the dim square of palest twilight where the door had been.

But over him he could faintly see the stairs and the balustrade, winding away to what seemed immeasurable height. That stairway must lead to the top of the building, and thence there should be some access to the amphitheatre. Jim turned toward it.

S

uddenly a tremendous uproar filled the streets, yells, the clicking grunts of the Drilgoes, the screams of the panic-stricken populace. The invaders had arrived, and they were sweeping all before them. No chance[272] of recognition in that darkness. Lucille! Shouting her name, Jim began to ascend the stairs in leaps of three at a time.

But long before he reached the top he was ascending one by one, with straining limbs and laboring breath. Red slaughter down below, a very inferno of sound; above, that shadowy stairway, still extending almost to the heavens. Step after step, flight beyond flight!

Jim's lungs were bursting, and his heart hammering as if it would break his chest. One flight more! One more! Another! Suddenly he realized that his task was ended. In place of the stairs stood a vast hall, and beyond that another hall, dim in the faint light that filtered through the glass above.

Jim thought he remembered where he was. Beyond that next hall there should be the tongue of flooring, crossing the amphitheatre and joining the platform of the idols. But he stopped suddenly as he emerged, not upon the tongue, but upon still another stairway.

He had gone astray, and out of his bursting lungs a cry of rage and despair went up. For a moment he stood still. What use to proceed further?

And then, amazingly, there came what might have been a sign from heaven. Down through a small, square opening overhead, no larger than a ventilator, it came ... a glimmer of violet flame!

And Jim hurled himself like a madman against the stairs, and surmounted them with two bounds. There were no more. Instead, Jim found himself looking down into the amphitheatre.

The thick walls had cut off all sound from his ears, save a confused murmur, but now a hideous uproar assailed them. The whole floor of the amphitheatre was a mass of moving shadows, of slayers and slain.

The Drilgoes had broken in and trapped the multitudes that had taken refuge there. Their fearful stone-tipped spears thrust in and out, to the accompaniment of their savage howls and the screams of the dying.

N

ever has such a shadow-play been seen, perhaps, as that below, where death stalked in dense darkness, and the slayer did not even see his victim. Only the thrust of spears, the soft, yielding flesh that they encountered, the scream, the wrench of stone from tissue, and the blended howl of triumph and scream of despair.

Yet only for a moment did Jim turn his eyes upon that sight. For he knew where he was now. He had emerged upon the other side of the amphitheatre, upon the platform where he had seen the priests and dignitaries gathered when he was led forward to be sacrificed.

There, in the rear, were the hideous, shadowy gods, looming up out of the darkness, their outstretched arms interlaced. And there upon the platform was the Atom Smasher, a little thread of violet light seeping out of the central tube.

Beside it stood a group of figures, impossible to distinguish in the darkness, but of a sudden Lucille's scream rang out above the din below.

With three leaps Jim was at her side. He saw the girl, Tode, and Parrish, struggling in the grasp of a dozen priests. They were dragging them toward the idols, and Jim understood what that scene portended.

In despair at the irruption of the Drilgoes, the priests were seeking to propitiate their gods by sacrificing the three strangers whom they held responsible for all their woes.

Jim caught Lucille in his arms, shouting her name. She knew him, turned toward him. Then one of the priests, armed with a great stone-headed club—for no metal is permitted within the precincts of the god Cruk—struck at him furiously.

Jim leaped aside, letting the club descend harmlessly upon the floor. He shot out his right with all his strength[273] behind it, catching the priest upon the jaw, and the man crumpled.

hirling the club around his head, he fought back the fanatics, all the while shouting to Tode to start the Atom Smasher. In such a moment he only remembered that Tode was a white man, and of his own generation.

He struck down three of the priests; then he was seized around the knees from behind, and fell heavily. The club was wrenched from his hand. In another moment Jim found himself helpless in the grasp of the Atlanteans.

As he stopped struggling for a moment, to gather his strength for a supreme effort, he heard a whir overhead, and saw the arms of the stone gods begin their horrible revolution. The priests had started the machinery. And high above the din below rang out the wild chant of the high priest.

Jim saw him now, a figure poised upon a platform behind the arms, his own arms raised heavenward.

"Aiah! Aiah! Aiah!"

Jim was being dragged forward, with Lucille beside him, old Parrish following, still making a futile struggle for life, while pitiful screeches issued from his mouth.

Jim saw the revolving arms descend within a foot of his head. One more fight—one more, the last.

Suddenly, with loud yells, a band of Drilgoes leaped forward from the head of the stairs and rushed upon the struggling priests and victims. And, dark as it was, Jim recognized their leader—Cain.

And Cain knew Lucille. As the priests rallied for a desperate resistance, Cain hurled his great body through the air, landing squarely upon the shoulders of the priest nearest the revolving arms, and knocking him flat.

Then the arms caught priest and Drilgo, and the steel hooks dug deep into their flesh. A screech of terror, a howl that reverberated through the amphitheatre, and nothing remained of either but a heap of macerated flesh.

But in that instant Jim had fought free again. He caught Lucille and dragged her back toward the Atom Smasher.

T

ode had already broken from his captors and was working at it frantically.

"Hold on!" screeched old Parrish. "Hold on!"

They had a moment's leeway. The Drilgoes had driven the priests back into the hooks. With awful shrieks the fanatics were yielding up their lives, in the place of their selected victims.

But more Drilgoes were pouring up the stairs. A moment's leeway, and no more, before the savage band would impale the four upon their stone-pointed spears. There was not the slightest chance that they would be able to make their identity known.

"For God's sake hurry!" Jim yelled in Tode's ear.

The wheels were revolving, a stream of violet light, leaping out of the central tunnel, cast a lurid illumination upon the scene.

But it was too late. A score of Drilgoes, with leveled spears, were rushing on the four.

"Hold tight!" screeched Parrish. He thrust his arm into his breast, and pulled out a little lever. Jim recognized it and remembered. It was the instrument of universal death—the uranium release of untold forces of cataclysmic depredation.

"Take that!" screamed the old man, inserting the lever into the secret groove in the Atom Smasher and jerking it in the direction of the priests.

CHAPTER XI

Tode's Last Gamble

A roar that seemed to rend the heavens followed. Roar upon roar, as the infinite momentum of the disintegrating uranium struck obstacle after obstacle. The Drilgoes vanished,[274] the amphitheatre melted away, walls and roof.... Overhead were the moon and stars.

And proud Atlantis was sinking into the depths of the sea.... Not as a ship sinks, but piecemeal, her walls and towers crumbling and toppling as a child's sand-castle crumbles under the attack of the lapping waves. Down they crashed, carrying their freight of black, clinging, human ants, while from the sea's depths a wave, a mile high, rose and battered the fragments to destruction. From the crater of the volcano a huge wave of fire fanned forward, and where fire and water met a cloud of steam rose up.

A boiling chaos in which water and earth and fire were blended, spread over land and sea. And then suddenly it was ended. Where the last island of the Atlantean continent had been, only the ocean was to be seen, placid beneath the stars.

The Atom Smasher was vibrating at tremendous speed. Jim, with one arm round Lucille, faced Tode at the instrument board. Near by sat Parrish, watching him too.

"That took a whole year," said Tode. "That pretty little scene of destruction we've just witnessed. The good old Atom Smasher has been doing some lively stunts, or we'd have been engulfed too. We're not likely to see anything so pretty in history again, unless we go to watch the destruction of Herculaneum and Pompeii by lava from Vesuvius. But that would be quite tame in comparison with this."

Tode's jeering tone grated on Jim's ears immeasurably.

"I don't think any of us are craving any more experiments, Tode," he said, trying to keep his voice steady. "Suppose you take us back to Peconic Bay. We'll dump the Atom Smasher into the pond, and try to forget that we've had anything except a bad nightmare."

"Don't trust him, Jim," whispered Lucille.

Tode heard. "Thank you," he answered, scowling. "But seriously, Dent, we can't go back with nothing to show for all our trouble. Those fools tried to betray me, and then the Eye went out. Perhaps I have you to thank for that performance? However, the sensible thing is to let bygones be bygones. But we must make a little excursion. How about picking up a little treasure from the hoards of Solomon or Genghis Khan? A few pounds of precious stones would make a world of difference in our social status when we reach Long Island."

Jim felt a cold fury permeating him. Tode saw his grim look and laughed malignantly.

"Well, Dent, I'm ready to be frank with you," he said. "The game's still in my hands. I want Lucille. I'm willing to take you and Parrish back, provided you agree she shall be mine. I'll have to trust you, but I shall have means of evening up if you play crooked."

"Why don't you ask my girl herself?" piped old Parrish.

"He needn't trouble. He knows the answer!" cried Lucille scornfully.

"There's your answer," said Jim. "Now, what's the alternative?"

"The alternative is, that I have already set the dial to eternity, Dent," grinned Tode. "Eternity in the fifth dimension. Didn't know I'd worked that out, did you? A pleasant little surprise. No, don't try to move. My hand is on the lever. I have only to press it, and we're there."

J

im stood stock still in horror. Tode's voice rang true. He believed Tode had the power he claimed.

"Yes, the fifth dimension, and eternity," said Tode, "where time and space reel into functionlessness. Don't ask me what it's like there. I've never been there. But my impression of it is that it's a fairly good representation of the place popularly known as hell.

"You fool, Dent," Tode's voice rang out with vicious, snarling emphasis, "I gave you your chance to come in with[275] me. Together we'd have made ourselves masters of Atlantis and brought back her plunder to our Twentieth Century world. You refused because of a girl—a girl, Dent, who loved me long before you came upon the scene."

"That's a lie, Lucius," answered Lucille steadily. "And you can do your worst. There's one factor you haven't reckoned in your calculations, and that's called God."

"The dark blur on the spectral lines," old Parrish muttered.

Tode laughed uproariously. "Come, make your choice, Dent," he mocked. "It's merely to press this lever. You'll find yourself—well, we won't go into that. I don't know where you'll find yourself. You'll disappear. So shall I. But I'm desperate. I must have Lucille. Choose!" His voice rang out in maniac tones. "Choose, all of you!"

"Lucille has answered you," Jim retorted.

"And how about you, old man?" called Tode to Parrish.

Parrish leased forward, making a swift movement with his hand. "Go to your own hell, you dev—"

A blinding light, a frantic oscillation of the Atom Smasher, a sense of death, awful and indescribable—and stark unconsciousness rushed over Jim. His last thought was that Lucille's arms were about him, and that he was holding her. Nothing mattered, therefore, even though they two were plunged into that awful nothingness of the fifth dimension, where neither space nor time recognizably exists. Love could exist there.

CHAPTER XII

Solid Earth

e's coming around, Lucille. Thank God for it!"

Jim opened his eyes. For a few moments he looked about him without understanding. Then the outlines of a room etched themselves against the clouded background. And in the foreground Lucille's face. The girl was bending over Jim, one hand soothing his forehead.

"Where am I?" Jim muttered.

"Back on earth, Jim, the good old earth, never again to leave it," answered Lucille, with a catch in her voice. With an effort she composed herself. "You mustn't talk," she said.

"But what place is this?"

"It's Andy Lumm's house. Now rest, and I'll explain everything later."

But the first explanation came from Andy Lumm. "Well, Mr. Dent, my wife and me sure were glad to be on the spot when you and Miss Parrish got bogged on the edge of the Black Pool," he said. "Mean, treacherous place it is. Thar was a cow got mired thar last month, up to her belly. If us hadn't found her, and dragged her out with ropes, she'd have gone clear under. Granpop Dawes says thar's underground springs around the edge, and that it runs straight down to hell, though that seems sorter far-fetched to me.

"Yessir, and if I hadn't heard WNYC giving Miss Parrish on the list of missing persons, and as having been seen near here, I reckon I'd never have found you. Made me and my wife uneasy, that did.

'Andy,' she says. 'I got an inkling you oughter go to the Vanishing Place and see if she ain't there.' And there I found you two, mired to the waist, and Mr. Parrish dancing around and fretting, and his clothes burned to cinders.

"It sure seems strange to me, to think Mr. Parrish got away safe after that explosion five years ago, and of his wandering around with loss of memory, till you found him, and brung him back here to restore it, but thar's strange things in the world—yes, sir, thar surely is!"

In the happiness of being back on Earth once more, Jim was content to let further explanations go. The return of Parrish had been duly chronicled in the newspapers, and had provoked a mild interest, but fortunately the public mind was so occupied at[276] the moment with the trial of a night club hostess that, after the first rush of newspaper men, the three were left alone.

D

ay after day, in the brilliant autumn weather, Jim and Lucille would roam the tinted woods, recharging themselves with the feel of Earth, until the memory of those dread experiences grew dim.

"Well, Jim, I reckon I'd better tell you and get it over," said old Parrish one morning—Parrish, quite his old, jaunty self again. "Tode had got the dials pointing to the fifth dimension—eternity, he called it, though actually I believe it's nothing more than annihilation, a grand smash. Well, he pressed that lever. But something had gone wrong.

"You remember how poor Cain seemed to take great interest in the Atom Smasher. There's no way of telling what had been going on in that brain of his, but it looks to me like he'd known that that lever meant death. It was sealed up in wax, and Tode had got it free on the way out of Atlantis.

"Well—this it what I made out from examining the thing afterward. Cain had been monkeying with the lever. He'd pried loose one of the wires that hooked to the transformer, and short-circuited it, not knowing, of course, just what he was doing. The result was that when Tode pressed that lever, instead of blowing the whole contraption to pieces, he got a couple of billion volts of electricity through his body, combined with a larger amperage than has ever been imagined. It burned him to a few grease spots. He simply— vanished. You don't remember what you did at the moment, boy?"

"I don't seem to remember anything," said Jim.

"Well, your response was an automatic one. You jumped him. Luckily you were too late, for Tode vanished like that!" Old Parrish snapped his fingers. "But you must have got into the field of magnetic force—any way, you were almost electrocuted. Lucille and I thought you were dead for hours.

"We laid you down and set a course for home. I used those dial numberings Tode had given me. He'd said they wouldn't work, but he'd lied. They did work. They brought us back to the Vanishing Place.

"We carried you out, and then I saw your eyelid twitch. We worked over you with artificial respiration till it looked as if there was a chance for you. Then I shut off the power and let the waters rush in over the Atom Smasher, and swam ashore. And there it lies at the bottom of the pool, and may it lie there till the Judgment Day."

"Tode was a genius," said Jim, "but he never understood that character counts for more than genius."

"Let's think no more about him," said Lucille. She had come up to them, and the two looked at each other and smiled. Love is self-centred; other things it forgets very quickly.

"To-morrow we go back to New York," said Jim. "You think you're able to face the world and take up life again?"

"I think so, Jim," said Lucille.

"You're not remembering him after all?"

"No, Jim. I was thinking of poor Cain. He died for me."

"But that was twelve thousand years ago, my dear, and to-day's to-day," said Jim. "And to-morrow a new life begins for you and me."

He drew her closer to him. No, he would never quite forget, but that was twelve thousand years ago ... and to-morrow was his wedding day.

---

[277]

A Meeting Place for Readers of Astounding Stories

The Readers' Corner

An "Astounding" Career

Dear Editor:

A friend introduced me to your new magazine, and it is wonderful. The best story in the magazine, or, rather, the one I liked best, outside of the serial, which I didn't read, is "The Cave of Horror," by Capt. S. P. Meek. Next comes Ray Cummings' story of the Fourth Dimension, "Phantoms of Reality." Other good ones are, "Tanks," "Invisible Death," and "Compensation."

I did not like "The Stolen Mind." It seemed to me to be a mixture of superstition and magic. A fairy tale. I am glad that you are publishing this magazine, and I think that it is worth double its present price. You have my good wishes to the magazine for a long and astounding career. My way of reading a serial is to save copies and to read the story at one time. I do not like to wait a month for a story to end or continue.

Your next issue seems to sound quite interesting. "The Spawn of the Stars," a very interesting and, I am sure, a fit name for the story. "Creatures of the Light" is a very vague name—you don't know what to expect. The others will prove to be as interesting as any that I have named. I prefer interplanetary stories the most, as any amount of science can be injected in them.—Nathan Greenfield, 318 East 78th St., New York, N. Y.

Prefers Long Stories

Dear Editor:

I got your first issue of Astonishing Stories, and, although I like the stories, I do not like the way you have it bound. (This is supposed to be criticism, so don't take it to heart.) The pages are uneven and hard to turn. But the stories in the first copy were good. And you'll have a swell magazine if you have stories by Harl Vincent and Ray

Cummings. The aforesaid men are two of the best in the science fiction field. Another thing: don't have any short stories. If you have about 3 or 4 l-o-n-g stories, I'd like it better. I hope your magazine enjoys much success!—Linus Hogenmiller, 502 N. Washington Street, Farmington, Mo.

Another Who Likes Interplanetary Stories

Dear Editor:

I have read the first issue of Astounding Stories with much pleasure, and if the first issue is any indication of what is to follow I will continue to be a reader.

You inquire as to the kind of stories that your readers think should be published. I think you will find the most popular brand to be interplanetary stories and stories along the line of the "Beetle Horde."[278] Best wishes for success in your new endeavor—F. C. Cowherd, Room 333, L. & N. Railroad, Louisville, Ky.

Attention, Joiners!

Dear Editor:

I have just finished one of the stories in your magazine, and could not resist the temptation to write and tell you how much I enjoyed it. The stories are great and are just the thing to give one rest and recreation. At the same time they fire imagination and are not trashy love stories.

The main purpose of the letter is to revive an old idea and see if I can put it through. I propose to organize a correspondence society for readers interested in science. We would use Astounding Stories as our official medium. Each member would receive a list of members' names and addresses, a quantity of official stationery for inter-correspondence, and a certificate of membership suitable for framing.

The object would be the discussion of scientific topics and the latest advances.

I would suggest an annual fee of $2.50 to cover the cost of printing stationery, certificates, application forms, copy of the constitution, lists of members and official pins.

All those interested in the formation of such a society are earnestly requested to write me, giving suggestions as to a suitable name, etc. They will receive full information, and a sample of the certificate of membership and an application form.

I trust you will publish this letter at your earliest convenience—M. R. Bercovitch, B. Sc., 4643 St. Urbain Street, Montreal, Canada.

Sound Criticism

Dear Editor:

You ask for readers to write you regarding types of stories desired. Well, I am an electrical engineer and of course like my yarns to have a touch of science in them. Also I like my authors to make an original contribution to whatever theory of science they develop fictionally. This Ray Cummings doesn't do in his very interesting story, "Phantoms of Reality." His beginning is palpably borrowed from Francis Flagg's story, "The Blue Dimension," which appeared in a Science Fiction magazine in 1927. Flagg developed the theory of vibrations, reverberation, etc., and contributed something new to speculative science. Cummings merely seizes this point and dives into a series of improbable adventures.

Now I am not quarrelling with their improbability: I like my stories improbable, but I am asking for something more original than the old rehash of kings and queens, intrigues, and returning princes, etc. Again, Cummings seems to lack enough scientific acumen to make his other world different than this. Even a superficial thinker will readily see that the terrain of the other world would not faithfully follow our own in its salient features. However, forgive me for knocking—the story wasn't so bad, and Cummings doubtless can do better than this—or has.

"The Beetle Horde"—so far—is a gem, and holds the interest. Furthermore, its science is splendid. I am looking forward to its conclusion. "The Cave of Horror" is a damn good yarn, well written, interest sustained: but I didn't care for "The Stolen Mind." The truth is that that particular story didn't hang together very well. It left one up in the air, as it were, and far from satisfied me. Too, the science involved, to say the least of it, was not very sound or plausibly put. In reading the story I felt that the author was one who should be encouraged to write more—nothing wrong with his imagination or ability to fling words—but that he should be gently coerced into writing with better continuity and intelligence. "Compensation" didn't click—too loose—not compact enough. Splendid idea ruined by hasty writing. Another author needing a gentle hint. But "Tanks" was another sure-fire hit with me. Held me to last word. The story sounded real.

So for the stories in your first issue. You see, on the whole, I liked all of them. Still, I also like variety. Can't you give us some of the Francis Flagg type of fiction? H. Hyatt Verril is another of my favorites, also Dr. Keller and Clara Harris. I have read mighty good tales by those authors. I believe you could do worse than to run an occasional H. G. Wells story, and if you gave us "The First Men in the Moon" serially, I for one would be delighted. I have tried in vain to get that story and never have. Well, I guess I have said enough. Best wishes for the New Year. May Astounding Stories grow and prosper—and its Editor.—C. Harry Jaeger, 2900 Jeedan Road, Oakland, California.

Likes Interplanetary Stories

Dear Editor:

Having read the first issue of Astounding Stories, I am about to pronounce a sentence on it. It is guilty of being "Astounding" to the Nth degree!

I enjoyed all the stories immensely and will be anxiously awaiting the next issue.

Now as for some suggestions which I think would improve the magazine.

I. Try to have an interplanetary story in each issue.

II. Publish a number of interesting letters concerning Astounding Stories in each issue.

III. Have several illustrations in long stories.

I think this would improve the magazine, although it is perfect just the way it is.

Hoping Astounding Stories has a long and successful life!—Forrest Ackerman, 530 Staples Avenue, San Francisco, Cal.

Watch the Coming Issues, Miss Miller!

Dear Editor:

Saw your new magazine at the newsstand and bought it at once. I like the following[279] stories in this issue: "The Beetle Horde," "Phantoms of Reality," "The Stolen Mind." I did not care much for the others, and least of all for "Tanks."

I believe that readers, like myself, who are interested in scientific fantasies, prefer stories of interplanetary travels and fourth dimensional stories, and variations of these themes. Such as various space-ships and vibration machines for visiting other planets and traveling backward and forward in time. Stories of lost continents and of strange races of people living in unknown places on our own Earth are interesting also.

A magazine of this kind has unlimited possibilities for stories of the aforementioned types, and I believe that readers who buy magazines of these subjects expect to find therein really Astounding Stories.

Best wishes for the success of your magazine!—Ruth Miller, St. Regis Hotel, Cleveland, Ohio.

"The Scienceers"

Dear Editor:

This is to inform you that we have formed a club which we named "The Scienceers." The object of this club is to bring together members who are interested in science in general, also to talk the stories of your magazine over. We have no means of reaching those who are interested except through your magazine. We hope you will grant us space to print this letter in your magazine. We would appreciate it if every reader of your magazine living in New York City or nearby towns would drop us a card with his name and address. We then would be able to send him information of our club. We hope you will print this letter, as we are all readers of your magazine.—Louis Wexeler, 1933 Woodbine Street, Brooklyn, New York.

We Examine All Science Very Carefully

Dear Editor:

In the first edition of your periodical, you invite criticism from its readers. I am extremely pleased to note that Ray Cummings is among its contributors. His short crisp sentences and word pictures are most interesting. As to the type of stories, I would not be particular; but there is one thing which must be observed: Since this magazine is about science every story must be examined to discover any false statements by the author concerning present-day science.

I think that discoveries and inventions to be made in the future—by the author, of course—cannot be censored.—James Brodent, New York, N. Y.

Young Mr. Wright Writes In

Dear Editor:

I am accepting your offer to write and tell you what kind of stories I like. So I did.

I prefer stories of the Fourth Dimension.

I hope to find plenty of these fascinating stories in your coming issues.—Billy Wright, Age 11, Sheppard Place, Nashville, Tenn.

Likes His Science Fiction

Dear Editor:

Allow me to congratulate you on your fine magazine, it being one of the seven (more or less) magazines in print that are the best on the market.

I am glad to say that I can't throw you any brickbats, only bouquets, and thought I would tell you the kind of stories I would like to see in "our" magazine, if I may take the liberty of calling it that.

I like stories of the type A. Merritt and Edgar Rice Burroughs write, particularly A. Merritt, and if you could reprint "Through the Dragon Glass," by A. Merritt, I wish you would, and give it a cover illustration, as I have everything by him except that one. Please give it a cover illustration as well as any by Merritt and Burroughs you ever print.

You certainly have a good title, and in my opinion the magazine need not be changed one iota, except perhaps you might have the background a different color every month; that is, the background of the cover, using every color in the solar spectrum, which might make it sell better, and, at any rate, would make a nice looking magazine in my opinion. Everything in Science Fiction that comes out I have to get, and pretty soon I will have so much that I will probably have to pay storage space for it. I have a pretty good amount now; four stacks two feet high each, but I can't resist it and will keep on buying as long as there is anything in that line to buy, and as long as I can.

Put this in the proverbial waste-basket if you don't want to print it, as that is probably its ultimate destination anyway, as my ideas are not worth much or less than that. But I do wish you would read it through and act on my suggestions soon.

Thanks—from an ardent devourer of Science Fiction, who reads everything in that line he can get his hands on, your and our magazine being one of the best in that line.—Worth K. Bryant, 406 North Third Street, Yakima, Washington.

"A Great Magazine"

Dear Editor:

I have just come across a copy of your new magazine Astounding Stories, and to say that it is a great magazine is putting it mild. I enjoy stories of the distant future. The first instalment of "The Beetle Horde" by Victor Rousseau was great. I hope to hear more of this author in coming issues. I would like to see stories by such authors as Edgar Rice Burroughs, Harl Vincent, Otis Adelbert Kline, Garret Smith, also Ray Cummings. I wish Astounding Stories a long life.— Wilbert Moyer, 533 N. 7th Street, Allentown, Pa.

Mr. Anderson's Favorites

Dear Editor:

Just a word referring to your "What kind of stories do you like?" in Astounding Stories. I like stories with some facts based[280] on true science of to-day, but let the author's imagination wander a little, because anything might be possible to-morrow. I do not like love stories or much humor in this type of stories.

Stories of other worlds or of the Fourth Dimension always interest me, because there is no limit to the imagination there.

Why not have a discussion column and print some of the letters? It would encourage more to write, and give you their opinion: and, whether good or bad, should help you please the majority.

Some will maybe say the cover is too vivid—but that was what attracted my eye when I picked it out from among many others.

Most of your stories in the first edition were good. I liked "The Beetle Horde" and "Phantoms of Reality" best. Also noticed the "Spawn of the Stars" next issue, which sounds O. K. Hoping you all success in this type of stories.—C. E. Anderson, 3504 Colfax Avenue, Minneapolis, Minn.

A Young Reader's Favorites

Dear Editor:

I am writing you, per your request in your first issue of Astounding Stories. They are most entertaining. I have read three of the stories and they are excellent. You asked the readers to tell you the kind of stories we liked best. I like stories that concern the future of aviation. I like interplanetary stories, also the stories about the Fourth Dimension. I like Cummings', Rousseau's, Leinster's Meek's, Vincent's and Starzl's writing. Your magazine is sure worth twenty cents. You could put more science in your stories.

Please hold H. Wesso, your artist. He can really draw. I have seen his drawings in other magazines. And you may console yourself with the thought that you have one continuous reader. I feel that your magazine is going to be a success. I am also expressing the thoughts of other readers. I am only 15 years old, but I like to read good science stories, nevertheless. I hope to see you in next month's magazine.—Ward Elmore, 2912 Avenue J. Ft. Madison, Iowa.

A Contented Reader

Dear Editor:

Congratulations on your new publication, Astounding Stories. I certainly enjoyed reading the January issue. I believe that this magazine is the answer to the prayer of those readers who are desirous of something different, something unique. Another feature is that you are charging only 20¢ a copy for a magazine that is really worth several times that amount. You may count on me as a steady buyer of the Astounding Stories as long as future issues are up to the standard of the January issue.

Let me urge you that you give us the magazine on time every month. I do not want to postpone my enjoyment of reading the Unique Magazine on the first Thursday of each month.

Keep up the good work, and remember me as a contented reader of your publication—T. J. Creaff, Jr. P. O. Box 734, Phoenix Arizona.

"A Lallapaloozer"!

Dear Editor:

Well, I've got to say something, and I might as well get it over with. Your new magazine, Astounding Stories, is a Lallapaloozer. I'm sorry I didn't get the first edition of the new magazine, but I suppose you have some in stock and I'm sending in my twenty cents in stamps to get one. I might as well tell you how I found out about this new wonder.

One dreary, dreary night I walked into my newsdealer's store to get a paper. While there I happened to glance upon the bookstand—I saw the word Astounding and, my curiosity aroused, I walked over to the stand and pulled the magazine out. Imagine my surprise and delight when I found out what it was! Well, I bought the book then and there without even taking a look inside. When I got home I opened the book, and the first story that caught my eye was "Old Crompton's Secret," by Harl Vincent. I knew the story was good before I read it, because I've read quite a few of Mr. Vincent's novels and they were all excellent. The best stories I like are interplanetary stories.

Why not have a "Reader Talks" in Astounding Stories, where each reader gives his point of view on the stories in the magazine? I know everyone would enjoy that, as it gives the readers a chance to comment on stories and, also, see what the other reader thinks about any story in particular.

I wish you success in your new enterprise and hope my first edition of Astounding Stories arrives soon.—Joseph Kankowsky, 35 Columbia Street, West Orange, New Jersey.

"The Readers' Corner"

All Readers are extended a sincere and cordial invitation to "come over in 'The Readers' Corner'" and join in our monthly discussion of stories, authors, scientific principles and possibilities—everything that's of common interest in connection with our Astounding Stories.

Although from time to time the Editor may make a comment or so, this is a department primarily for Readers, and we want you to make full use of it. Likes, dislikes, criticisms, explanations, roses, brickbats, suggestions—everything's welcome here: so "come over in 'The Readers' Corner'" and discuss it with all of us!

—The Editor.

UNIQUE
GIFT

FOR KIDS, PARTNERS
AND FRIENDS

Timeless books such as:

Kids

Alice in Wonderland · The Jungle Book · The Wonderful Wizard of Oz
Peter and Wendy · **Robin Hood** · The Prince and The Pauper
The Railway Children · Treasure Island · A Christmas Carol

Romeo and Juliet · Dracula

Visit
Im TheStory.com
and order yours today!

Lightning Source UK Ltd.
Milton Keynes UK
UKOW06f1956190617

303701UK00012B/1551/P